Jakarta, Drawing the City Near

] Jakarta, Drawing the City Near [

AbdouMaliq Simone

University of Minnesota Press
Minneapolis • London

Portions of this book have been previously published in AbdouMaliq Simone and Vyjayanthi Rao, "Securing the Majority: Living through Uncertainty in Jakarta," *International Journal of Urban and Regional Research* 36 (2011): 315–35, copyright 2011 Urban Research Publications Limited; in AbdouMaliq Simone and Achmad Uzair Fauzan, "Making Security Work for the Majority: Reflections on Two Districts in Jakarta," *City and Society* 24 (2012): 129–49, copyright 2012 American Anthropological Association; in AbdouMaliq Simone and Achmad Uzair Fauzan, "On the Way to Being Middle Class: The Practices of Emergence in Jakarta," *City: Analysis of Urban Trends, Culture, Theory, Policy, Action* 17 (2013): 279–98, reprinted by permission of Taylor and Francis Ltd., www.tandfonline.com; in AbdouMaliq Simone and Achmad Uzair Fauzan, "Majority Time: Operations in the Midst of Jakarta," special issue on Urban Rhythms, *Sociological Review* 61 (2013): 109–23, copyright 2013 the authors and the Editorial Board of *Sociological Review*; and in AbdouMaliq Simone, "Cities of Uncertainty: Jakarta, the Urban Majority, and Inventive Political Technologies," *Theory, Culture, and Society* 30, no. 7–8 (2013): 243–63.

All photographs were taken by the author.

Published by the University of Minnesota Press
111 Third Avenue South, Suite 290
Minneapolis, MN 55401–2520
http://www.upress.umn.edu

Library of Congress Cataloging-in-Publication Data
Simone, AbdouMaliq, author.
    Jakarta, drawing the city near / AbdouMaliq Simone.
    Includes bibliographical references and index.
    ISBN 978-0-8166-9335-1 (hc : alk. paper) — ISBN 978-0-8166-9336-8 (pb : alk. paper)
    1. City planning—Indonesia—Jakarta. 2. Jakarta (Indonesia)—Social conditions. I. Title.
    HT169.I54J3775 2014
    307.1'2160959822—dc23

                                                                        2014002380

Printed in the United States of America on acid-free paper

The University of Minnesota is an equal-opportunity educator and employer.

20 19 18 17 16 15 14   10 9 8 7 6 5 4 3 2 1

Contents

Preface

I first came to Jakarta in 2006 at the invitation of the Urban Poor Consortium, an organization famous in Jakarta for its battles with the governor of the city at that time. UPC was a collective that tried to be many things and avoid being many things at once. Part social movement, part umbrella body for community-based organizations, part militant advocate, it tried hard not to institutionalize itself in one form as a way of addressing both the strengths and the needs of the urban poor. Even with its focus on the poorest residents of Jakarta, UPC was one of the only organized vehicles fighting for urban change in Indonesia. But it always had to play down its reputation for "going it alone," for wanting to maintain the absolute integrity of its work, which in the end limited its effectiveness as an interlocutor even among its "natural" constituencies.

I had been to Jakarta only once before, in 1982, and then just for a few days. I was invited to work in a city that I did not know. UPC fashioned itself as a vehicle through which poor communities could advocate concerns important to them, as well as a means by which they could valorize their own skills and contributions to the city. My introduction to Jakarta was through its poorest, tensest, and grittiest locales. While homogeneous pockets of poor residents certainly exist in Jakarta, the majority of poor residents live in intense contiguities with people of other social classes. Despite this proximity, diverse groups often do not really "see" each other or, more important, do not see their intricate interdependencies.

UPC was convinced that it was important for the poor to stand on their own, that their presence was critical to the city, and that they possessed determination and skills to improve their lives in their own ways without large measures of external support or technical assistance. After all, much of the isolation and passivity experienced by the poor, UPC claimed, was self-imposed. There was no denying all of the ways in which the city waged "war" on the poor, undermining their efforts to be full citizens of the city; yet, it was important for poor residents to take greater charge of their own communities. UPC believed that, given the several decades I had worked with the urban poor in many African cities, I could be of some use to strengthening their approach by helping their members document the ways in which they survived and eked out some kind of livelihood, meager as it was. But what struck me were the intensive contiguities of different walks of life and kinds of residents. Unlike many cities where proximities are managed through sharp segregations affected through the strategic use of highways, railways, topographies, and walls, Jakarta's infrastructures of segregation were more ephemeral and in some ways more porous. Additionally, while it was evident who the so-called absolute poor were, the demarcations and gradients above were not clear, particularly in terms of having well-defined geographic locations. While UPC frequently engaged residents whose residences were situated in particularly precarious circumstances and who were vulnerable to imminent eviction, and, as such, may have embodied a more well-defined marginality in relation to the larger surrounds, most of the larger districts in which its members were situated were mélanges of material and social conditions.

My work with UPC then was focused on working with residents in eight different locations across North Jakarta, the part of the city with the largest concentrations of poor people, to map out the local economies and key power relations of the larger districts in which they lived. In other words, the focus was to be less on the residents themselves and their immediate conditions and more on the heterogeneity of conditions that prevailed in the larger immediate surrounds. After all, many of these poor households were located in these areas because they were close to work and other income-earning possibilities. Many provided cheap labor and services to better-off nearby neighborhoods. If these households were to more effectively appreciate the importance of their role in Jakarta and more effectively mobilize from it, then their relationships with the various facets of economy, politics, and social life taking place within the larger districts in which they were located—in terms of administration, everyday interaction, and more symbolic senses of belonging—would be critical. While some resident-researchers were bewildered by the task of having to focus on situations that were not theirs, most engaged the opportunity with great inventiveness and flair.

Up until then, UPC members would frequently claim that they had little in common with neighboring localities, that their isolation was imposed by the harsh judgments made about their presence, their illegal status, or their impoverishment. But in this project, many resident-researchers displayed substantial tactical reach deep into neighboring locales, documenting the operations of key industrial plants, markets, local government operations, criminal organizations, and public institutions. Of course, they often played with other people's expectations that they would be incapable of finding out anything significant or troubling the operations being "investigated" in any important way. But in order to do the job, resident-researchers had to cultivate existing networks of contacts or forge new ones, and so they indeed had concrete vehicles of movement accessible to them.

Funds were available for two years to keep this project going, and participants eventually had to get back to their jobs or to their ongoing searches for new ones. But what was striking was that these poor residents, often overwhelmed by the labor-intensive demands of putting bread on the table and constantly confronting the precariousness of their everyday lives, managed to penetrate the workings of district life and ply a range of contacts and networks while having so few resources to work with. What might happen if these individuals and households had more resources and opportunities at their disposal? As UPC, like many such social movements, experienced some debilitating internal realignments and many participants moved on to different efforts, I began on my own to pursue an understanding of how intensely mixed districts worked. I focused on households conventionally designated as the working poor, the working class, or lower-middle class. In the early stages these were small investigations; I helped out graduate students at different local universities as well as some Jakarta nongovernmental organizations (NGOs) while "rounding up" collaborators along the way.

The subsequent projects have operated under the rubric of an urban laboratory administered jointly by the University of Tarumanagara and the Rujak Center for Urban Studies. The lab has concentrated most of its efforts on working with local councils in the three central-city districts of Senen, Kemayoran, and Johar Baru. Work has also been done in other central-city districts, particularly Tambora and Anyer. The emphasis over the past five years has been to engage residents as coresearchers in a process of trying to understand the practices, politics, and economies that have made these districts what they are today. This history of the present has focused on the continuous recombination of different operations of data—that is, intersecting different actors with different spatial mappings, archival documents, resident memories, records of registered changes in built environments, audio and video recordings of events and particular places, and historical trajectories of the use of specific architectural forms and building materials, and emplacing residents in different forms of dialogue, argument, and recollection.

The point has been not to establish definitive narrative lines of development but to chart out the range of intervals—that is, intensive spaces and times where things could head in many different directions—actually and potentially at work in the shaping of these districts. This has been a critical line of exploration, since some districts began with the provision of uniform grids and built environments and have greatly diverged from this pattern over the years, others began with a plurality of different constructions and have converged over time, and still others have oscillated between these patterns. From the design and construction of residences and commercial spaces to the sequencing of occupational choices to the oscillating compositions of household income and membership to the complexion of households' primary social networks to the overall characteristics of the district itself, the question has been "How did things get to be this way?" and the range of responses has become material to be queried and explored by other residents, local experts, and outsiders from other areas.

Much effort has been devoted to drawing attention to all of the ways in which the city works despite its glaring challenges. We have encouraged individuals and institutions in Indonesia and around the world to take up their own projects and to maintain an exchange of information and knowledge. We have conducted scores of workshops in schools throughout Jakarta to incite student interest in taking up various facets of life in the city as school projects. Our concern has not been to develop a coherent overarching picture, and we acknowledge that at times different efforts have worked at cross-purposes. Our commitment is to lend visibility to a broad range of efforts, primarily on the part of Jakarta's residents, to contribute to the popular knowledge of the city and to suggest ways in which residents from different walks of life can get involved in witnessing and documenting those aspects of everyday urban life that have particular value for them.

My engagement with Jakarta over the past eight years has been a process of enabling one thing to lead to another, of reaching across the city from different vantage points, working in different sectors, multiplying starting points to see if and where the subsequent pathways generated might intersect. Thus this book is not a report of a systematic research study, but rather a circulation through various experiments, provocations, studies, interventions, and advocacies that have progressively folded in larger numbers of collaborators. While various national sentiments, political administrations, and multilateral influences, as well as infusions of private capital, have been important, a large swath of Jakarta has been produced by the efforts of its residents. Working for decades under severe political constraints, these efforts have given rise to local economies, cultures of inhabitation, and material environments that testify to the enormous commitment and skill of those who built them. My commitment has been to identify concrete ways for research to demonstrate fidelity to these efforts, to heighten the appreciation for their complexity, contradictions, successes, and failures.

The projects at the center of this book were realized by people from many different walks of life in Jakarta. They shared their time and thoughts and did all of the concrete everyday things that make research and social action possible. I cannot individually acknowledge them all, but I do express special thanks to Jo Santoso, Marco Kusumawijaya, Dian Tri, Rika Febriyani, Achmad Uzair Fauzan, Rizqi Muhammad Ghibran, Elisa Sutanudjaja, Noer Fauzi Rachman, Kemal Taruc, Wardah Hafidz, and Bahwani. The abiding friendship of Filip de Boeck and Edgar Pieterse has been critical to this project. I am indebted to Karin Santi, without whose support, wisdom, and patience none of my work would have been possible. Finally, my gratitude to the curiosity, sacrifices, and love of my daughters, Zaira Simone and Na'ilah Simone.

Introduction

Rehearsal for an Urban Commons in Jakarta

Jakarta is a city full of deceptive appearances. It contains large swaths of unequivocal desperation, of people facing constant scarcity, caught in the exhausting daily struggle to put food on the table. No matter how much the government may extend subsidies or promote empowerment, at least two million Jakartans live in substantially deteriorating conditions with which they can do little. In contrast, the machineries of megadevelopments work their way across the metropolitan region, promising all-in-one living environments designed to concentrate the accumulation of a growing middle class. Much of the city remains an ambiguous landscape, difficult to read. Places are not necessarily the way that they look, and looks represent intricate decisions as to what to do with available resources that are not necessarily meager.

Urban life entails a wide range of investments and decisions about where to put time, effort, and social and monetary capital. While the absence of clear readings may make assurances of important rights and services difficult, and may impede the consolidation of a sense of urban commonality, it also indicates the existence of intricate intersections of people, practices, spaces, and materials that have forged viable working relationships among residents who otherwise might not have bases or techniques for dealing with each other. These ambiguous landscapes are the main object of my discussion in this book. This discussion builds on important past engagements, particularly those of Abidin Kusno (2000, 2012), Rudolf Mrázek (2002, 2004, 2010), Peter Nas (1992), Gumira Ajidarma (2008), Jo Santoso (2011), Goenawan Mohamad (1994), and Marco Kusumawijaya (2004, 2006).

Jakarta is widely considered part of the "Global South." This designation has long had diminishing returns as a means of pointing to something specific or unique about cities such as Lagos, Jakarta, Johannesburg, Mexico City, São Paulo, Mumbai, Cairo, Casablanca, or Karachi, to name a few. The elements of a set designated "Global South" can seemingly be added and subtracted at will. In a global urban landscape, where intensive urbanization describes processes of interconnection that both include and go beyond cities, how is it possible to think about the ways in which all cities, regardless of location, increasingly look alike but significant inequities and disparities in life trajectories exist within and among cities? The array of tropes long applied to consider these conundrums seems increasingly inadequate. Terms such as *postcolonial, modernization, development, neoliberal urbanism,* and *sustainability,* while still salient and resonant as pieces of a popular vernacular, do not quite get at the complex processes of urban change or the multitude of practices that different residents and institutional actors use to eke out niches and spaces of operation.

In each of the following chapters I focus on one "inventive" concept that attempts to shed light on how the processes through which the city affects its residents, and the residents their city, create moments and places of suspension whereby the city exists in ways that are not fully accountable at any scale or in any specific narrative of structuration. As such, Jakarta has many modes of existence, none of which necessarily rules the others, even as differentials in power may circumscribe or potentiate specific terms for what each mode may be able to do.

The concepts rehearsed here emerge from the field, from the often convoluted and ambiguous circulations of people, economies, and understandings, as well as the material intersections of social life, urban infrastructure, and politics. The intersection of field and concept thus mirrors the circuitries of reciprocal shaping taking place between city and resident. Then these conceptualizations are "fed back" as a means of telling stories about Jakarta and its complex urban dynamics.

In chapter 1, I posit the notion of the *near-South,* offering a theoretical formulation that explores the ways in which major metropolitan areas of the Global South remain near to the conditions of urbanization usually associated with this designation and near to the contemporary trends of urbanization everywhere. More important, they also remain near to a wide range of complexions, economies, and practices that are useful as instruments for situating and developing themselves within a globalized urban world. In chapter 2, I consider the *urban majority* as an assemblage of people of different backgrounds operating in close proximity to each other. The proximity means different things—sometimes closeness, sometimes distance, coordination, or separation—but the oscillation is important. There is no underlying commonality. Things do not fit easily. But the sheer diversity of ways of doing things provides a basis for collaboration, constitutes a "working majority," and offers individuals the concrete potential to alter their course of action. In chapter 3, I take up the concept of *devising relations.* People figure themselves out by figuring out arrangements of materials, by designing what is available to them in formats and positions that enable them to take different vantage points. What it is possible for people to do with each other is largely a question of what exists between them and how this "between" can be shaped as active points of reference, connection, and anchorage. How do markets, public spaces, and infrastructure attract things and people, draw them in, coalesce and expend their capacities? By taking materials out of their usual contexts, uses, and meanings and then piecing them together, residents can produce unforeseen and not readily controllable ways of existing. This is a politics that goes beyond specific claims, interests, and agendas. Finally, in chapter 4, I explore processes of *endurance.* If communities and institutions are to endure, they must constantly build bridges between what they do and what others are doing. These are not always bridges that link distinct entities into a common purpose, resemblance, or mutuality. Bridges also point to the breaks and frictions created when different operating systems attempt to work together. Without such frictions those involved have little motivation to work out ways of associating things that have no overarching reason to be associated. Endurance means conjoining with others in the possibility of "saying something" that need not be summed up, that need not have specific parameters of efficacy or objectivity, something that keeps people going in and through transformations that are without precedent in the sense that they need not represent the culmination of a goal or necessity. Endurance is the capacity to risk what is familiar, because what is familiar may not be what it seems to be; every ground and appearance is deceptive.

In light of these concepts, Jakarta becomes not so much a culmination or destination of clearly delineated city-making processes, but more what Édouard Glissant (1999, 130) would call "a place you pass through, not yet a country." As Allewaert (2013) points out in her discussion of African American identity, this absence of destination, far from being an insufficiency, rather reiterates the city as full of twist and turns, plural genealogies, and "strange" gatherings of fragments, efforts, and forces. Through these four concepts—near-South, urban majority, devising relations, and endurance—I try to come up with formulations that themselves convey the oscillating, unstable, and vibrant sense of Jakarta as always seemingly on the verge of becoming many things at once while at the same time exuding the appearance of heading in the same direction as every other city. So the concepts here are to a large extent unstable. They are provisional formulations less interested in "tying things down" than in trying to find ways of "keeping up."

The overall gist of this book, then, is how residents live with uncertainty and how life emerges from it; city life, as Lefebvre's (2004) later work explores, is replete with different rhythms propelled by the intersections of "passing bodies," human and inhuman, materials, and force. Rhythm does not stand still; it continues to push things in new directions, creating new frictions, with new attendant devices to pave the way, softening or amplifying the collisions and, for many Jakarta residents, keeping different moments, experiences, and techniques they have found vital near to them.

By exploring how residents from different walks of life consider each other, how they work together or keep their distance in order to make the districts in which they live endure, how they trade, build, adjust, and seek out new opportunities for livelihood, I will try to chart out these practices of drawing things near, of keeping things in play in a city whose horizons, like those of cities everywhere, seem narrow and prescribed.

Throughout this discussion I want to avoid what Ash Amin (2013) calls a "telescopic urbanism," which zeroes in on particular territories of efficacy and resourcefulness at the expense of examining how the city as a whole is to be integrated and made common. At the same time, these landscapes, or what I refer to as districts, where lives are simultaneously separate and intermeshed, where complex circuits of

exchange and collective undertakings coexist with highly differentiated destinies and ways of doing things, constitute in practice a constantly burgeoning, if not fully accomplished, commonality. In the
tendencies of Jakartans to amplify the polarities, to disentangle themselves from actual complementarities in their imaginations of well-
being, many of these rehearsals for an urban commons are dismissed.

An aspect of an urban commons would seem to entail the capacity
of residents to reach each other, to know what to do to engage with
each other's concerns, capacities, and limitations. It is about how different aspects of the city connect to each other, take responsibility for
each other, and ensure that the ability to make viable livelihoods is
protected and that residents have the space to become familiar with
different positions and perspectives. The city as a whole does not
exist unless people are able to see it and feel it, and such sensibility emerges only from the ability of residents to maneuver their way
across the city's heterogeneity with as few impediments as possible.
Throughout the work that my colleagues and I have conducted in
Jakarta, many residents have repeatedly emphasized the importance
of movement—movement not in the conventional sense of physical
or social mobility, but in the sense of being able to circulate through
different relationships, stories, scenarios, and events, even if they occurred primarily within highly circumscribed geographic domains.

As I indicated in the preface, my work with the Urban Poor Coalition made me aware of just how prolific and wide-ranging the connections among different residents could be, the lengths to which
residents would go to downplay these connections in representations
of their everyday lives, and the intensive mixtures of tentativeness
and endurance that characterized these links. In terms of time and
resources, the poor do have a lot going against them in terms of their
ability to extend themselves into their surrounds. They also tend to
internalize the harsh judgments others who are less poor make about
them. Indeed, many of the members of UPC seemed caught in imper-
meable bubbles in the midst of spaces and economies that were much
more robust and whose terms of access were too difficult for them.

Those whose participation in the project was most substantial
were young people who banded together in their determination to
be formally employed somewhere, scheduling participation in demonstrations and social movement activities with job applications and

scouring a wider terrain for all kinds of opportunities. They recognized that in order to gain access to particular spaces, institutions, and politics they had to act as if they were not already poor; they had to operate against their inclinations with a certain doggedness and inventiveness for which they were not well prepared and that often produced limited results. This was resilience put in service of finding out the details of how districts worked, not so much to create a life based on resilience but simply to join the mundane world of low-level steady employment. But along the way these young people were able to notice and learn many things. Perhaps most important was the way in which some minimal guarantees—steady income, reasonably secure tenure, close proximity to transport and markets—created things residents could work with.

In order to expand their opportunities of any kind, residents had to have some assets to work with. These did not have to be monetary—they could take the form of skills, connections, or status—but they did have to be made visible in some way. People had to be able to take note of the residents' assets, and this necessitated relatively open-ended venues and times for mutual watching. The stories that unfolded would have to be sufficiently interesting and diverse to keep people watching, as the maneuvering of people around each other obligated everyone to keep on their toes and not step on too many others along the way. So the common here is not so much an outcome or disposition as it is a work in progress. Given this fact, I became more and more interested in those parts of Jakarta where it was possible to see how this "work" has progressed over time. This meant shifting focus from the urban poor per se or exclusively to the residents of areas of the city where the heterogeneities in social makeup and economy seemed to be most elaborated. These were areas such as Senen, Kemayoran, Johar Baru, Anyer, Tanah Sereal, and Jembatan Lima.

The Indonesian government marks the year of Jakarta's official origin as 1527, when Fatahillah took back the Sunda Kelapa port from the Portuguese, who had established a beachhead there five years previously. According to the 2010 census, Jakarta spans an area of 662.33 square kilometers and has a population of 9,588,198, which suggests a density of 14,464 people per square kilometer—the ninth-highest urban population density in the world. The population of Jakarta rose from 1.2 million in 1960 to 8.8 million in 2004, counting only its

legal residents.   The city also spills over into an urban region that includes the cities of Tangarang, Cilendek, Depok, Bogor, Cianjur, and
Bekasi; with nearly 26 million people, it is one of the largest urban
regions in the world.

Important Signposts for Jakarta

LAND

The extensive planning literature on Jakarta, most effectively embodied in works by Firman (1999, 2002, 2004) and secondarily in works by
Silver (2008), Leaf (1993), Winarso (2011), Cowherd (2002), Colombijn
(2010, 2011), Hutabarat Lo (2010), Lim (2008), and Soegijoko and
Kusbiantoro (2001), portrays the ways in which a systematic consolidation of an urban commons, providing affordable and judicious infrastructure and service delivery, is constantly hijacked by the inability
of politicians and planners to fully grasp who actually resides in the
city and the different uses to which it is put. This is most incisively
reflected in the city's relationship to land.

Land is still governed by the Basic Agrarian Law of 1960, which
was the first piece of legislation enacted after Indonesian independence. As the provider of the essentials of life, the state was to control
land as a public trust, a guarantee of the fundamental rights of its
citizens. Based on the notion of common good *(ulayat)*, autonomous
customary communities *(adat)* could attain access to land for the
purposes of their sustenance. But given the practicalities of an increasingly urbanized, industrialized, and capital investment–receptive
society, Indonesia has enacted many different individual pieces of legislation that have been used to appropriate land and bring it within
the confines of private ownership. This process has also spurred
various forms of documentation and rights, including the rights of
ownership, exploitation, building, use, and opening up of land—all
of which may fall under different jurisdictions and may be met with
countervailing laws and authorities (Firman 2004; Thorburn 2004).
There are also various versions of *girik ketitir*, proof-of-ownership
documents issued by local authorities to residents.

In Jakarta, the initial inhabitants on a piece of land would register their occupation with the relevant local authority (the composition and scale of such authorities have been revised continuously

over time). The authority would issue the *girik* status, and this status could be transferrable to other subsequent occupiers. If a resident is in possession of *girik* status, can demonstrate continuous occupancy for a period of five years, and has paid all prevailing land tax, the resident is eligible to apply for *hak guna banguan* (HGB), long-term use rights. This is the mechanism of securing property claims used by residents, businesses, and developers. It is a process that requires formal land certification, which is the purview of the Badan Pertanaman Nasunal (National Land Agency). Another provision exists, *hak pengelolaan* (HPL), through which state management rights are given to specific government institutions that use the land to develop facilities and engage in activities relevant to their remit. Although HPL land is supposed to revert to the state when the government institutions no longer have need for it, a common manipulation of the framework is for the land to be sold and converted to HGB status for private corporate uses. The acquiring corporation then uses the acquisition of land, land that is not legally within its possession, as a form of collateral in acquiring mortgages and other bank loans. Thus intricate collusions among politicians, developers, and finance institutions have circumvented the law and transferred much strategically located land into the hands of private corporations for long-term use. These same manipulations have been applied to large-scale evictions of Jakarta's urban poor (Human Rights Watch 2006), justified as an essential step for maintaining public order and the integrity of the public good.

Even at smaller scales, such conversions are facilitated by unscrupulous district authorities charged with witnessing the formal assignment of rights. An important facet of *girik* status is that conversion cannot proceed without a clear statement from the family that holds this status that there are no competing claims on this land. If any immediate or extended family member can demonstrate that he or she expended either resources or labor to acquire or develop the land and the buildings on it, the family is entitled to a formal decision regarding the ultimate disposition of that land. Thus many land holdings are subject to protracted disputes.

As the majority of land in Jakarta retains *girik* status and is not officially certified with the national government, municipal authorities have no official basis on which to extract payment for municipal services. While both officially certified land and *girik* land are subject to land tax, the latter avoids various forms of assessed valuation that otherwise constitute a key element in how municipalities budget and deliver public services. The very composition of land thus reinforces the ambiguities of the urban landscape that I emphasized before. While circumventing the official registration and conversion processes introduces vulnerability in relationship to the long-term security of resident occupation, it is also, in the short to medium term, the most effective means of slowing down the capacity of more powerful actors to acquire land. Without the certification of land, the municipal government has few devices for extracting value from it, and this complicates the capacity of the local state to effectively administer the urban territory under its jurisdiction. But as Jakarta's metropolitan government has acted in a predatory fashion in the past and is subject to vast complicities between major developers and national politicians, avoiding certification remains an important strategic decision for many residents. Here, residents attempt to reconcile competing forms of security, integration, and vulnerability.

STREETS

Jakarta's residents are always trying to reconcile their often conflicting needs for conviviality and security. They tend to extensive family and kinship obligations while pursuing more individualized styles of accumulation, sustaining a sense of integrity to their pursuits and ways of organizing themselves while living in the midst of often very different kinds of other residents (Jellinek 1991, 2000, 2002; Houweling 2002; Tunas 2009).

While the many interviews I have conducted and meetings I have attended have been indoors, the streets are the sites of really trying to figure things out, of seeing how the connections unfold among disparate backgrounds and practices. Many streets in Jakarta are sites of constant usurpation, continuously worked-out contests among differing interests and needs. They are the sites of various kinds of incursions—places to work, park vehicles, run markets, cook food, extend houses. They are sites of information exchange, sociality, and witnessing—an arena of paying attention. They are full of publicity and secrets, places where many residents escape stultifying interiors and implosive domestic routines but are also often reminded of necessary decorum and the need to toe the line. Streets are thus conjunctions of disparate authorities, expectations, limits, and possibilities (Lee 2007). The growth of a new middle class has been linked to a move that attempts to depoliticize Indonesian society in part by moving a great deal of this working out of everyday life away from the street (Leeuwen 2011). This does not mean that residents of Jakarta sit silently by. Rita Padawangi (2013), in an important piece, documents the ways in which the city is a space of constant contestation, witnessing almost daily demonstrations by various groups dogged in their persistence to give voice to both protest and alternatives.

Given the fact that Indonesia was ruled for more than three decades, 1965–98, by a government characterized by a combination of military demeanor, rampant cronyism, arbitrary violence, bureaucratic tedium, and, most important, a cunning appreciation for Indonesia myth and history, a government that also curtailed most forms of democratic expression, the streets became the arena where more "silent" forms of collective collaboration were worked out, but always under close scrutiny. The government's watchful eye was constantly manipulated and often tricked, but this required various forms of both "muscle" and tactical skill (Siegel 1998; Wilson 2006; Barker 2009b).

The regime also systematically took apart any semblance of lower-class political movements (Hadiz 2000). Fear of the streets became an increasingly critical element of Jakarta's spatial organization, and compensation for this fear reproduced conditions in which it was difficult to address the traumas of the past (Nas and Pratiwo 2003; Tadie 2006). Because Suharto ruled with oscillating repression and tolerance, it was difficult for any sustained, well-organized opposition to emerge, with the result that many of the key political figures from that era remain powerful today (Aspinall 2005).

POLITICAL TRAUMAS

It was on the streets where some of the key traumas that shaped the "spatial mentalities" of Jakarta occurred. In the period since 1949, when Indonesians wrested independence from the long-term colonial rule of the Dutch following five years of national revolution and decades of incessant struggle, several key events stand out: the 1965–66 political crisis, military coup, and liquidation of the Communist Party

(Partai Komunis Indonesia, or PKI); the so-called Petrus killings of the early 1980s; and the rise of Reformasi and the May riots of 1998. During the latter stages of his time in office as Indonesia's first postcolonial president, Sukarno increasingly subsumed power to himself, but this aggrandizement depended on the support of the Nasakom, a shaky coalition of interests and parties that had long been antagonistic toward each other: the military, the Islamic parties, and the Communist Party. While the PKI had been the critical platform for organizing mass-based resistance against Dutch control, even launching a disastrous revolution in 1926, it shared the space with a large number of popular groupings, many of them rooted in various Islamic organizations. Sukarno considered that the Nasakom was necessitated by the urgency of fighting Western imperialism. The PKI used this as leverage to become an increasingly dominant force, with its power largely based on its swelling numbers and its long-term efforts to organize across Java's agricultural plantations and the industrial workforce. These efforts directly challenged Islamic customary systems of land use and agrarian economy. As Sukarno progressively shut down the political space for democratic contestation among divergent trajectories of nation building and economic transformation, clashes among competing parties grew more violent. On September 30 and October 1, 1965, a group calling themselves the 30 September Movement killed the country's top six generals. Almost immediately, Suharto, one of the top surviving generals, took control of the military. He would progressively, within the following two years, replace Sukarno, already stripped of most of his powers, at the top (Anderson 1972; McVey 2006; Roosa 2006; Strassler 2010).

Shortly after the initial coup attempt, the military launched a massive propaganda campaign blaming the PKI for the assassinations and destabilization of the country. A campaign of killing and imprisoning PKI cadres began in Jakarta and spread across the country; it has been estimated that one-half million people were killed and another million were imprisoned (Anderson and McVey 1971; Vickers 2005).

In the years subsequent to these events, a cultivated reign of silence prevailed. Many surviving PKI members went into hiding, changing their identities and cutting themselves off from their families. The events are still not talked about in any official way, and they do not show up in school history lessons except in the form of highly truncated citations. Only recently have some tentative efforts been made to initiate public discussion about this period.

Of particular relevance to my work with the urban poor, both in Jakarta and in more socially mixed areas of the city, are the effects of these events on the composition of informal local authority systems and the shaping of figures who were, in varying degrees, gangsters, entrepreneurs, security guards, community activists, and religious leaders. While operating parasitically on the communities they might claim to protect and develop, these figures often played critical roles in interlinking different kinds of residents and their activities. Vilified for spreading crime and insecurity, they also, to an important extent, embodied the efforts of particularly low-income groups to make their mark on the city. For this reason the Suharto regime, increasingly nervous about the security of the city, came to perceive them as a threat.

As Joshua Barker (2001) points out in his masterful account of the events known as the Pembunuhan Misterius (Petrus), or Mysterious Killings, the state attempted to subsume all informal extrajudicial security operations in the country to the system known as Siskamling, under which informal providers of security would be integrated into the state bureaucracy. Legislation in 1982 banned the renting out of security guards and mandated the state to set up its own local security branches. Those elements that could be reformed were to be integrated into these branches, while those deemed incorrigible essentially could be legitimately killed.

In this regard the state established surveillance mechanisms that constituted secret and immutable lists of those persons determined to be beyond hope of reform. As those with backgrounds in gang activity did not know whether their names might be included on these lists, they were forced to scrutinize themselves using the terms of reference issued by the state, for failing to recognize oneself as possibly included on the lists could be fatal. Across the country, some ten thousand purported incorrigibles were killed. While those carrying out the killings certainly used the lists, it is also likely that persons bearing tattoos were indiscriminately targeted. The prevailing assumption was that individuals who wore tattoos signaled their willingness to be "anything"; their tattoos identified them as persons who made a point of operating outside the state. Such claims were backed up by widely held beliefs about the relationship between tattoos and the possession of magical power and charisma.

As the killings were themselves extravagantly performed, Barker asserts that this was a means for the state to deploy its own "magical powers." As thugs, criminals, and various *preman* (figures of street authority and charisma) were often subject to vigilante killings by local communities, this systematic violence exerted by the state operated as a means for the state to reach out into local communities and express solidarity with them. Thus anyone who took an interest in magical powers, as many Indonesians do, would come to associate such powers with the state. This practice intensified the popular sense that not only was the state immune to popular resistance, but it could also operate at a distance, reading people's minds. If residents of Jakarta, for example, were then to open up spaces of autonomous operation, they would have to couch their activities in layers of opacity. Ironically, it was the actual figures of the new local community security forces, with their uniforms and sense of being part of the powerful state, that often were the weak links and could be the purveyors of the needed deception, as the state, swollen with the sense of its own special powers, came to pay less attention to the actual situations of those supposedly providing surveillance and security on the ground (Wilson 2011, 2012).

Following the Asian economic crisis of 1997, the Indonesian economy, already weakened by inflation, cronyism, large private foreign debt, and bad investments, nearly collapsed (Robison and Rosser 2000). Students, workers, and an emerging strand of political activists, already increasingly active in the immediately preceding years staging protests at universities and factories, took bolder steps, organizing massive demonstrations against the regime. This capacity to fight the regime was reinforced by the development of important links between Indonesian civil society and organizations across the world (Uhlin 1997).

The economic crisis marked a point of intense behind-the-scenes realignments in the political class, with many concluding that the regime needed a major overhaul to cushion the accumulating strength of popular resistance, culminating in the Reformasi (reform movement) in May 1998. Thirty thousand, mostly student, protesters occupied the grounds of the parliament building. Suharto stepped down that month. The uncertain political atmosphere and increased violent clashes between student demonstrators and the military produced an increasingly volatile situation, fueled by incidents of rioting and looting. It is widely believed that much of this chaos was fostered by remnants of the regime looking for a reason to impose martial law (Sidel 1998a, 1998b).

During the riots, thousands of mostly Indo-Chinese residents of Jakarta were killed and many Indo-Chinese women were gang-raped. Nearly 150,000 Indo-Chinese quickly fled the country, and many districts where they were concentrated were burned to the ground. The members of this group were targeted because of the common assumption that they were the economic power of the city. For a long time popular jokes referred to the capacity of most Jakartans to entertain each other with bawdy and irreverent stories about the way the city worked while the Indo-Chinese were busy working to make the economic life of the city. While the Indo-Chinese as a whole certainly exert economic power disproportionate to their numbers, there are many poor and working-class Indo-Chinese throughout the city, and this group is often more stratified by class than are other ethnic groups.

Jakarta retained a highly uncertain political atmosphere in the months following Suharto's resignation, with continuing mass unemployment and an intense jockeying for power among the military and ascendant forces from major Islamic groups. In November 1998, while protesting the new government's failure to address the economic crisis and the immanent ratification of new emergency powers for the military, eighteen students were shot dead in what is known as the Semmangi tragedy.

A culture of silence prevails in Indonesia in regard to all of these incidents. The traumas are covered up with discourses of unity in diversity, and the perpetrators of the violence have not been brought to justice. Further, the government has attempted to cover over spaces of tragedy with new construction featuring bland facades that emphasize the capacity of the state to integrate its differences (Kusno 2003). The invocation of commonality then is based on a systematic lack of recognition of the capacity of those in power to act with arbitrary impunity. Although Indonesia has now become a model of democracy, the country's political elite still is largely made up of individuals with military backgrounds and is dominated by a generation thoroughly steeped in the New Order regime. These systematic policies of elision contribute to an urban culture that constantly values the process of moving on, of running away from the past and from conflict.

RELIGION

In Jakarta remembrance largely takes place through the vehicle of religious devotion. The worship of God and the solidarity of congregants are the means of expressing faith in the city, in the capacity of the city to carry individuals beyond the confines of their increasingly individuated struggles to make viable lives. This is true not only for the Muslim residents who make up the majority but for other confessional communities as well.

Some Muslims who have found affordable housing in newer settlements at the periphery of the city, without long traditions of living in close proximity to members of different religious groups, have adamantly sought to deter the construction of new churches. Most of Jakarta, however, exhibits religious tolerance and has avoided the Christian–Muslim violence that has been a continuous problem in Sulawesi and the Moluccas particularly. Given the systematic shrinkage of public space, in respect to both political atmosphere and built environment, prayer and teaching groups—from large-scale public gatherings to smaller assemblies in households—usually become more than just strictly religious occasions. They are important conduits for the circulation of information, mutual witnessing, and expressions of discontent and opinion, and they provide arenas where various kinds of group efforts are organized.

Islam has many singular expressions in Indonesia; the ability of urban residents to take their faith seriously has not dampened enthusiasm for a wide range of more secular concerns and engagements. At the same time, Islam has been a nexus around which diverse populations in the nation can intersect and mobilize. It operates as a way through which an emergent middle class can fashion itself through a series of moral precepts, social attitudes, and comportment (Hefner 1993, 1999, 2006, 2011).

But, as it does everywhere, Islam also becomes a "brand." For example, the fabrication and sale of *jilbab* (women's head coverings) and other forms of Islamic dress are a huge business. Some areas of Jakarta are marketed as being particularly "Islamic" in their orientation. Some populist Muslim groupings act outside the law to intimidate aspects of cultural expression that they don't like, and largely get away with doing so.

Tremulous Navigations

In this book I seek less to reinvent Jakarta than to continue in the vein of understanding how residents make a life in the midst of things, how they navigate confluences and contradictions. My goal is to take a particular slice of Jakarta's urban life and use it as means of thinking counterintuitively about the continuing importance of notions of "the city" and of how, in the midst of clearly significant problems, near disasters, and challenges to sustainability, a certain "liveliness" persists. This liveliness does not stand separate from the dubious decisions and inequities in power and opportunity that preclude effective and just planning and governance. My intent is not to make undue claims for the resourcefulness of residents in the face of or despite policies and structures over which they exert little control. All attainments are ambiguous. There are few clear stories. Take violence, for example.

A critical point to emphasize at the beginning of any discussion of Jakarta is that except in moments of political crisis, the city has largely warded off the violence that characterizes many other large metropolitan areas. In many respects this is counterintuitive given that the city, while predominantly Javanese, does bring together distinct peoples from across the far-flung archipelago who have long chafed at the dominance of the former. It is a city of nearly two million poor people, minimal safety nets, massive government corruption, and few avenues of broad-based political participation. It is city where Islam is overwhelming the majority religion, but also where Christians are particularly well organized and thus economically and professionally influential beyond their numbers. While not a stringent city in terms of moral rigidity, it does not provide a large number of outlets for frustration, particularly for youth.

Despite increasingly systematic, multiscalar research on violence in Global South cities (Moncada 2013), clear determinants of such violence remain elusive, for both why it appears and why it does not. Although Jakarta is hardly immune to vast manifestations of criminal activity, police and military corruption, arbitrary and extra-parliamentary manipulation, and sexual assaults against women workers, everyday fears about individual and household security do not overwhelm the city. Additionally, there seem to be a number of fallback mechanisms capable of interceding with varying levels of force and efficacy. The proliferation of mosques, with their quotidian rhythms of public gathering; the Javanese reticence regarding social disruption; the involvement of households and local authorities in exerting control over the streets, often in the face of provocations by policing agents; the generalized desire of residents to avoid the traumatic explosions of collective violence that have appeared at critical moments of political crisis in Indonesia—all of these intersect to attenuate possibilities of violence.

While large numbers of Jakarta's young men lack sufficient education, training, and opportunities to gain formal employment, many participate in informal jobs that have deferred the consolidation of large-scale criminal syndicates, which anyway have largely been shaped by the military. With big military figures in the background, criminal gangs are usually made up of the descendants of those from Ambon and Flores who were recruited into the army by the colonial regime and whose racial and religious complexion accords them a strictly minority status. These gangs are careful not to let violent conflicts among themselves or the deployment of violence as an instrument of securing territory get out of hand for fear of prompting mass reactions from local populations.

If only periodically actualized, violence seems nevertheless to hover in the background. The Indonesian state has often diffused the scope of potential internecine conflicts among street gangs, criminal syndicates, and extraparliamentary groups by incorporating these groups' symbolic power, demonstrating the state's capacity to act not only like a state but also in the guise of popular, mystically tinged warriors that play an important role in the Indonesian cultural imagination. Thus, while it has long tolerated complicities among various criminal groups and the police and military, the state nevertheless makes sure to find ways of asserting that it remains the "toughest gang in town." In part this assertion serves to domesticate a sometimes highly fractious state, where strict demarcations between military and civilian do not hold and where power over the city of Jakarta is constituted along many different scales that intersect public institutions, religious associations, ethnic networks, and economic sectors in oscillating ways, so that it is difficult to know precisely where power lies in any particular instance.

Thus the state manages to affirm its role as the state by often depending on ways to not act like one. At the same time, it must continuously find ways to insist on its prerogative to act beneficially and judiciously across specific social divides—something only a state can do. Alternating civic-mindedness with ruthless street smarts, the state manages to divide and rule, not only in terms of large-scale and significant political contestation but also in terms of the complexion and economies of the street.

There is much that is not known about how Jakarta operates, and those who seek to find out encounter many difficulties. Store owners, local politicians, street vendors, and civil servants, for example, can often be reluctant to say much of anything about their understanding of events and realities within their own purviews, let alone about their ideas concerning the larger city. Jakarta is a city where for many years the daily events of local life were closely scrutinized by an array of policing agents. In many cases these agents, in reality, did not do much about anything, but the sheer fact that they had a presence and could take actions that often were arbitrary and for which residents had little recourse to appeal was often enough to keep residents from saying what was on their minds. Land could be confiscated and livelihoods shut down. While the severity of such surveillance largely disappeared with the end of the Suharto New Order in 1998, formal municipal institutional arrangements have not changed much, and there remains little democratic political competition. Thus the mechanisms through which residents of particular areas can make their needs and interests known have to be put together through deals among police, local military officials, local government bureaucrats, endogenous informal authorities, prominent religious figures and businesspersons, local "defense" organizations (which are often ethnically defined), and national politicians.

In some areas of the city there may be individuals among these entities or outside them that have sufficient experience, historical authority, or cunning to ensure that certain arrangements are secured over time and can guarantee a semblance of equity to residents of different backgrounds and livelihoods. In other areas of the city such arrangements may be constantly changing, particularly as opportunistic figures seem to come from nowhere, entering the fray and shifting delicate balances of power.

From petty traders to major business figures, there are many people who must be paid off. Many of the deals that are brokered locally have to do with limiting the scope of such payoffs or maintaining them more as gestures than as any significant outlay of money. Complex interdependencies develop among local officials formally charged with performing a range of administrative tasks and unofficial brokers who negotiate small deals among, for example, local street traders, store owners, suppliers, and transporters to make local economies run smoothly in light of, and often in spite of, whatever official regulations exist. These interdependencies extend to "big patrons" placed in government, in business, or both. There are duplicities of all kinds. Organizations that officially look like they do one thing sometimes end up doing something completely different. Individuals who are "actually" in charge of a market, construction site, factory, or sector of artisanal production may not be the official managers, supervisors, or designated functionaries, but rather persons who seem to be marginal to the entire enterprise, such as parking attendants, drivers, or security personnel.

In the past, in order to get things done, to secure some semblance of stability over time, as well as economic possibility and social peace, residents did not simply have to take matters into their own hands; they also had to actively find ways of "checkmating" the authority of different officials, operators, and policing agents. They had to fold these figures into the local arrangements of economic cooperation and space sharing they came up with, and they had to do so in ways that ensured that no one particular set of officials, "big men," patrons, or military personnel, for example, would gain excessive advantage. Further, they had to continuously revise the ways in which they accomplished this. This process gives Jakarta a strong sense of being a city of many different kinds of districts, each defined by its relative capacity to deal productively with the constraints the residents faced.

For example, some districts developed on land that has been tied up in legal disputes for decades—where most of the residents and buildings are "unofficial," but where the very peculiarities of the districts' legal status have worked to the advantage of residents, since the shaping of available land and what takes place on it can move flexibly in terms of what is occurring economically in the areas surrounding it. There are some districts in the heart of the city that seem not to have changed much for many years, that continue to have an almost rural feel. Much of the diversity of complexion of course has to do with differences in morphology, geophysical structures, and the political circumstances of initial settlement. But in a city full of blockages and hesitancy, how blockages are overcome and how subsequent initiatives may prosper, whether it be a dynamic night market or a thriving small- or medium-scale industrial sector, often remains a mystery. One can trace the origins of things, but quickly the relevant events and details seem to spread out in many different directions and constitute many stories.

The stories that follow concern specific parts of Jakarta. They take place in the central city and within districts that have existed for some forty to sixty years. During this time, these districts have been largely built and inhabited by residents from different parts of Indonesia with a wide range of incomes, occupations, settlement histories, and ways of doing things.

As indicated earlier, most observations here are drawn from the work of an urban laboratory operating in three central-city districts of Jakarta. The University of Tarumanagara, the Rujak Center for Urban Studies, and the district councils of Senen, Kemayoran, and Johar Baru jointly administer this lab. The focus over the past five years has been to engage residents as coresearchers in a process of trying to understand the practices, politics, and economies that have made these districts what they are today. The thrust in much of contemporary urban research is to consider the ways in which organizations, systems, and institutions establish the grounds for a particular availability of resources and possibilities of action on the part of residents, associations, and neighborhoods (Allard and Small 2013). Still, these small projects in Jakarta attempt to shed new light on the systematicity of district life and how districts intersect with the larger city, how they fold in various presences and absences of organizations into efforts to integrate themselves within larger flows of material and political resources while also designing strategic enclosures capable of attaining synergistic densities among local efforts and competencies, not necessarily distributed across different organizational fields, such as those of health care, social welfare, education, and urban services. At the same time, the work does not pretend to be anything it is not. It does not go inside many organizations, does not analyze particular sectors or fields. It does not examine the economics of Jakarta's position in the broader context of Indonesia and its articulation with regional and global transactions.

So it is clear that my discussion of Jakarta leaves many things out. I make no attempt to be comprehensive, although I do try to provide the reader with enough overall information about the city so that the details presented here make sense. My aspiration is to unfold a reciprocity—a way in which the details of one particular city can generate significant concepts that lead to a better understanding of urban processes in general and that serve as instruments for uncovering aspects of a city that may otherwise be opaque or simply ignored.

As indicated throughout this introduction, Jakarta is a city replete with ironies and deceptions. Nothing seems to work, but somehow residents find ways to make things work, while these efforts often spell more trouble. Yet Jakarta is full of a diffuse busyness that one colleague, Marco Kusumawijaya, describes as "the inexplicable mysteries of full-speed ahead development; you think you know exactly what all of the dimensions are; it seems obvious, but when you start trying to look closer, through all of the official lenses and ideological conventions, no one seems to know exactly what they are doing." So, in some ways, these conceptual devices also reflect this sense of uncertainty—how to work with it so that uncertainty becomes a resource, a mode of travel.

] 1 [

THE NEAR-SOUTH
Between Megablock and Slum

Ambiguous Locations

Recently, I lived for one year on the thirty-ninth floor in one of the fifteen towers making up Podomoro City in Jakarta. I rarely saw my neighbors and even more rarely had any kind of conversations with them. The first person on my floor with whom I ever spoke was a middle-aged woman from Abidjan. I stupidly asked how it was for an Ivorian woman living in Indonesia, and she replied that on the thirty-ninth floor, "where are we really anyway?" As the fascination and exigency of vertical living becomes more extensive throughout the world's cities, does this woman's somewhat throwaway remark have anything to say about our seemingly growing sense of dislocation and uncertainty about the spaces we inhabit? Or is identification of location simply a pragmatics, a way of pointing to a relation of difference or similarity without it mattering what the content of those contrasts might be? Where advances in the technologies of reachability render vertical living viable in the first place, do they not also obviate the need to have a clear sense, when we say, "I am here, and you are there," of clear-cut implications of that distance? So was an urban theory infused with political meaning about first and third worlds, North and South, simply a function of the streets, of a street sensibility concerned with divvying up spoils and allegiances?

Across the upper stories of urban living there is at least an implicit communion of dissociation. This is perhaps what is meant in advertisements for superblocks or megadevelopments that invite people to be a "part of the world." This is a world that is no longer burdened by differences, or at least is able to smooth their rough edges and cleanse them of controversies. We all know that we will have to go up. We know that if intensive urbanization, now encompassing most of the world's population, is to be sustained it will have to reduce its footprints and carbonated atmospheres. This will require densities that no longer will allow people to "space out." Putting people and identities into territories will hardly cease, but the usual spatial crutches and tricks that conventionally distinguish people on the basis of nation, region, and ethnicity will require readjustment.

Of course, many will simply be relieved to escape the mess below. Dealing with traffic gridlock, bad air, bad manners, collapsing infrastructure, and corruption seems to take up inordinate portions of people's lives. Meeting the exigency of personal efficiency and constant makeovers would seem to require more socially rarified environments, where the idea of sociality—the counting of friends, the mapping of networks, the unencumbered profusion of constant chatter—prospers away from fumes, sweat, and noise.

At the same time, sitting on a balcony on the thirty-ninth floor, looking into hundreds of living spaces in three directions, one develops an appreciation of the ability of these upper stories to contain just about anything. The contiguities of all kinds of "household compositions," from three-generation families to packs of singles crowded into a small two-bedroom apartment to "rent a piece of floor by the day," seem to domesticate or soften the inevitable tensions and clashes. From here it is possible to register the scope of urban life in its various textures and as a patchwork surface, at least in idiomatic fashion. On the street, one has to decide quickly and arbitrarily what to pay attention to and what to leave out. One has to filter out what in the immediate surround is relevant to one's efforts to navigate a particular route or task and what is not. Quick rundowns on who people are and where they come from remain important, but they are only shortcuts for trying to determine what these people might be capable of doing. These shortcuts become instruments for revitalizing the viciousness of fights over race, class, gender, and sexual orientation. Most people think they know what takes place on the streets. But these shortcuts glare like headlights in part because residents, like the colonialists of past, are running away from them to ever higher regions.

The Disappearing South

During recent years, considerations of cities in the Global South have again taken on a significant role in critiquing the basic assumptions of urbanization. But the striking irony is that this occurs as the "Global South" seems to disappear as a useful designation of particular conditions or geographies. Current mapping of socioeconomic development in the world does not support general notions of a basic divide between a developed "North" and an underdeveloped "South." Examination of the basic economic indices reveals significant disparities in the economic capacities of countries grouped together as North and South. The kinds of impoverishment that are popularly associated with an underdeveloped world tend be concentrated in sub-Saharan Africa and the northern part of South Asia. The conventional bifurcation also occludes intensities of poverty across parts of Eastern Europe and North America (Shin and Timberlake 2000; Peck and Theodore 2007; Sparke 2008; Lewis 2010; Edensor and Jayne 2011; Roy 2011a).

Individual cities and urban regions are often dissociated from their larger national contexts in terms of economic indices of well-being as contrasts between urban and rural areas widen. Distinctions of capacity within different urban regions themselves widen as social segregation and economic polarization increase the gap between the earning and purchasing powers of the rich, middle-class, and poor. Thus it is possible for some nations to experience lingering underdevelopment while that description is not necessarily applicable to major metropolitan areas within them. This is particularly the case if the relative rates and degrees of impoverishment in these areas are not substantially different from those of large metropolitan areas in general (Jones 2002; Coe et al. 2004; Smith 2004; Sassen 2006; Bourdeau-Lepage and Huriot 2008; Scott 2009; Hirsch and Kannankulam 2011; MacLeod 2011).

The circuits of transmission and assemblage at work in the design and implementation of urban policies also obscure conventional divides. Ideas and programs move simultaneously in many directions across intensive forms of institutional layering and hybridization. "Top-down" and "bottom-up" designations carry less meaning, as do clear-cut hierarchies in which it is possible to attribute power and influence to a small and specific set of multilateral institutions (Peck and Theodore 2010a).

Transnational circuits of consultation, experimentation, evaluation, and funding coincide with contextual contingencies and national complexions to produce specific orientations to how urban populations are governed and developed. These orientations do not simply mirror each other but also lend opportunities for reciprocal and simultaneous reinventions. Brazil learns from Mexico, Mexico from the United States, the United States from Brazil, and so forth. As municipal governments increasingly rely on monitoring and evaluation techniques, empirical studies of development solutions, and performance indicators as "neutral arbiters" of what works, the particular history of where particular policies and orientations "got their start" no longer establishes any particular authority. Ideas and effects reach across conventional hierarchies and boundaries, constantly recirculating and carrying the different experiences of their adaptations with them (McCann and Ward 2011).

Yet any cursory examination of cities such as New York, Los Angeles, London, Frankfurt, Beijing, Shanghai, Mexico City, São Paulo, Cairo, and Jakarta would result in the obvious sense that these cities "feel" different from one another. Among these particular cities, those toward the front of the list feel more connected to each other, as do cities in the latter part of the list, with Chinese cities perhaps constituting a kind of "swing state." The emphasis here is on the way cities "feel," their impact on all of the senses, as well as an intuitive knowledge, because constructing sets of cities based on strings of variables cannot quite get to the grounds of a distinction (Bridge 2008; Anderson 2009; Thrift 2009).

While the intensity and composition of squalor in Cairo may well outdo anything present in New York, the intensity of contrasts between the well-off and the poor in cities of the "North" may be basically equivalent. Distributions of income, employment, and relative purchasing power within the major megacities of the "South," in terms of proportionality and with some African and South Asian exceptions, do not vary greatly from those within major megacities in the "North." Across indices concerning infrastructure capacity, resource access, gross urban product as a proportion of national output, physical and communication connectivity, and diversity of economic activity and cultural assets, sufficient evidence does not exist to justify a North–South divide in terms of the world's major cities (Burdett and Sudjic 2007; Friedmann 2007; World Bank 2009; Bunnell and Maringanti 2010; Mahon and Macdonald 2010; Ancien 2011).

Still, São Paulo seems different from New York, as does Jakarta from Los Angeles, Mumbai from London, and so forth. These differences have conventionally been attributed to distinctive temporalities, such that major cities of the South are still catching up in terms of a linear-scaled trajectory of urban development. They have also been attributed to colonial histories and the complicated and volatile projects of subsequent postcolonial nationalisms that have overburdened cities with too many readjustments. Of course, simple differences in time do not hold. Mexico City, for example, is one of the world's oldest urban areas, and one would think that after 486 years, Jakarta, whatever its history, would have finally emerged with a viable transportation system and a governance process capable of running the world's second-largest, and by far "messiest," urban region.

Colonial histories do count. Cities in the colonial world were heavily constrained from pursuing lines of urban productivity that would have far outpaced their current dispositions if they had been "left alone" to do so (Dick and Rimmer 1998). Colonial cities were domains of experimentation. Not only were their productive powers subsumed into increasing the efficacy of cities and nations elsewhere, but also their residents were forced to serve as guinea pigs for experiments in population control and spatial design, the results of which were imported back to the metropole. The ideas and aspirations entailed in these experiments were not aimed at making colonized cities work better, at least not at the outset. Nor were the experiments ended when they proved to be problematic to local environments. Rather, they were cultivated as instruments of rule to be applied to crises of urban consolidation back home. European cities were rife with various antagonisms and intrigue, always seeming to teeter on the brink of being ungovernable. As such, lines of common interest needed to be drawn among urban residents that had little to do with each other (King 1991; AlSayyad 1992; Wright 1992; Çelik 1997; Robinson 2004; Kipfer 2007; Stoler 2009).

Still, these legacies of colonization do not quite get at the matter of persisting differences among cities, North and South. In cities such as São Paulo or Mexico City, colonialism is of a distant past, at least in terms of official references and sensibilities. Residual orderings, such as those based on race or ethnicity, may remain in terms of fundamental social and economic divides, with the production of overall urban wealth and capacity located in more narrowly drawn bands of the overall population. Yet there has been a steady, progressive history of increasing well-being for most of the population.

Then there is the issue of the residual status of the countries in which some of these cities are situated. These countries persist primarily as the suppliers of raw materials to the industrial North, or as the largely failed locus of the former import substitution policies for emergent or resurgent nationalist regimes, or as the only viable places of residence for individuals migrating from exhausted rural economies. Such residual status, no matter its specific characteristics, has produced an urban economy heavily dependent on various modalities of informal production and work. The profitability of this informal economy in turn depends on a lack of regulations, so that it can take all forms and shapes, thus affecting the built and social environments in highly heterogeneous ways (Alonso-Villar 2001; Davis 2005; Chant and McIlwaine 2009; Centner 2010a, 2010b; Peck, Theodore, and Brenner 2010; Birch and Wachter 2011; Sidaway 2012).

If many cities of the Global South depend on informal economies—or, more precisely, a plurality of modalities of work, economic accumulation, governance, and social design—many forms of irregularity have also shaped the cities of the North. Ordinary economic life in cities like New York, London, and Paris—the ways in which people are housed, put food on the table, and access various services—often depends on various sequences of deals, improvisations, and questionable legalities (Le Galès 2002; Jensen and Richardson 2004; Dikeç 2007; Kothari 2008). For example, there are parallel realities in terms of accessing housing. Renting an apartment in New York conventionally involves the presentation of massive amounts of documentation, including employment history and past residential references, as well as a thorough credit check. At the same time, especially within various diaspora networks, significant supplies of housing pass through all kinds of hands and uncertain ownership structures, where the use of actual stock exists in a nebulous world of informal leasing and usufruct arrangements (Thery 2012).

In addition, the earning capacities and availability of opportunities for those ensconced in "informal" labor markets may not be all that different from those of persons laboring in formal jobs, albeit the methods entailed in ensuring security of livelihood are different. At the same time, histories of unionization, labor mobilization, and popular municipal politics show up across all cities of the South, no matter how constrained. Residents of cities subjected to colonial rule often became particularly proficient in exploring various forms of organization to make their interests known, elaborate social support, and aggregate economic activity. To a large extent, histories of apparent informality do not represent an absence of capacity to deploy and live through the more formal labor market (Lomnitz 1977; Jacobs 1996; AlSayyad 2004; Blundo 2006; Lund 2006; Legg 2007; Whitson 2007; Lindell 2008; McFarlane 2009; Banerjee-Guha 2010; Brown, Lyons, and Dankoco 2010; Dosh 2010; Jáuregui 2010; Meagher 2010b; Segre 2010; Wigle 2010; Roy 2011b).

The characteristics of urban politics have also been invoked as an element explaining the differences between North and South. Notions such as "deficits in democracy," clientelism, and patrimonial rule are deployed to account for the skewing of urban resources to an elite, as well as the concentration of land and fixed and mobile assets within a small set of hands. Without recourse to effective political participation, there was little urban residents could do except constitute themselves as a threatening force, through periodic but almost always heavily repressed rebellion, or do their best to look after themselves. Access to urban finance, in terms of infrastructure development and economic expansion, often came at a high price. It was usually availed to governments, which had sufficient authority and control to guarantee returns. In addition, policies of the major multilateral institutions from which significant finance was available tended to fluctuate, and these institutions were seldom available to address the recurring costs entailed by the major interventions they forced governments to adopt. Many also had strong antiurban biases and concentrated development finance in rural areas (Escobar 1995; Mitchell 2002; Pieterse 2008; Hanlon, Barrientos, and Hulme 2010).

The urban political histories of Mexico City, Bangkok, Jakarta, and São Paulo, for example, have never been "exemplary" cases of widespread democratic participation. These cities' nations have certainly faced difficult challenges posed by unworkable economic policies, neocolonial constraints, and excessive debt obligations, but in all cities politics is seldom straightforward. From New York to London to Los Angeles to Paris to Toronto, there are plenty of examples of critical tipping points—moments when cities virtually collapsed under the weight of dilemmas, bad politics, corruption, and restructuring plans that residents bore little responsibility for and had little power to do anything about (Savitch and Kantor 2002; Nicholls 2006; Shih 2010; Keil 2011; Kirkpatrick and Smith 2011; Phelps and Wood 2011).

More important, attributions of particular political characteristics to Southern cities as causative factors for particular states or stages of development tend to depoliticize the processes at work in the consolidation of global cities in the North. Here there remains a limited understanding of the politics that has produced the ways in which these cities attempt to maintain agglomeration effects that produce their central role within the nexus of global capital and that ensure returns to scale. The rescaling and restructuring of the state have not simply been technocratic exercises (Evans and Marvin 2006; Boudreau 2007; Curran 2007; Low 2007; Swyngedouw 2009; Marcuse 2011). Rather, municipal, regional, and national authorities have to make critical choices concerning the kinds of investments they will attempt to mobilize, how they will maximize connections among existing economic advantages, and the kinds of legal and administrative mechanisms they will put into play to coordinate and cohere different sectors and jurisdictions. All kinds of interests are at work, and managing the antagonisms is always a difficult process. Here, interrelationships between setting macro-level monetary policy, deregulating capital controls, and liberalizing financial markets and the ways in which the outcomes are spatialized become critical (Brenner 2004; Pries 2005; Jones 2009; Ancien 2011). Who gets to do what, under what circumstances, with what authority and reach constitutes the crux of urban politics, and this politics has largely been occluded by particular discourses of efficacy, democracy, and growth. The "real politics" concerns the many different imaginaries and material advantages that have continuously enabled cities of the North to ensure the unevenness of opportunities, resources, and authority to effect urban change.

Devising the Near

Still, cities of the apparent South continue to feel different. Perhaps there is no way around the absence of a precise account. Perhaps it does not really matter anymore that cities like São Paulo and Jakarta, strikingly different as they may be, feel more connectable to each other than either does to New York or Los Angeles—or Beijing, for that matter. Perhaps one of the characteristics of any city is that it will be different from all other entities also designated as "cities." For the time being, perhaps only an intensely artificial device will serve to keep the differences "in view" while, at the same time, not making too much of them. Perhaps we need such a device to hold them in place as we wait to see how much they are moving toward or away from each other—or, more precisely, to see on what kinds of parameters these movements are taking place. In this case, such a device might be simply to designate these cities as the *near-South*.

What I mean by *near-South* is the sense that these cities are not located within the rubric of "the South" as it has been conventionally known—that is, the locus of underdevelopment, of a development still catching up to cities of "the North," or of places composed of large degrees of unfulfilled economic aspirations and capacities. Instead they are, in fundamental ways, "near" such connotations— near in the sense that, although they do not represent these conditions and are not examples of them, the policies and politics of these cities must be conscious of the ways in which the present dynamics of urban life there border on these realities. Within these cities, enormous challenges remain in terms of providing platforms for viable urban lives. Significant proportions of their populations could, without too many complicated provoking factors, slip into pockets of debilitating impoverishment for which there exists almost no functional cushion (González de la Rocha 2006; DiMuzio 2008; Dawson 2009; Roberts and Wilson 2009; Rodgers 2009; Sassen 2010; Vargas and Alves 2010).

Still, inequality, spatial segregation, economic skewing, and inadequate infrastructural and social supports do not immediately threaten the functioning of these cities. These factors do not keep them from a continuous process of overall development and do not mark them as fundamentally distinct from most other major cities. Rather, these cities are near conditions, inversions, and tipping points that could make them different from the other major cities to which they are compared. This does not mean that London or New York is immune from multiple crises or social disasters. It simply means that through a combination of all the factors identified above, none of which singly or in various combinations is sufficient to establish a marked difference between cities of the South and North, these cities of the South could be nearer to a wider range of "tipping points" than are their Northern counterparts. This is the case despite the fact that, in terms of certain kinds of resilience and resourcefulness, gained through the vagaries of their colonial and postcolonial pasts, they may be better equipped than cities of the North to address many kinds of crises.

Accordingly, *near-South* also means not simply the proximity of these cities to conventional "Southern conditions" but also the proximity of the South to the conditions of the city everywhere. Major cities of the South have grown spectacularly during the past decades, not just in terms of population size but also in their ability to mirror cities of the North in terms of infrastructure, wealth, amenities, cultural assets, urban vibe, and social and economic dynamism. This mirroring and jump in capacity have enabled improvements in urban conditions for many inhabitants, but they have also left in place substantial spaces of localized practices, shadow economies, marginality, and social and economic domains for which it is difficult to find adequate labels. "Informality" is the usual placeholder label applied to these spaces. In their leaps and bounds, these cities bring a sense of the South closer to the urban realities of the North (Ghannam 2002; Yeoh 2005; Emrence 2008; Huyssen 2008; Chu 2009; Goldman 2011).

This proximity connotes several things. First, the ways in which Northern cities attained modernity and the capacity levels associated with it are not the *only* ways. This notion has less to do with debates over the existence of multiple or alternative modernities than it does with processes of equifinality—that is, varying routes can wind up at the same destination. Cities are indeed moving together, for better or worse, along particular paths and face similar economic, social, and ecological challenges largely posed by processes of planetary urbanization structured by global capitalism. By demonstrating the ability to construct urban policies, environments, and economies that are not that different from those of Northern cities, but on the basis of different histories and conditions, these Southern cities bring close the contingencies entailed in Northern cities' own development. In other words, things could have turned out differently, or turned out as they did, simply because of responses to contingency and not because these cities were the necessary imperatives of, for example, the structures of capitalism. In other words, there is no one-to-one correspondence between overarching context—the context of contexts—and the particularities of the urban form that ensues.

If, as Brenner and Schmid (2013) argue, urbanization at a planetary scale reflects a pluralization of urban form and process, its extensiveness and intensity would seem to depend on the inscription of volatility into domains, metabolisms, cultures, and the earth itself. As such, this volatility cannot be commanded or channeled exclusively into a definitive and circumscribed range of effects. It disrupts, dispossesses, and reorganizes according to the logics and actors capable of mobilizing sufficient force and articulation. The dominance of capital is not obviated. But the very processes through which urbanization has attained its reach and diversity would seem to indicate the existence of a manifold virtual domain incapable of exhaustion and from which multiple potentialities for urbanization might be drawn. The "mixed-up" complexion of Jakarta that I attempt to detail throughout this discussion is not simply the embodiment of the contradictions of capital but also a result of the way cities seem to bring together so many (half-baked) notions about how people are supposed to live.

Second, cities of a near-South bring closer attention to realities embedded within cities of the North, such as their own "Souths." Of course, cities of the North have been greatly affected by situations elsewhere, some cities for longer durations than others. For example, New York has always been largely a city of immigrants. These changes have accelerated in recent decades so that many cities of the North no longer even have a majority of inhabitants that can claim to have been born there or even share the same national background. The intensive articulations of economies and spaces, coupled with the multiple volatilities of various nations facing one kind of short-term or structural crisis after another, have resulted in Northern cities with increasingly diversified residential compositions. These cities thus also find themselves incorporating a more diverse range of economic activities, livelihood practices, and cultures of inhabitation.

The translocal character of many of these activities and practices places them out of range for a comprehensive, direct, and controlling engagement by municipal authority. The "nearness" that is then brought into view is the potential recognition on the part of cities such as London, Paris, Chicago, and Frankfurt that the ways in which they have deliberated past futures and governed accordingly cannot be the ways of their present. In order to sustain themselves, they may have to better familiarize themselves with assembling, coordinating, and cohering highly diverse mixtures of formal and informal, licit and illicit, ordered and chaotic, clear and opaque, spiritual and secular, the wide diversity of everyday practices and the commonalities of citizenship, as has often been the overarching task of cities of the near-South. The methods will not necessarily be the same, but a sense of similarity will come in the intersections of different kinds of effort that cities of *both* the near-South and the North make in order to address these challenges.

So the designation *near-South* is simply a device that points to an interstitial space, neither of the North or of the South, one that challenges the solidity of both designations yet nevertheless is proximate to them. It does not yet claim to be something else definitively, as it operates here as an instrument of translation among distinctions that do not really exist but still have purchase on our ways of knowing about the urban world. It also signals that relationships among Jakarta, Cairo, Karachi, Lagos, and São Paulo do not have to constitute a clearly defined platform of associability. These cities are indeed very different from one another, but here their differences substantiate the notion of a near-South rather than detract from it. These differences widen and thicken the spaces of the interstitial from which will emerge more heuristic and productive terms of comparison and articulation. This does not mean that there are not significant differences among Northern cities or among the megaregions of the South and thousands of smaller secondary cities.

The process of qualification could go on and on. Certainly São Paulo is not Karachi is not Jakarta—the cities' colonial, national, and geopolitical situations differ, as do the particularities of their municipal histories. Yet beyond the more glaring problems of segregation, speculative urban investment, and enormous urban growth are the less visible similarities grounded in how large numbers of residents in each city manage to put together workable lives, largely on their own. The approaches to this process of autoconstruction may vary among cities, but these differences supplement the repertoire of how it is possible to make cities in the face of the indifference or incapacity of city and national governments, so that when states are finally convinced or compelled to do more to build an urban commons, these efforts can be complemented by a wide range of popular contributions from "below."

There is no need to consolidate a specific "thingness" for the "near," as the latter becomes a relational device. This does not mean that "thingness" in urban theory is not important, and I will explore some aspects of this dimension in the next section. Rather, the idea here is to clear the decks for a more sensory-filled engagement with these cities, to make a space in which the feeling of them as different can generate new ideas and concepts. In this sense, everything is kept "near," whether it be modernity, colonialism, postcolonialism, neocolonialism, informality, translocality, development, or underdevelopment—all of the labels that are not quite sufficient for engaging interurban differences and similarities. They are kept in view, not discarded or discredited, but also not completely relevant or operable.

So I pose an operation that deals with the collapse of old binaries and still maintains a sense of plural urban pasts and futures. The challenge of this operation is to create the possibility of an emergence of something else for urban thought and action, a something else that draws from a wider range of affective engagements and social practices.

The Resilience of Inhabitants and the Conditions of the Larger City

If the "near" refers to an interstitial space, a way of elaborating a sense of intimacy among divergent pasts and futures, practices and potentials, then who occupies this space, or, more important, whose actions have helped shape it as more than a structural vacuum or zone of incommensurable variables? In other words, the sense of the "near" refers not only to acts of comparison among cities and processes of urban change but also to the context in which certain residents have the opportunity to build specific ways of life. How do they negotiate the aspiration to be just as good as any other urban residents of the world yet, at the same time, remain close to the toolboxes of practices, sensibilities, and tactics that enabled them to keep adjusting to the changing realities of the city? If residents once made significant accomplishments in building districts that worked for them, then what now? How are their practices of autoconstruction related to the unwillingness or inability of municipal institutions to conduct basic planning and delivery of services, which only dedicated institutions with clear authority and capacity can do at the scale necessary? What has to be considered in order for these accomplishments not to exist as mere relics or shadows of themselves, but to constitute a source of influence on subsequent events? What kind of institutional assumptions are prevalent about who residents are and what they can reasonably or legitimately do? What does urban policy attempt to do as an instrument of relating to the residents of the city? The organization of land is particularly important here, since residents have to elaborate ways of life on a physical platform. Who are the big actors that command the resources and authority that can make their interests the purported interests of the city as a whole? Given the constraints on what residents can do to secure places for themselves in the city and aspire to particular ways of living within those places, what are residents willing to risk? How are practices of making the city tied up with notions of risk? While this discussion will be focused primarily on Jakarta, many of these issues are salient for other similar metropolitan regions.

Decades of convocations on urban development have emphasized the need for effective decentralized and transparent governance and the importance of broad-based participation in urban development. They have attempted to address the need for the sustainable use of resources, the deleterious impacts of unrestrained carbon emissions, and the exponentially increasing footprints of urban resource use. The imperatives of sectoral and spatial planning have been inculcated into politicians, managers, engineers, technicians, policy makers, and public officials. Everyone has largely come to speak the same language. The results are of course varied, but overall these efforts have registered limited impact.

While such variance reflects the singularity of urban morphologies, histories, and politics, it also reflects the unfounded overconfidence that actors often possess that things will turn out all right. Conversely, it signals dejection. Trying to get a handle on the city is such a daunting task that the only thing possible is to make sure that on a day-to-day basis things do not get too far out of hand. In between these assumptions are highly textured understandings and behaviors, but what they have in common is a general reluctance to compel urban inhabitants to fundamentally alter the ways in which they have come to measure success and well-being—particularly those with the least economic means to do so.

At best, appeals to behavioral change embodied by new urban policies are translated as multipliers of the interests of the more privileged. Take, for example, the ways in which supplemental green space increases land valuation or the ways in which protracted social conflict may depreciate important assets. Enrolling the support of the most powerful actors in the city has too long been predicated on enabling them to attain a heightened confidence about the decisions they make. In other words, where the powerful put their money and projects, and what is likely to ensue from this placement, will not be subject to the messy interference of a messy public. These investments will not have to work their way through complicated social relationships, reciprocities, and obligations. They will not have to work their way through different ways of doing things or efforts to steer things in different directions (Peck, Theodore, and Brenner 2010; MacLeod 2011; Ward et al. 2011).

This is not to say that municipal officials in Jakarta have always deferred to the most powerful. Jakarta's visionary governor Ali Sadikin (1966–77) was determined to turn the city into a modern metropolis. For him, this was an agenda that meant dismantling many preexisting neighborhoods of the poor, but then simultaneously providing the residents of those neighborhoods with mechanisms of redress and rights to operate within the city. In maneuvers fraught with contradictions, the city was to transform the poor into citizens by dislodging them from the very places they inhabited so that they could then more properly assume a viable place in a city now modernized. What is important here is that a series of propositions were pursued, full of twists and turns, as Sadikin attempted to coordinate a wide set of divergent interests and needs without being deterred by them. He tried to clean up a city that for him was not a real city by making it more of a mess. In the process, he discovered that he could not do everything.

But he pressured different actors to pick up the slack, particularly in the provision of basic housing developments that anchored self-built housing radiating around them (Silver 2008).

But the way policy "talks" may not necessarily need to make sense for the policy to be effective, and it need not reflect conditions as they "really are." Policy is an anticipatory discourse. It anticipates the kinds of concepts and language that are potentially resonant with disparate actors so that they think that what is being said appeals to them directly and they do not feel compelled to defend familiar versions of themselves. The apparent need for policy always to be faithful to an accurate reading of the reality of any given situation masks the way in which all policies generate either unintended effects or effects that run counter to those the policies are supposed to produce (Sandercock 2003; Healey 2007). For example, the sacrosanct notion of private property, intended to deliver the most efficacious value to a piece of territory, often produces vast zones where property lies fallow. In Jakarta, as in many large cities, buildings, factories, and plots lie empty because of unpaid property taxes, prolonged property ownership disputes, or problems of irregular documentation. The criterion that brings full eligibility to the use of a particular asset in the end keeps important assets from being used, and thus disrupts the fabric of the city.

In fact, much of the provision of security of tenure across cities in the near-South has been based on ruse, on the appearance of guarantees that are unable to demonstrate indisputable connections between the users of land and the land itself. Rather, the ambiguity of the ruse—the very lack of clarity about just who has superseding claim— ends up being the only available, albeit never permanent, guarantee. This ambiguity has a lot to do with the impossibly high standards enshrined in many municipal land regulations, under which only plots of a certain size and character can be bought and sold. Thus the regulatory framework established to govern a land market misses many of the land transactions that actually take place, involving small plots of land, subdivided land, or land of uncertain status in terms of either legal definition or geographic location (Durand-Lasserve and Royston 2002; Fernandes 2007; McGranahan, Mitlin, and Satterthwaite 2008).

In Jakarta, few pieces of land are designated for freehold title, with the bulk of land titled according to the specific use for which it is eligible. As such, land registration is exceedingly complicated, involving multiple agencies and adherence to strictures regarding not only the land's proper use but also rules governing eligible materials and size. Nearly two thousand distinct pieces of legislation exist to govern the disposition of land. With so many affiliated documents in circulation specifying distinct types of claims and procedures for resolving disputes, extensive backlogs in the courts, and the near absence of judicious regulatory enforcement, any regularization of land transactions and development is largely contingent on the ability of parties to pay large amounts of money to do whatever they want. Otherwise, residents flood the field with all kinds of materials and uses that are formally illegal, a kind of security through illegality (Santoso 2011).

Given that the vast majority of land development in Jakarta is illegal in one way or another, the invocation of illegality as a justification for any authority to act is arbitrary; such arbitrariness is most often seen in the eviction of poor inhabitants from self-built areas. While poor communities may illegally occupy certain land, most gas stations in the city are also illegally situated, as their owners have failed to secure the required permission of the residential areas in which they are located. This is why many residents' associations are filing civil suits against gas stations as one mechanism to press for the rationalization of legal authority in relationship to land issues. More important, the filing of civil suits consolidates these residential associations as official parties to deliberations concerning land regularization. This is a status that does not precede them, so these suits become mechanisms for converting otherwise "fictional" entities into entities that have some say in how land is used in their areas.

While an aim of policy may be to provide clarity as to the rights particular kinds of residents may have, as well as the circumstances in which a specific resource or opportunity can be legitimately used, policy need not act only in the interest of clarity. Rather, it considers the kinds of information and incentives that will compel particular kinds of inhabitants to act in a given way, to take the risk of expanding what they consider to be issues or practices directly salient to them (Hillier 2002).

Given shrinking public resources and governmental autonomy to configure income generation at scale, urban policy must increasingly target the latent capacities of various collectives—or conglomerations of inhabitants thrown together by territorial proximity, historical affiliation, or related interest—to become the coaffiliates of low-energy-cost provisioning systems through actively tending to the environmental conditions in which they are situated. Policy must aim to effect trade-offs in terms of time savings—that is, reduce the amount of time individuals have to spend getting to and from work and other key institutions, as well as the time they spend securing a basic basket of material and informational goods, and then use this freed surplus as a series of credits applied to various community services or local economic incubators. Policy makers cannot simply tell people that this is in their best interest, that it will produce better living conditions in the long run. Rather, they must tell a story that proceeds on the basis of defining new versions of self-interest. In other words, they must put together new vehicles through which individuals and households can build platforms that enable them to access worlds and opportunities they have not previously seen as available. Here, policy requires new forms of accreditation and sanction, new ways of recognizing and rewarding efficacy.

But above all, the efficacy of these approaches requires a more textured understanding of the conditions of the city, the complexion of its residents, and the major shift under way in terms of the use of space and environment. The intent of this chapter and the ones that immediately follow it is to provide such a textured understanding of Jakarta, a city replete with contradictions, problems, and potential. It is a city that unfolds along the globalized trajectories of megadevelopment and inward investment but retains significant repositories of substantial residential skill in city making. Megadevelopments are self-contained residential and commercial centers, cities within cities that include residential and office towers, shopping malls, leisure zones, and hotels. While each megadevelopment attempts to be more spectacular than those that came before, all basically mirror one another in terms of look and operation. This contrasts with the highly diversified built environments that working- and lower-middle-class residents in Jakarta have built largely on their own.

The Impact of Big Actors

Throughout this book a premium is placed on the efforts and strategic practices of city inhabitants who have largely been left out of urban theory. I call these residents, who are neither strictly poor nor middle-class, the "urban majority." This is a way of referring to another kind of in-between that often shifts in terms of the kinds of conditions and resources it has to work with. I emphasize these residents' intricate entanglements of self-interest and collaboration, reciprocity and opportunism, as well as their political acuity in the management of heterogeneous relationships and their cynicism in regard to many formal institutions. While it is often tempting to get lost in the orchestration, it is important always to keep the aspirations and understandings of the performance in mind.

But the urban majority on which I focus here does not live in the city alone. There are, and always have been, other actors who play dominant roles in the shaping of the city. In Jakarta, for example, the development of "new towns" has been the locus through which property developers such as Ciputra, Podomoro, the Sinar Mas Group, Lippoland, and Summarecon Agung have come to play a dominant role in dictating the city-making process. These developers have maintained close links to the Jakarta provincial government over the past decades. By demonstrating the capacity to deliver showcase projects that added something special to the city's emerging modernity, the big developers established themselves as symbols of the city's modernity and not just as entrepreneurial vehicles that realized specific projects. In terms of affordability, new town residential areas are accessible only to upper-middle-class earners. While provisions were made to set aside at least 20 percent of residential units for low-income residents, this regulation has been universally circumvented, especially as unit prices have increased on average 1,000 percent over the past decade (Winarso 2011).

The symbolic capital of developers was parlayed into the acquisition of large tracts of suburban land at cheap prices. This land provided the developers with unimpeded territory in which to elaborate "fully formed" visions of urban living. These visions contained not only residential structures but also schools, roads, hospitals, recreational and community facilities, and shopping complexes (Dieleman

2011). These self-contained infrastructures have been catapulted into the predominant way the city visualizes its own modernity. In order to maintain their viability, developers are authorized to collect taxes in the form of service fees and to maintain control over major infrastructural inputs such as water treatment plants, sewage systems, and electrical grids. The developers' influence extends even to surrounding areas, particularly the poorer kampongs from which much of the lower-end service labor for new towns is drawn.

The deregulation of the banking system in 1988 also facilitated the proliferation of megadevelopment projects through partnerships with foreign banks and the increase in the number of banks that ensued from greater competition in the financial sector (Winarso and Firman 2002). By the time of the financial crisis in 1997, nearly three-fourths of the one billion dollars lent to the property sector consisted of nonperforming loans. This financial crisis created the platform that launched the overthrow of the thirty-year regime of Suharto, a transformation accompanied by intense violence and attacks on the symbolic edifices of the rich. Ironically, the fear generated by the riots helped relaunch a substantial capitalization of the property market (Hadiz and Robison 2005).

As the elaboration of new towns also coincided with the decentralization of municipal authority, nascent local governments were more prone to cultivate various complicities with greenfield developments than they were to think about long-range economic development plans. While the BKSP Jabodetabek exists as a coordinating forum for the Jakarta metropolitan region (consisting of Jakarta, Tangerang, Bekasi, Cianjur, Bogor, and Depok), it has no formal planning or administrative powers. Unless such a body is empowered to manage regional transportation systems development, watersheds, solid waste, and spatial development, it has few mechanisms available to force different sectors and territories to deal with one another. The situation then accentuates the practice of displacing one municipality's problems to other areas.

As the price of land escalates with each new megadevelopment in the urban core, districts where the heterogeneous urban majority have resided not only lose space for the extension of economic activities that require their own spaces of agglomeration and upscaling but also are increasingly priced out of existing home bases. Often

Kebon Kemayoran, a self-built neighborhood whose residents have faced imminent eviction for more than two decades, is located next to an empty megadevelopment. Backers of the megadevelopment attempted many different schemes to keep it viable after the project went bankrupt just prior to its completion.

households transplanted to the periphery operate in more spacious and competition-free conditions but without access to multiple markets.

Especially with new town developments, what counts as effective urban development is largely established outside the public sphere, with government relegated largely to the role of onlooker. Still, the twenty major new town developments in the Jakarta metropolitan region house just under one million inhabitants in a region where the population borders on twenty-five million. This means that, despite all the attention the developments have received, the enormous expenditure that has gone into these satellite, self-contained cities has made only a small dent in housing the overall population.[1]

As developers have taken up the space to define efficient urban residence, other sectors' willingness and capacity to deal with the very implications of these developments have become marginalized. One example is in the area of subsidence, where groundwater extraction, construction load, and the consolidation of alluvium soils are producing shrinkage rates of up to twenty centimeters a year in some parts of the city (Abidin et al. 2011). While the fragmentation and frequent interruptions of municipal water supplies compel groundwater extraction in myriad household wells across the region (where only 35 percent of households have access to piped water), the most substantial impact on subsidence comes from the deep-well extractions of major superblock developments, whose locations along the fringes of the region have also seriously curtailed the volume of green space.

The other area of ineffectual action is in the provision of affordable housing for poor and middle-class residents. While the property market in Jakarta retains occupancy rates averaging 85 percent for commercial space and residential developments geared to upper-middle-class and higher incomes, much of this is based on the calibration between current demand and available stock. Megaprojects continue to come onstream, but more and more of these are being taken over by large foreign investors who then manage their own subleasing of space. Even though there is increased emphasis on building for the lower strata of the residential market, take-up rates of below 75 per-

---

1. These data come from research in progress by Suryono Herlambang, who is completing a study at the University of Tarumanagara on new town developments for the Ministry of Housing.

Megadevelopment at Bakrie Land.

cent do not exert sufficient pressure to stimulate more comprehensive coverage. The construction of new apartments to lease for the lower strata is slow in developing. The provincial government has declared a moratorium on the construction of new shopping malls, since their viability so far has largely been linked to tie-ins with large residential complexes (as well profit-sharing agreements through which tenants can accrue a share of overall income generated by the project) and the steady profusion of international retail outlets (Colliers International 2011).

At the same time, property developers often lie about occupancy rates on projects where "formal completion" is delayed. Any cursory examination of second-tier shopping malls in the region will uncover substantial vacancies and/or turnovers. Except for the large "international trade centers" (clothing and electronic markets), popular for their inexpensive prices, and the premier shopping malls, most other retail spaces are in trouble, as are a wide range of district-level traditional dry markets. Bringing bodies into shopping malls is largely the work of scores of restaurants, coffee shops, and supermarkets. These are places where families can make one stop to "stock up" on basic consumption needs and entertain the kids. Shopping malls count on the increase in valuation added to land to make up for initial lags in retail volume. The malls that are the most successful are those that provide "atmosphere" approximating public squares and that also contain annexes that remain open for adult leisure during late hours. As Jakarta doesn't really have a "downtown" or shopping and entertainment districts separate from the malls, the malls constitute a plurality of "downtowns" distributed across the city.

This particular dimension of an approximate public space is reflected in the proliferation of twenty-four-hour convenience stores across the city, such as 7-Eleven, Kmart, Alfamart, Family Mart, and Circle K. Referencing their success in other Asian countries, these convenience stores have been converted into hangout locations, with facilities providing tables and chairs, usually just in front of the stores themselves. Nothing is changed in the basic operation except that the stores provide spaces where customers can linger, thus enabling inexpensive social gatherings. As thousands of these convenience stores are distributed across the city, residents do not need to go to shopping malls if they simply want spaces where they can socialize and snack. Additionally, convenience stores have a popular atmosphere, given that they are affordable to almost anyone, and thus customers can count on finding a colorful mixture of people there.

While the profusion of convenience stores certainly represents a significant incursion of corporate retailing throughout the city, it offers an affordable prolongation of the day to many Jakartans, as well as a brightly lit alternative to all of the almost empty, lethargic, and dreary eating places that rush to close by 10:00 p.m. It is difficult to discern how this plenitude of restaurants manages to stay in business. While many cater to lunchtime customers from surrounding businesses, most workers prefer to grab quick meals from the scores of *kaki lima* food stalls that congregate around most enterprises of any kind. Nevertheless, these conventional restaurants continue to take up significant amounts of space. Many make enough money only to cover their property taxes; many are parts of chains that simply are interested in maintaining a foothold on valuable urban core property. Even though Jakartans are fond of eating out, these restaurants, most of which are now ten to twenty years old, stand out as anachronisms in the conversion of popular tastes toward something else that has yet to be completely defined.

This uncertainty is not unrelated to the ways in which the process of building economies is increasingly centered on buildings both as objects and as locus from which to explore new intersections among tax regimes, brokers, intermediaries, investment platforms, securitization, shareholding, and regulation. Buildings are then not just buildings, but projects and occasions to experiment with bringing together different streams of money, as well as different mixtures of rights. In other words, who gets to use a project in particular ways is not necessarily the person or company that owns it. Sometimes publicly financed and owned projects are leased to private managers; at other times, shareholders hold projects publicly. Private ownership, trusts, public holdings, and development rights come together in mixtures where no one modality dominates in a broadened domain of real estate. Although these mixtures may produce uncertain dispositions when it comes to the relationship of specific projects to different regulatory authorities, they also force a reexamination of these very relationships. Sometimes they proliferate exceptions to the prevailing rules. At other times they create new forms of public revenue and taxation. In this way, financial systems are not integrated into the designs of the city so much as the city is built as a "corroborator" of financial prospecting (Aalbers 2009; Pryke 2011; Desai and Loftus 2013).

Partnerships in a project can be easily unraveled, leading to a rapid downward spiral of credit problems, construction and service shortcuts, and discounted sales that pass on maintenance problems and other issues of sustainability to another set of actors. These are most often those whose financial security enables them to convert problematic holdings into advantageous losses. These are actors who also tend to acquire large holdings and build projects without much concern about the projects' long-term profitability, since they simply need to stake their claims; such actors are prepared at the outset for the properties they purchase to be flexibly converted into a wide range of possible uses. Often this conversion is anticipated in advance with the complicity of public officials who provide certain advantages and exemptions in exchange for the possibility of "coming in" at a later date to shape the conversion process in the event that things do not work out with the project officially proposed.

Tricks of the Trade: Dancing around the Consolidation of "Bigness"

In Jakarta, the construction of some of the major shopping malls has been a means of cleaning "hot money." If one of the major implications of the profusion of shopping malls has been to diminish the sales volume of older retail outlets, some of these outlets have been revitalized through the procurement of their own illegality. Jakarta has become one of the world's key centers for the pirating of optical disks and software. In the absence of legislation to prevent the practice, camcorders are widely used to record movies right off the screen; these copies are then sold to "source labs," where they are duplicated, packaged, and passed along to various bootleg distributors. Pirated movies are widely available throughout Jakarta, and certain markets in the city are known for particular specialties. Even though the source labs are continuously raided, each operation usually has converted multiple residences throughout the city into labs, so that when one shuts down, there are only temporary lapses in overall production.

Markets specialize in the retailing not only of pirated CDs, VCDs, DVDs, and CD-ROMs but also of a wide range of pirated software and published materials, including copyrighted files, music, ringtones, and applications for mobile phones, as well as digital scramblers and access to cable television signals. Around this modality of piracy, the trade of fake brand goods, most often clothing and fashion accessories, has grown. In some markets almost the entirety of the stock, even if the content is not pirated or counterfeit, entails some form of illegality, as "official" goods such as electronics and household items have circumvented existing customs regulations. While the shopping mall has become a widely replicated symbol of Jakarta's modernity, the markets at Glodok, Mangga Dua, Kunigan, and Fatmawhati, to name a few, remain hotbeds of retail activity. They are invigorated not only through the discounting that illegality brings but also through a thickening of forward and backward linkages across various retail and renegade production centers, warehouses, transport systems, and the port. The cultivation of particular tastes is thus made possible through the widespread distribution of materials, information, experiences, and images that would otherwise be beyond the affordability of the vast majority of the consumer market (Juliastutti 2008).

These operations also know how to stage their illegality. From extensive interviews with retailers in this trade, I know, for example, that the retailers sometimes initiate bogus raids on their own operations to convey the sense that the government is indeed cracking down on this sector. Since these raids are self-staged, they end up generating anxiety within the official bureaus responsible for policing the sector. The bureaucrats are forced to speculate as to what other agencies might assume about their own complicity in this trade. As a result, the bureaucrats look at each other with increasing suspicion, and this immobilizes their initiative. Sometimes the retailers stage these raids to curtail overproduction or to enforce more equitable opportunities for players.

There are also deceptions on deception. For example, in the markets across the city that do a brisk trade in various forms of piracy, travel agencies have grown up, usually with small groups of young women in full Muslim attire working the front desks. This display of "innocence" has come to be considered a ruse for the travel agents' talents as the movers of hot money across different destinations, and so the public secret about Islamic travel agencies as glorified "boiler rooms." But now this reputation has been put to work even by those travel agents who intend to work simply as travel agents. They seek locations close to where "the action" is as a way to draw in potential customers—for even pirates need to make religious pilgrimages and take vacations.

At the same time, this reliance on illegality affirms a popular assumption that the infrastructure for the city's global functions will be built without much being done for anyone else. This infrastructure reflects the widespread confidence investors and firms have in the Indonesian economy. While the materialization of this confidence will enhance the aggregate consumption power of Indonesians in general, it does not address the issues of where the majority of Jakartans are going to end up living, how much they will pay for living spaces, and the kinds of adjustments they will have to make so that an infrastructure for global functions is secured. Despite commitments on the part of the state to build "one thousand towers" of low-cost housing, the state-owned housing company, Perum Perumnas, constructed only 786 new units of housing in the period 1997–2004, and many of these units are occupied by residents with incomes higher than allowed under established eligibility criteria (Human Rights Watch 2006).

Substantial housing deficits exist across the urban world, not only in terms of a shortfall in the number of available units but also in the widening need to repair existing stock in order to retain its viability. In a study of sixty-four Latin American cities, Cristini and Moya (cited in Lora 2010) calculated the costs of existing deficits in terms of the qualities of materials based on local standards, as well as access to water and sanitation, and then calculated the costs of maintaining existing homes and connecting to services. They determined that eliminating deficits would on aggregate cost 8 percent of the gross domestic product (GDP) of these cities.

It is no wonder that in Jakarta, as the state and the major developers fail to provide adequate housing stock to low- and middle-income households, there is a thriving market in unofficial land development for new residences, particularly in the eastern parts of the city, Bekasi and Bogor. As industrial estates move in this direction, many small-time developers are informally trading in small plots of land, usually acquired in bulk by other investors who may register the land under a variety of different auspices.

The residential districts of many Jakartans have largely been protected because they are inaccessible to cars, if not motorcycles, or are accessible to cars but not to flow-through vehicular traffic. Most large developments are situated along major thoroughfares, and the intricate webs of narrow lanes and nongridded small roads that make up the bulk of the city make it difficult for developers to stray far from these main arteries. But with high density levels in most central-city districts, what are the implications for converting largely single-family dwellings into multistory, multifamily dwellings? Such conversions have already been under way for a long time, but if they were to take place in a much more sweeping fashion, what strains would this place on the existing infrastructure, given the problems of piped water and overtaxed drain and sewage systems? Institutional facilities such as schools and clinics would also have to be expanded.

Additionally, there are questions concerning the extent to which securitizing low- and middle-income districts in the urban core— through the revision of existing regulations, the adjustment of master plans, and the addition of new bylaws—means entrenching structural inequalities across the city system. For example, while Brazil's official urban development policy, the City Statute, formally recognized the particularities of low-income districts in São Paulo in order to lend them legitimacy, it also reinforced the notion that different norms of acceptability were to prevail for different parts of the city (Maricato 2010).

Currently there are many controversies in Jakarta's residential districts about mixing commercial and residential activity. Most districts in the city have never been either strictly commercial or solely residential; the lines between these kinds of activities have always been blurry, but now maintaining a delicate balance appears to be growing more difficult. While these mixtures bring new economic vitality to districts and, when commerce is registered, bring new infusions of money into local government coffers, they also create problems in regard to neighborhood cohesion. While most Jakartans have grown up in districts with such mixtures, the intensification of commercial activity in an area sometimes pushes out residents who can no longer afford to live there. While tight zoning regulations may be in place, they are frequently ignored or do not really deal with the complexity of some neighborhoods that need a mix of commercial and residential activity in order to remain viable.

In residential districts surrounding some of the major commercial areas of the expanding central business district, many property owners have substantially supplemented their incomes by providing rental accommodation to single workers with jobs in the central business district. Additionally, thriving night markets have grown up along the small thoroughfares that run through these neighborhoods. In their proximity to the central business district, they become significant conduits of vehicular traffic, and this sets up a nearly unworkable collision of uses and interests. There is not much opportunity to widen the roads unless the bylaws governing frontage are altered, and even if the roads could be widened, improved vehicular circulation would come at the price of removing the food stalls on which this large pool of temporary residents depends.

There are also many tracts of vacant and underutilized land in the urban core. For example, the PT Kereta Api Indonesia, the parastatal railway company, owns a huge piece of land in Manggarai, right in the center of the city. While the company has designated this area for workshops, administrative buildings, and worker housing, very little of it is actually used. It is now tied up in various intrigues around competing land development projects. Unresolved issues keep large swaths of land unused across the city, although with a more aggressive land development policy the city could resolve many of these disputes, which are sometimes simply cover for speculation. In major cities across the world, the numbers of empty properties stand in stark contrast to the growth of low-income areas at the cities' peripheries. In São Paulo, for example, nearly 15 percent of the total housing stock remains unused (Maricato 2010).

This raises the question of what kinds of actors might be cultivated to operate in the zones between the large developers and the small-scale individual and group efforts at the neighborhood and district level. In cities like Jakarta, large volumes of underutilized buildings exist in older commercial and residential areas. Although many are in need of serious repair, they remain functional infrastructure. In some instances these spaces are seized by nefarious characters who, through a combination of physical toughness, cunning, a few good ideas, and sophisticated manipulation of local political games, create successful projects that often violate all kinds of rules. The weekend night produce market that has been held on the streets around the formal wet market at Tambora for the past several decades is basically an illegal operation. Even so, local authorities in the surrounding subdistricts have invested heavily in the market, bringing a "legal order" to its functioning in the absence of any official sanction from above. People come from all over North Jakarta, both the poor and the well-off, to buy fresh fruits, vegetables, and meat delivered direct from outlying farms, bypassing the established wholesale markets and thus the conventional pricing structure.

This circumvention has caused disputes with the wholesalers, which continue to control retail sales within the established market at Tambora, which is why the night market operates outside in the parking lot and on the surrounding streets and after the wholesale market is officially closed, even though it largely remains unofficially open during these weekend night hours anyway. As trucks load and unload, and customers throng the night market, the streets are virtually impassable, creating yet another few jobs to be doled out by the *preman* (gangsters-cum-local politicians, entrepreneurs) who run the market (which is not a market).

The nearly empty official market at Pasar Tambora, in front of which a vibrant night market specializing in fresh produce operates from 2:00 p.m. until 4:00 a.m.

Produce sellers in front of Pasar Tambora.

Although there is no official tally, according to comparative estimates made by the Urban Lab through observations over several months, the yearly weekend night market's sales exceed the total yearly output of the official market. As similar markets have spread to other parts of the city, they have been able to maintain premium prices for some sectors of agricultural land in the periphery. While the proliferation of these unofficial markets may not make a big dent in the official produce distribution system, it constitutes a direct critique of the poor management and backlogs that characterize that system, which has priced smaller retail operations out of competition with the larger supermarket chains.

The challenge is how to turn effective small and medium-size players into big players, not through the expansion of discrete business projects but in terms of forging ongoing complementarities among them. It is important also to keep major corporate entities at some distance, at least at the outset, so they do not manipulate or colonize the new markets opened up by these projects. Governments could provide this protection by specifying the content of partnership structures, sanctioning moratoriums on the takeover of start-ups by corporate entities of a certain level of capitalization, and fostering different forms of collective local ownership and profit sharing. Instead of offering exemptions to foreign direct investment, governments could make access to markets contingent on investment in various forms of local composition or the promotion of local subsidiaries, especially in rapidly expanding emerging markets such as Indonesia.

None of this will bring about any major results in Indonesia, however, if the current level of corruption throughout public and private institutions persists, eating up, as it does, nearly one-third of public expenditures (Henderson and Kuncoro 2004). Given a GDP of roughly $25 billion, a provincial budget of $3.5 billion, and pressing investment needs—transportation, seawall, housing, flood control—of nearly $30 billion, the Jakarta metropolitan region needs to be a much more active "choreographer" of partnerships to generate finance and infrastructure (Krank, Sarosa, and Wallbaum 2009). One initial step would be to stop wasting all of the money currently spent bribing local officials to circumvent the rules around the conduct of local enterprise and let much of that money run unimpeded and thus taxable, as long as basic sets of safety and environmental rules are adhered to.

The "Enchantments" of Occupation
and the Spectral Dimensions of Property

One illustration of the dilemmas connoted by the notion of the near-South is the accelerating development of megaprojects as ways to address the need for both affordable and upscale living spaces and as mechanisms to continuously "socialize" and govern urban populations. Megadevelopments are important to consider because they represent an inevitable response to the exigencies of intensifying the density of cities—necessary for the mitigation of the adverse ecological footprints of cities—and accomplishing this task in a way that is affordable to both residents and municipal institutions. They are also important in their traditional capacity as instruments for maximizing the value of land and the ways in which this modality of valuation affects the practices of municipal governance.

Further, megadevelopments embody the conundrum of residents who seek to embrace the largely externally imposed imaginaries of worthy urban lives but are also reluctant to forgo the labor-intensive yet highly resourceful orientations and ways of doing things that characterized their inhabitation of heterogeneous districts full of the messy intermeshing of commerce and residence, of daily contact with others of diverse backgrounds. If the *near* in the near-South indicates the often precarious proximity of potential and dysfunction, of quiet solidarities and noisy fragmentation, of the intimacy among discordant trajectories of development and contested spaces, then megadevelopments offer important sites for looking at the ways in which cities of the Global South attempt to "meet" their Northern counterparts, but in a way full of interruptions and staggered rhythms that, by default, lend visibility to other ways of thinking the city's future—ways that have been embedded all along in the practices of autoconstruction. This is not to say that location is destiny. No matter where residents are located in the city it is still possible to conceive of many different outcomes deriving from people's interactions with each other within a given space. But by initially focusing on the megadevelopment, rather than on the heterogeneous popular districts that are otherwise this book's major interest, I wish to imagine ironically the ways in which these districts could be the future of the megadevelopments rather than exclusively constitute their past.

Although Jakarta seems to follow in the footsteps of other major

Southeast and East Asian cities, and to out-West the Western city, in its determination to flood the city with megadevelopments, there have been hesitations and interruptions along this seemingly smooth path. Sometimes the irruption of resistance, where a city "fails" in its seamless imitation of global urban imaginaries, appears in a series of small, inexplicable events. In the following, I want to trace some of the things that have not gone according to plan in Jakarta's pursuit of supermodernity as a way to further illustrate the sense of the near-South. Here, Jakarta stays near the image implicitly expected of it but, in the process, experiences moments when things go astray.

In this project, the Urban Lab was interested in what actually takes place within new megadevelopments. The following is a synopsis of information gathered from residents, planners, managers, technicians, custodians, and security guards, as well as the few property developers who were willing to talk to us.

Custodial jobs within the proliferating megadevelopments of Jakarta come at a premium these days, as such jobs offer workers plentiful opportunities to supplement their otherwise meager salaries. Many of these developments certainly were hastily constructed, since profitability requires adherence to strict schedules and price scales for material inputs. Considerations of market volatility maintain fast construction speeds, as the relative success of a given project depends heavily on the rate of turnover in units before they are even completed. So within completed buildings, things go wrong and need to be repaired; this is all in a day's work. But events also take place for which the efficacy of available interventions is much less certain, and some of these stretch the capacities of the developments' technical personnel.

Before we turn to this domain of strange events, however, we need to take a long detour to look at some of the important features of these megacomplexes, for these strange events are related to the contingencies of occupancy. In a city where thousands of new high-rise residential units are coming onto the market every year, the modalities of how they are actually occupied vary. It is well-known that the economics of such developments already factor in absentia. In other words, some units may never be occupied or may be occupied only at some future time when personal situations, money, and even the stars are in some kind of optimal alignment.

One recently built development for middle-class households on Jalan Casablanca in central Jakarta, an avenue that attempts to model itself explicitly on Singapore's famous Orchard Road.

Before anything, many of these projects exist primarily as claims—claims on space that are calculated to posit significant gains only at some future time, yet have to be concretized and "implanted" now in order to access such future possibilities. Additionally, prospects of more integrated and systematic infrastructural planning always loom on the horizon. These prospects force developers to interweave their projects within existent and emergent articulations to contiguous territories, whether the form of articulation is that of infrastructure reticulation, cross-subsidies, or land-use planning. As it stands, most developers pay little heed to how their megaprojects relate to and affect the surrounding areas. They strive to create projects that can function as much off the grid of public service provision as possible, in keeping with their offering of self-contained and enclosed environments. While each development may be marketed as a singular experience of consumption, in reality there is little to distinguish one from another. What counts is the offer of a withdrawn, or at least recessed, world of living even as the supposed self-sufficiency relies on the modular provision of the same retail outlets, design standards, recreational facilities, and so forth.

Marketing pitches offer developments as the platforms undergirding specific lifestyles. These are the lifestyles of the members of highly individuated professional households, disentangled from the continuous complications of extended family livelihoods. These are individuals who have their eyes squarely on the procedures necessary for self-advancement. They are equipped with the accoutrements necessary to convey their accruing status and capacities to networks of known and yet-to-be known peers. In the recessed environment of the megadevelopment, there are theoretically no messy neighborhood management issues to be deliberated; the experiences of other residents are to have little impact on how individuals conduct their affairs. Despite the high density, residential experiences are heavily codified through the very act of the development's withdrawal from the local surrounds. Conversely, articulation to those surrounds is specified through strictly delimited modes of access, and through the inclusion of most of what residents need to consume within the confines of the development itself—the usual supermarkets, cinemas, coffee outlets, and retail stores. The potentialities of density are also structured through the specification of available spaces, where very little in terms of possible use is left to chance.

While the megadevelopment is marketed as a way of living in the midst of a chaotic, vibrant city while enjoying the security and ease associated with suburban life, spillages of all kinds seep across the lines that otherwise attempt to divide inside from out. While residential megacomplexes may withdraw themselves from entanglements with the larger surrounds, they do so in part to effect a heightened connection with the larger global urban world. This is a world whose specificity rests largely in the simultaneous proliferation of such megacomplexes. A resident of Jakarta seeking professional mobility and status competes not only with fellow Indonesians but also with a larger world of urban professionals whose relative capacities are important criteria for the circulation of investment, services, and opportunities.

The more such professionals distance themselves from the vagaries of day-to-day negotiations over different obligations, expected reciprocities, and involvement with the problems of family, neighbors, and associates, the more they are able to concentrate on better positioning themselves in a larger world of increasingly abstract work. This entails dealing with a potentially larger pool of people whose contours and conditions are not readily available to be scrutinized directly. By situating themselves within the enclosed worlds of residential megacomplexes, professionals can anticipate what those contours and conditions are and what their competitors are capable of doing, because what they all have in common is a highly standardized residential environment.

Professionals in Bombay, Taipei, São Paulo, and Jakarta do not actually need to deal with each other directly to acquire a confidence that they all fundamentally share a similar world, and that their actual transactions, if they ever take place, will be informed primarily by equivalent sets of aspirations and commitment to particular practices and an ethos of self-presentation. Residents of such complexes then implicitly know that the specific conditions of history, culture, and politics that characterize their individual cities, while of course remaining determinant of individual character and possibility in many ways, are not the overarching determination of what they will come to be. Without direct evidence of who people are, convictions about their characters are a matter of speculation. Day-to-day transactions over how best to provide for one's household—how to take advantage of new opportunities for information, material inputs, and potentially important social connections—which once dominated everyday life across Jakarta's districts, then give way to speculation. Residents of megadevelopments hedge their future possibilities on how well they are able to conduct themselves in a world where most of the people they need to know in the long run they will never know directly. They must act as if they are "all in the same boat." But without evidence of who those other people are exactly, they must speculate as to their commonality, and so the megadevelopment becomes a relatively "safe" venue through which such speculations can be made.

Still, this form of conveyance and transurban consolidation remains an abstract sense of conviviality and mutual recognition. Disentangling individuals from the complications of street-level urban life and placing them in employment that puts a premium on innovative calculation, personal demeanor, connectivity, niche markets, and the management of increasingly abstracted relationships do not in themselves offer fully formed information about how those individuals are actually going to operate in a globalized urban world. Occupation and residential form have concretized a means of disentanglement through which a continuously revised and supplemented domain of performance management criteria can be elaborated. Adherence to these criteria would then seem to ensure professional success, security, and accumulation. But these are insufficient to the challenge of individuals' being able to register effects uniquely attributable to their participation in this world. As Ferdi, a thirty-year-old media consultant living in the Oakwood complex in Kunigan, pointed out, "We all know what it takes to do the right thing, but then if everyone is doing it, what is my particular advantage, how do I stand out?"

In other words, simply doing the right thing, living in the right place, and dissociating oneself from insignificant attachments and preoccupations does not in itself provide one with the highly individuated performance necessary to innovate rather than comply, to create rather than proficiently calculate, and, more important, to speculate on the possible configurations of connections that could be possible in this state of disentanglement. Speculation is not simply a rational, calculative act. Speculation always entails a certain amount of risk that anticipations and actions will produce outcomes that have little or nothing to do with the dispositions aimed for. To exert risk, we need devices for carrying, packaging, or embodying risk. As noted by Ferdi's roommate, Riaz, a thirty-five-year-old marketing executive, "In Indonesian society we were always taught not to create any chaos; people could run over each other at times with disrespect and nothing would happen, so we learned to be careful, not to rock the boat, but I find myself now always tempted to do impetuous things, even foolish things that might get me into trouble, but might open roads I never thought of before."

Risk Is Not Something Only Finance People Do

Risk is thoroughly woven into the fabric of everyday urban life. Throughout the popular economies of Jakarta, residents commonly seek to exceed their incomes, livelihoods, and social positions through initiatives of all kinds, by doing something out of the ordinary. They know that whatever is sufficient for now—shelter, provisioning, social security—is unlikely to be sufficient in the long run, given the volatility of urban life. This is a volatility that ironically is intensified through their very means of hedging against it. As Vicki, a fifty-year-old nurse, indicated, "Everyone felt the urgency not to get left behind, to show others that they knew how to be in the city, how it worked, and that meant always making something else from what you had." Subranto, a sixty-year-old mechanic, put it this way: "Sometimes it was important just to do something, anything, no matter if you had anything specific in mind; it was a way of seeing what else could happen in one's life without risking too much, but of course you could never know just how much it was going to cost you in advance."

For a younger, disentangled professional class, risks lie not only in the disentanglement itself but also in a self-fashioning that does more than simply increase financial savings, pursue continuous training and educational opportunities, become proficient in the use of social media, or make sound but potentially high-profit investments. Everyday "epistemology" for them also requires a kind of self-fashioning that can be deployed in highly visible ways but the outcomes of which are usually not going to be productive of anything in particular. As Sandyawan, a twenty-eight-year-old computer engineer, stated, "Sometimes I waste a lot of time dealing with people who seem to be headed somewhere, but then it seems that they make a full-time occupation out of giving this impression."

More young professionals may now live in megacomplexes, with their enclosed, withdrawn environments, where residents need not go anywhere except to work in order to have almost anything they need. Yet there is also a "rolling out" of many disparate "projects" into the larger environment. Across older working- and lower-middle-class districts, properties are bought up and become small coffee houses, dance studios, video clubs, boutique fashion shops, lounges, specialty food stores, galleries, and artisanal workshops. These are familiar signs of gentrification. Even when they are relatively short-lived, these projects revalue the areas in which they are situated, paving the way for larger real estate developments and bigger money. But this has yet to happen in many of the areas of Jakarta where these projects take place. It may eventually happen, but for now, the projects' relative significance rests in the expansion of these seemingly unproductive expenditures, with their hit-or-miss impact on specific areas and consumers in the city.

A wide array of forums and workshops at various levels of government and private enterprise have noted Indonesia's need to identify more creative forms of productive investment. Now that the country's skill base is well developed, it is widely acknowledged that greater emphasis should be placed on developing new industries and service sectors and identifying innovative entrepreneurial solutions to the critical needs of urban management. These needs include infrastructure development, transportation, and consolidation of the energies and skills of the vast informal economy into more efficient and lucrative organizational forms. It is an argument not dissimilar to the criticisms leveled against big developers over the years: Why are they not able to use their technical capacities and available financial resources to develop more adequate water, sewage, power, and transportation systems? Why are they not at least more concerned with using their own projects as means of pioneering more sustainable provisioning technologies?

Even if some developers have signaled their desire to make gestures in this direction, infrastructural revisions are enormously costly and complicated. As Abdee, a planner with the Agus Podomoro Group, indicated: "The entire operation [of building one megacomplex after another] is a future-forward thing; you need to keep building in order to cover the costs of past projects, and there is no time or financial base to really innovate. . . . Most of what we do has to take place in-house because it is so complicated to work with other organizations, and this encourages standardization and replication of basic techniques already put in motion." In cities with multiple networks of pipes and cables, often constructed of highly differentiated materials, as well as divergent measuring and specification systems, coming up with interventions that can integrate and cohere existing infrastructure, extend existing capacity, and make provisioning more equitable across different population groups requires the harmonization of many different sectors of expertise as well as policy and management institutions.

Most of the time, developers are simply allowed to do their own thing regardless of whether it fits into existing spatial development plans, adheres to municipal bylaws and zoning requirements, or meets resource management guidelines. This practice prevails in part because it results in living environments where residents do not have to pay attention to the complexities of the city's material articulations and disarticulations. With their recessed and vertical optics, the megadevelopments provide an overview of the city that obscures the messiness on the ground and underneath it. This ocular politics sustains the illusion that as long as the creative, professional, political, and expatriate class is housed and serviced in environments vulnerable only to minimal interference from the larger city, then that larger city's effect on the burgeoning supermodern city is reduced.

The slums, the working-class districts, and the industrial zones cease to matter as much. The new developments then become sites where actions undertaken in that larger city do not matter much. As Dina, a communications specialist in the Jakarta provincial government, pointed out, "'Foke' [the nickname of a former Jakarta governor] was so determined that Jakarta have its own Orchard Road [a major upscale commercial area in Singapore] that no matter how many problems it would create that it would magically make everything all right."

Of course, such dismissal of the larger city is not that easy. Whereas in recent decades there have been many attempts to remove the poor, the working-class, and the lower-middle class from the equation of urban productivity and growth, there is now widespread recognition among economists, policy makers, and politicians that these segments of the population need to be factored back in. This recognition is reflected in the current predominance of widely institutionalized policy mechanisms that provide conditional cash transfers to the poor as long as they adhere to specific disciplinary guidelines, such as sending their children to school and making sure their children have adequate diets (Grant 2004; Beall and Fox 2009; International Housing Coalition 2010; Peck and Theodore 2010b; McCann and Ward 2011).

One of the major concerns raised by the near-gridlock traffic situation that exists in Jakarta is the deleterious impact of this problem on the small- and medium-scale economies that large segments of the urban population rely on to put food on the table. There is widespread concern about what kinds of work opportunities will be available in the future, especially as more residents are squeezed out of the central city and thus lose the locational advantages of living there.

Still, even with this renewed concern about the "urban question"—
that is, how to shelter, feed, educate, and service an urban population
whose presence is needed to keep the basic machinery of the city's
physical and economic infrastructure going—there is a general conviction that the highly textured and complex ecological and social
systems of Jakarta's heterogeneous districts do not matter. As they
do not matter, they are available for the expression of risks by those
who do not live in these districts but, instead, consider themselves to
be living in a world whose ecologies are simultaneously transparent
and opaque. These people can take risks in these districts without
risking too much. They can acquire properties as temporary play-
grounds, as arenas where they can experiment with different kinds of
construction and use. While these activities can be criticized as an absence of productive investment, productivity is indeed itself a costly
and complicated venture. Rifki, a forty-year-old financial consultant
to several multinational firms, indicated that "eventually the entire
city is going to change, not just the Golden Triangle [the business
district developed over the past decade along the Surdiman-Thamrin-
Kunigan axes]; many families will be priced out, but there is an enormous amount of still viable housing stock and plenty of opportunities
for incubation; the prices are pretty cheap now, so the idea is to buy
now, get something, anything going, knowing that in five to ten years
you will have to remake everything."

The City Left Behind

Like the challenges posed by large-scale infrastructural development,
productive activities require negotiation, planning, and integration of
different actors, agendas, practices of calculation, and ways of doing
things. Much of the reason historical, heterogeneous neighborhoods
in Jakarta worked as "economic machines" was that they configured
built environments that concretized different channels of accumulation, aspirations, materials, designs, and implications for how bodies and senses would be instantiated within the same place. This required continuous recalibration and adjustments that could not be
initiated and performed by any one group or individual, but necessitated the participation of different "teams" of varied social compositions. Differentiated strivings and assessments took concrete form.

The resultant volatility engendered long-term histories of conflict and collaboration that in turn provided work and circuits of interchange while maintaining certain autonomous responsibilities for individual residents and households (Barker 2009a; Tunas 2009).

In attempting to engineer productive investments, outsiders, whether new to the city or returning to the districts of their childhoods, confront more than the difficulties of piecing together the requisite permits, finances, cooperation, organization structures, and capacities necessary to make the investments work. They must also impose organization that is not readily consonant with long-standing practices of efficacy. While international policy trends have long emphasized the need for the rationalization of investment procedures, governance, and legal frameworks, "real" governance in cities like Jakarta has long depended on the subcontracting of management to a wide assortment of authorities, both formal and informal.

When sizable amounts of income are produced through multiple forms of official and unofficial payments—for rents, fees, licenses, certifications, authorizations—to the various strata that connect or avoid discrete agencies and institutions, it is nearly impossible to impose an overarching rationalization of the governance system. Haryo, a thirty-seven-year-old successful entrepreneur in the textile sector, points out that "there are untapped possibilities throughout the central city, underutilized space, large amounts of labor that is not necessarily skilled now but which could be easily trained, and local markets strengthened by increased purchasing power. . . . But it is hard for businessmen to work with entrenched ways of doing things on the ground; there are too many players that want to get profit, and not enough patience on the part of new investors to work with the old systems and turn them into more useful directions."

Still, things can happen quickly when these local authorities are either aligned at a specific local level or, conversely, isolated from getting involved at all. But the kind of protracted planning, deliberation, and bureaucratic navigation necessary for most so-called productive investments requires lengthy time horizons. A project can be interrupted and set back at any moment by the sheer number of regulations and players involved. The tendency in Jakarta is instead to inject these districts with a wide range of small, seemingly unproductive projects. Even if these projects do not turn out much profit and absorb significant amounts of their creators' disposable income, they are devices of speculation. They seek to attract and consolidate not only already existent networks of friends and associates but also others in the city both like them and, potentially, different from them.

The play among these older, often declining properties would be much greater if not for the anachronisms of Indonesian property law. One of the ironies of the rapid expansion of high-rise apartment provisioning is that many properties across the city are either vacant or underutilized simply because inheritance and resale dynamics are so difficult to resolve clearly. If, for example, a married couple owns a house together, it is quite possible that after both spouses die the eventual disposition of the property will be tied down in protracted negotiations among the offspring and other close kin in terms of competing rights and claims. While it is possible for individuals to draw up wills that specify inheritance rights, this is rarely done, as the drafting of a will is widely viewed as an expression of an immanent death, something that is not to be recognized. While the family position of firstborn accords certain priorities to an individual in terms of the disposition of property, that person's specific intentions to sell can be challenged by any family member who can demonstrate either a direct connection to the property or that his or her own resources were applied to acquire the property in the first place.

Families have conventionally attempted to avoid these dilemmas by relegating part of an overall plot to each child, with the remaining part designated as belonging to the parents, so that when the parents died their part of the plot would simply be sold and the proceeds equally divided among the children. In other instances, families have built properties large enough to accommodate the anticipated families of their offspring. Yet, despite these practices, many disputes do occur, as particular family members are reluctant to relinquish the ancestral home, insist on waiting for an eventual higher sale price, or seek some other way to have their needs or claims accommodated. The end result is that a large number of properties remain vacant or only partially used.

It is also not uncommon for residents of older inner-city districts to have other homes at the periphery of the city, where they may stay only on weekends or other special occasions. These houses in the periphery, or in areas that were once the periphery but now fall within a ring of inner suburbs, were built as "dream houses" on land that was cheaply available at the time. But because they were located at some distance from work and the social networks on which residents relied, they were not viewed as places of permanent residence, at least until the owners reached retirement age. In building these houses, some households may have spent all of their savings and/or borrowed against future savings.

As long as inner-city residents were able to build their dream houses, it did not matter much to them that where they actually lived most of the time was crammed and crowded, situated in extremely dense areas, and subject to rapid deterioration. Sometimes, having realized their aspiration for better physical circumstances elsewhere, residents were reluctant to expend time and resources improving the old neighborhood. Investing in improved living conditions was not as important as investing in the economic relationships that had largely funded their ability to build their dream houses in the first place. For those who now shift their residence to the megacomplexes, actual residence and dream can be conjoined. Here, the individual combines the locational advantage of being in the central city, close to work and amenities, with the possibility of occupying a dwelling that has status and prestige.

The local news media in Jakarta are full of stories about young entrepreneurs who hold down full-time jobs as investment bankers but also run small businesses, such as boutique cafés, on the side. Through their side jobs they are able to meet other professionals and have subsequent conversations about the possibilities of joint ventures or start-up companies. These projects constitute a kind of currency that is put into play as a means of forming specific groups of friends and associates within which new entrepreneurial activities might incubate, but also might not. Jakarta is a city where fine dining, clubbing, fashion design, media, and cultural events have been dominated by large business groupings, so the availability of underutilized spaces across the city has been an important means of decentralizing the grip on leisure time by the same groups that are major partners to the developers that build the complexes in which many of these young professionals now live. Thus the incursion of these small projects into districts surrounding the megacomplexes becomes a form of leakage away from the complexes' pretenses of self-containment.

The Vagaries of Occupation in Today's Megadevelopments

These pretenses, however, remain just that, for even as the mega-complex withdraws from its surroundings, it exerts a large footprint far beyond its confines in terms of the resources consumed as well as other environmental impacts. For example, it has been found to contribute to accelerating rates of subsidence (Rakodi and Firman 2009; Douglass 2010). But the megacomplex also has no intention to withdraw, as withdrawal becomes a device through which it is able to exert an impact on the city far beyond its means, vision, and ca-pability. The megacomplex takes up a sizable chunk of space, and it does so without adding much to the productive capabilities of the city itself. Its profitability relies on its deployment of various forms of modularity, in design, construction, and management (Firman 2004; Winarso 2005). What the megacomplex actually offers in terms of residential possibility rarely matches either real market assessments of need or the styles of varied potential occupancy. Instead, the mega-complex assumes a basic homogeneity in terms of how the spaces it provides will be used.

In some instances it can be argued that economic productivity is increased when developers and investors simply build self-contained industrial and commercial zones at the further outskirts of the met-ropolitan region, in part because this allows them to institute their own plans, rules, and operating procedures. But the disarticulation of such developments with the rest of the urban region creates serious problems of sustainability and cost. It is one thing to try to escape the messiness of Jakarta's ineffectual urban governance; it is another to think that large-scale economic activities can simply exist in autono-mous spatial bubbles (Hudalah and Firman 2012).

The value of what megacomplexes consume in terms of discounted land, tax abatements, infrastructure subsidies, and regulation re-laxation often exceeds the value of what they return to governmen-tal coffers. These complexes not only reshape how residents see the urban landscape but also act as devices that convince many residents that their old way of life in the city is soon coming to an end, even when there is no concrete evidence that this is so. Megacomplexes are also a testimonial to the weight of undomesticated money. As noted previously, even when most developers raise funds through legal, if not always transparent and accountable, means, such developments are also used to regularize illicit money.

Jakarta is full of examples of where corrupted funds end up. Thus, as indicated before, occupancy is not necessarily a required component of the "success" or viability of a given project. In some cases, a megadevelopment will have done its job regardless of whether anyone lives there or not. Of course, the management of impressions will require that at least a certain percentage of the building be occupied, and often the conditions of that occupancy will be flexible and provisional.

Because the financing of any given development project is hedged against the completion of a subsequent project, it is usually important for developers to demonstrate that a project is fully or nearly fully occupied. This is why intense marketing efforts are made prior to construction and with promises of marked discounts, often aided by property laws that allow resale without taxation prior to initial occupancy.

At the same time, occupancy can be managed in different ways regardless of the availability of bodies to actually inhabit the apartments. Property developers commonly report near-full occupancy rates on commercial and residential properties. It is often difficult to verify these claims, and even when available records seem to demonstrate their veracity, they may be untrue; such rates can be accomplished through various forms of financial sleight of hand.

One maneuver entails using holding companies established by the developers to purchase units in bulk, negotiate favorable mortgages from banks in which the developers themselves may be important investors, and then securitize these mortgages with an array of other loans. Some of these loans may include mortgages, but there are also loans for industrial and infrastructural development. These pay out at interest rates that exceed the costs of the mortgages themselves. This manufacturing of the "success" of a given project then allows the developers to entice other investors to pay premium rates for space that is supposedly "going fast." At times, potential prestige clients are offered cut-rate deals—such as payment deferrals on long-term fixed-rate leases or deployment of lease payments as investments in joint-venture accounts—in order to secure their tenancy, which is then used as a means to attract others.

As units are geared toward investment, with their actual occupancy a secondary consideration, what people do with their investments afterward is much less certain. But these developments are full of actual and potential frictions, as well as the circulation of discordant elements. It is exceedingly difficult to frame any space or activity within its own terms, and the same goes for the framing of the residential base of these developments. The developer of a complex may assume that those who live there will have specific social and professional backgrounds as demonstrated through affordability and background checks. But the results of actual occupancy display a different picture.

For example, instead of a two-bedroom apartment being occupied by a young professional couple, childless or with one or two children, that apartment may be occupied through multiple levels of subletting. Six to ten individuals, related through work or friendship, may share the unit, with the actual composition of occupancy shifting, perhaps even month to month. While existing local government regulations would seem to prohibit such forms of shared occupancy, the regulatory apparatus of local government is not geared to this form of high-rise living and can do little about what takes place inside these complexes. The primary renter may have to produce an official Jakarta identity card verifying his or her eligibility to live in the city, but once an apartment is purchased and then put out for rent, the owner does not really exert much control over what takes place there, particularly as rental contracts are paid for at least one year in advance.

In one of the city's primary high-end properties, Pacific Place, I have discovered a sophisticated Nigerian computer piracy operation in a luxury three-bedroom apartment next to an apartment where a Singapore fashion designer brings his secret male lover to Jakarta every other weekend so that his family won't find out next to one where the daughter of the former minister of finance runs a yoga studio for rich housewives next to one housing the estranged family of a clergyman of one of Jakarta's largest churches next to one that is home to the wayward daughter of one of the country's most militant Islamic politicians, who has no idea she is living there. Developments vary, of course, in the proportions of units sold, rented, occupied, and kept vacant, as well as in their histories of occupation. Some formerly high-end properties have now become affordable to lower-middle-class families. The multiplicity of stories and characters that occupy these complexes is in part attributable to the absence of any need for the residents to fit together. As the architecture of habitation and the provisioning of services are standardized, there is little need for the kinds of cross-negotiation and coordination among residents seen in the everyday practices of the city's older residential districts. Many different ways of life are accommodated because in significant ways they are "silenced." In other words, there are no occasions and platforms for the residents to speak to each other; the complexes do not produce built environments that singularly express their residents' needs, conditions, or aspirations.

Rather, the megacomplexes provide a veneer of anonymity that allows the insertion of many different expressions and conditions as long as they do not upend the capacities of others to prolong their own residency. Heterogeneity here is less an instrument through which to shape a large social space and more a process of individuation that enables residents to address a diffusely distributed or provisional world of actual or potential interlocutors.

Congregations do occur, but rarely in compositions and outcomes that are not predictable. Restaurants, lounges, and clubs attached to various complexes become venues of interchange, but they go through wild oscillations in popularity. Places that are packed one week as the designated favorites of a young high-society crowd may be empty the next, and it is usually not clear exactly what happened. The vast majority of venues are usually relatively empty, and it is often difficult to know where the crowds actually are, as they seem to disappear into increasingly privatized places. In fact, in one high-rise in Kunigan City, the entire penthouse, rented out by a businessman who got his start running a parking lot for a convenience store but is now known to dominate the nightclub security business, is styled as a mini–Las Vegas casino and is typically full of customers who work for the city's stock exchange.

The bulk of stories from the megacomplexes are certainly much more prosaic, full of minor differences in terms of background. But even here, as the majority of residential situations do not convey great exoticism, they do bring with them marked variations in terms of where the inhabitants come from, whom they choose to live with, what they are running away from, and what they are running toward. These complexes are full of different kinds of retentions, to use

Bernard Stiegler's (1998) term for what is held in view and remembered as a device for spatial orientation. What is it that a person pays attention to in a world where so many things compete for attention? How does a person create a space of operation when life can theoretically be moved and oriented in so many different directions? On one hand, the homogenizing environment of the megacomplex institutes a form of retention whereby residents, both those nearby and those who are far away but share a similar mode of habitation, come to see that they are actually "in the same place." This approximates what Stiegler has in mind when he writes about mnemotechnical systems and the synchronization of individual minds. But on the other hand, residents bring with them the residues of all the situations they have left behind. The newly formed residency then acts as a way of working out or, at least, eliding the conundrums entailed by these residues now settled in close proximity to each other.

Residents leave a plurality of conditions behind. Some of these are complicated familial dramas among households who can at least afford to displace them through taking up residency across the varied landscape of high-rises. Some involve histories of designation, where one family member has been implicitly selected to venture forth into the "new world" of a comprehensive professional lifestyle while the rest of the family remains ensconced in the messiness of self-produced livelihoods and an incessant dance with foreclosure. Some residents are escaping from troubles of various kinds in other parts of the country or world. Others opportunistically pursue high-paid expatriate jobs or the exploitation of various loopholes or niche markets. But equally important—in significance, if not necessarily in volume—are the exits produced by the workings of Jakarta's historic and working-class central-city districts themselves.

The Ambiguities of Jakarta's Pluri-districts

I have long been interested in the dynamic qualities of what I call pluri-districts and will say more about them in the chapters to come. I use the term *pluri-districts* because these areas are home to people of many different class and ethnic backgrounds and residential histories who take part in various forms of economic activities and ways of living in the city in general. I am interested in the ways pluri-districts function as complex machines for producing opportunities and intermingling different walks of life and economic practices.

In pluri-districts, households derive viable, if often limited, livelihoods largely from a multiplicity of incremental maneuvers undertaken to build upon and extend whatever they have access to. Households feel an urgency to go beyond what they are currently doing, whether this means using available financial savings, extra land or time, labor, or social connections. For salaried households, this extra could be the start or acquisition of a small business. For artisans and those in commercial activities, the extra might be a small expansion of current activities or, more often, an investment or working alliance with a trade, service, or commercial activity that has something to do with the current business. For example, small textile producers might go in together to buy a truck and hire their own driver to deliver goods to different markets across the city. Households might also expand their houses in order to rent out rooms or provide space for small commercial activities.

These maneuvers often involve positioning whatever assets households have—financial, social, and psychological—within new "neighborhoods" of association. In other words, households make these assets available to working relationships with people engaged in economic activities that are frequently different from those in which they themselves are engaged, or with people that they know intimately. Households often undertake these maneuvers just as much to expand their own relationships to the larger city as they do to make extra income.

As such, households speculate on the very conditions that consolidate them as social units. That is, speculative activities put into play the very conditions through which households recognize themselves as sharing a life together—a sense of predictable bonds, shared assets, and common collective performances. As Amrita, a forty-year-old local councillor, stated:

> Life wasn't easy for anyone, but neither was it full of hardships, just somewhere in between; families had to make sure they had what they needed, but usually they had a little something extra that they wanted to make grow for them. As a lot of things were going on in the neighborhood; people doing different things, coming and going, there was so much for people to pay attention

to, and so we had to figure out ways of getting people's attention without drawing too much attention to ourselves. But this meant we often had to do things we were not completely comfortable with, that went way beyond what we normally would do.

The initiatives undertaken often operate against the grain of what household members are accustomed to. They have to signal their willingness to participate in schemes and with actors they otherwise might shy away from. They must demonstrate that they can perform roles with others that might be discordant with the way they perform their relationships with each other. Instead of the wider neighborhood being an extension of household ethos, it is actively cultivated as a divergent arena of interests and operations, even when ties of belonging through ethnicity, common place of origin, or religious practice are maintained. Households know that they operate in a crowded field of various initiatives and that the best-laid plans will probably require continuous revision and adaptation to those of others if they are going to accomplish anything. As Rona, a forty-seven-year-old property broker, pointed out:

> Most of the time the extra things you wanted to do to get ahead were not really possible; others were either already doing them better than you could or they just didn't fit with what else was going on in the neighborhood; so you always had to be flexible and not expect that you were going to get your way, but then disappointment also was going to be no help, so you had to stay sharp. No one here could quite go it alone; you didn't necessarily help out your neighbors directly, but you knew that if they had more breathing space to work with, more opportunities to make their lives better, then the overall situation for you would also improve. You wouldn't have to worry about their making problems for you, or taking chances that would have a negative effect on your situation. Our idea was not so much to keep the city out of our neighborhoods, but to make them a larger part of the city.

Through this incremental approach, households secure many opportunities for work, improve their living conditions, and gain insurance against some of the dangers of urban life. But as with all experimentation, there are inevitable fallouts and failures, some of which cannot be compensated for, smoothed over, or forgotten.

That some former residents of Jakarta's pluri-districts now live in megacomplexes testifies to the success of such incremental practices of supplementing income and connections to the city. Some households have achieved substantial gains over the years. After all, an individual needs some amassed income in order to afford even a shared apartment. But in some ways, this new form of residence also conveys the relative failures of these practices, even when people are making money. The movement of residents from pluri-districts to megacomplexes reflects the tensions surrounding what actually makes up a sense of efficacy and viability; it reflects the draw of a larger world of cities to which urban residents everywhere are increasingly exposed. That larger world draws near as residents in a city like Jakarta increasingly sense that an urban world of enhanced individual consumption and infrastructure that works is within reach. But it a reassessment of the conditions in which the majority of Jakartans have lived that also entails a sense of people moving into this new scenario together, as a facet of being "modern Indonesians," even if the experience tends to individuate and particularize household identities and functions.

In our interviews, it was always interesting to note the extent to which the move to a development complex was accompanied more by comments about the past than about the future, as if the interviewees were keeping the past near even in this radical move to get away from it. Here, failure is expressed in the sense of individuals turning their backs on the contexts from which they came, of carrying with them experiences of betrayals and intense antagonisms or even boredom. Pluri-districts are full of both generosity and manipulation; they provide an intensely supportive, flexible environment for different ways of doing things, but they can be intensely critical and exclusionary as well.

It was often difficult to discern clear narratives of accumulation and loss as we conducted our interviews. It was not that the residents we spoke with were unaware of what people were doing, of who was making money in what way and who was not—there were few secrets. But in a thick mesh of interrelationships, it was sometimes difficult to make out clear narrative threads for what was indeed evident. The mystery rested more in the combinatorial effects than in the components themselves. What was murky was not what was hidden from view—which in neighborhoods of intensive mutual witnessing was very little—but rather what was in plain sight, the overflows of daily transactions and initiatives. As Rikwanto, a fifty-five-year-old police captain, put it:

> We would take small bits of money and put it in different places, and there were always new opportunities all the time, and our neighbors would do the same thing; so there was never a steady stream of things happening. I had my son run a corner shop, and sometimes he would get huge orders for things that he would have to run around and get from different suppliers, and it was not clear why they had asked him in the beginning, and then sometimes he couldn't even sell a few cigarettes on a given day. We never lost any sizable amount of money but we never could clearly understand when it came in large amounts or when it never came at all.

Budi, a fifty-year-old mechanic, stated that

> the more people you got to know, the more you would find out about small things to get involved with, but other people would get involved with these things at the same time, bringing their own expectations and connections, and so things would tend to pile up. Some days you would get a good deal on a large supply of rice at a particular market, but then it would disappear, or you could get supplies for your shop very cheap, and then people you didn't know would come and expect discounts as if they had found out that you had got the things cheaply.

Residents of the megacomplexes who grew up in these Jakarta working-class districts identified various affective qualities associated with their former lives. Some felt an intense sense of dejection, that somehow all the effort they put into creating viable lives amounted only to the capability to reproduce the game continuously—that is, to maintain the flexibility and resilience required to roll with the punches, to grab opportunities as they come up, or to make opportunities out of almost nothing. Instead of this resilience accruing in substantial accomplishments over the long run, it only keeps people going around in circles. Aisya, a twenty-five-year-old commercial designer, lamented: "People from my community were really smart and they accomplished many things from when I was a child, but they don't have the confidence that they have accomplished something.

They are always worried that everything is going to fall apart, and instead of using what they have gained to build more solid communities, they still are hunting for the small opportunities here and there."

These megacomplex residents sometimes dismissed even the gradual and progressive improvements they had experienced in homes, living conditions, and consumption for being precisely what they were—incremental. They seemed to view incremental improvements as signs of concession or defeat that promised no prospect of significant transformation, something that could come only through sweeping acts. However, even if most of these interviewees did not view their current residence as the culmination of any dream—far from it—they at least considered it worthy of the designation "transformation."

Others viewed the world of their upbringing as overly "Machiavellian," suffused with self-interest and always seeking the cloak of good neighborliness and social collaboration as a cover for more venal sentiments. Randi, a twenty-nine-year-old dental technician, complained that "our community always pretended that everyone had each other's interests in mind, but then you would find your neighbor stealing your water, or your uncle overcharging you for the cement he brought to your house, or other neighbors who would gossip to the police if they thought you were being too successful; it was always nerve-racking how everyone had to act as if they were one big family but would take any opportunity to undermine each other." Some cynically depicted relationships among neighbors as a vast "cover-up" that allowed individuals to view their own success as a guarantor for the well-being of others.

Our informants usually conceded that it was practically impossible for most residents to "go it alone" and that the viability of any entrepreneurial initiative required intricate collaboration. But they were often of the opinion that these were just preparatory phases for developing the capacity to eventually dispense with collaboration all together. In their present activation of professional careers and megacomplex residency, these individuals then professed to display a fidelity to the "real" sentiments that motivated their progenitors, saying that they were being more honest and direct about how they were conducting their lives. Rinaldy, a thirty-year-old accounts executive, professed: "I am no different than my parents; they just wanted to get ahead and saw the people that they had to deal with day by day as simply stepping-stones in that direction, and I think they wasted a lot time on being good citizens in order to do that, whereas I don't think I am pretending; I know what I want to accomplish and I am not going to depend on others in order to do it."

But perhaps the most interesting sentiment came from those who viewed their former home districts as repositories of wisdom before its time, implicitly imagining them as the future, not the past, of the megadevelopment. In this way, they kept the singular resourcefulness of Jakarta near by envisioning it as the critical aspect of a city yet to come. They appreciated having been immersed in this kind of urban life but felt that its real capabilities had yet to be discovered, that the time was not yet right for this experience to reach fruition. They did not dismiss its limited accomplishments or the ambiguities entailed in its moral practices. Rather, they felt that Jakarta was not yet ready to be a city of such reciprocities and intersecting initiatives. First, it had to pass through other phases; it had to develop greater overall economic capacity and political autonomy. It had to have more effective and judicious structures of governing and planning in place before it could incorporate these productions from below. These residents were simply participating in "the trajectory of the moment": they pursued the kinds of careers and residential situations that would expedite the development of such larger political and economic capacities, that would make them eligible to be taken seriously as the makers of the potentialities piloted by former generations.

Across these varying viewpoints of past life in the historical pluridistricts of central Jakarta, many different temporalities are at work. In alternating viewpoints, these districts are anachronisms, the essential kernel of now generalized neoliberal sentiment, or a future in waiting. They are thus vulnerable to the expansion of megacomplexes across the city. In part, the vulnerability of the city as a whole is relocated away from the hegemony of the major property developers to characteristics that are fundamentally those of the interior life of these districts. Whether they succeed or fail, whether they work or not, create thousands of new jobs and residential opportunities for those with limited means or simply warehouse the majority of residents in substandard conditions, in the end may not matter. As such, they are important touchstones for pointing out the ambiguities and conundrums of what I call the near-South.

These districts may count for little not because they exert something of little consequence, but rather because the stakes are so high in whatever it is they do. For the poor, the city offers a multiplicity of interconnected dangers, from environmental hazards to criminal and domestic violence to punitive violence by bureaucracies and police. The fundamental ambivalence of the economic and social practices of these working- and lower-middle-class districts is itself a source of endless harm, even if the historical position of these practices in the city has been uncertain. In other words, it is difficult to wade through the complexity of the social, psychological, and economic operations of these districts and view them with a clear lens. They are too messy. In a world where transparency, accountability, and efficiency are important values, as is the need to make determinant judgments about things, the ambiguity of these districts keeps them from offering clear, unequivocal lessons about how to develop cities like Jakarta going forward. This does not mean that Jakarta does not move, does not go anywhere, but rather that where it is headed may be in many different directions at once, keeping an entire gamut of possible futures near, as well as all the contradictory practices and ideas that compose these futures.

Ghosts in the Complex

This brings us back to the lucrative opportunities available to the maintenance personnel of the Jakarta megacomplexes, which have become the sites of strange occurrences. On some nights, the complexes' maintenance rooms are inundated with distress calls. Water appears out of nowhere, flashing lights continue even when the switches are turned off, elevators skip floors, mirrors suddenly dislodge from their mountings, car alarms go off by the hundreds in parking garages, doors refuse to open with the proper keys. The maintenance personnel sometimes see evidence of these events, but mostly they engage the panic of those who report having witnessed them, discovering nothing amiss themselves when they arrive at the scene. Iwan, a maintenance worker at Kunigan City complex, pointed out that "Jakarta is of course full of ghosts, and many buildings after a period of time do become haunted because of the things that took place within them, but here it seems that the ghosts moved in before the people."

At first, security and maintenance personnel thought that residents were simply taking them for fools and that they were unwitting participants in a collective joke proffered by the well-off at the workers' expense. But the alarm expressed by many residents was real, as were the lengths to which residents would sometimes go to avoid these events. Sari, who works in the management office of Gandaria City, related that spooked residents have tried to break rental contracts, arranged quick sales, or even hired private security personnel to watch over their abodes. Residents often slip maintenance workers sizable sums of money simply to keep their reports private. Fearing that they were being enrolled as the front line in some invisible war whose agendas and weapons were beyond their comprehension, the maintenance personnel I interviewed were reluctant to get overly involved, even though by the time I spoke with most of them, they had been dealing with these events for some time.

It was clear to them that something was wrong, that there was much more to these developments than met the eye. They were very familiar with the layouts, designs, and conduits of the complexes where they worked—after all, they were called upon constantly to deal with problems whose origins were quite clear. But they also reported that there was something about these developments that they did not quite grasp, that there were vacancies, "gulches," and other nebulous spaces that were to be expected of complexes this size. Given the expansiveness of the developments, it was difficult for them to anticipate the effects that the ingestions and exhalations of bodies and machines, the turning off and on of so many operations, and the frictions generated in the convergence of so many different technical operations and materiality could generate.

Additionally, many maintenance personnel, as well as domestics, cleaners, deliverers, and security guards, would come up with their own stories about what was taking place. They would argue among themselves not only about how the complexes functioned but about the sources of the difficulties as well. Consensus was difficult to come by, and sometimes mistrust developed among them over who might be "gaming" the system to their advantage.

Whatever the veracity of such occurrences, and whether they can be dismissed as a form of collective hysteria or an extension of the preoccupation with ghosts that sometimes sweeps over the entire city during moments of silent, gnawing crisis, these megacomplexes are full of varied retentions. They are infused with different memories, traumas, aspirations, and anxieties and markedly varied assessments of the past and the places in which that past took place. Residents see themselves as extensions, revisions, and abruptions of particular trajectories of making urban life work. All of these coexist uneasily in settings where there are few mediations and devices to translate them to one another. The overarching compaction of differences into a standardized lingua franca of residence that purports to speak to a globalized urban world far from Jakarta itself, across borders of culture, history, and politics, is often devoid of texture, since it is intended to subsume almost whatever comes its way. Relationships among residents are mediated largely through an abstracted form of ephemeral transurban professional-class solidarity, with its emphasis on individuation from social and historical specificity. But without much of a content of its own, this solidarity has little ability to prevent the discordant dramas and baggage that residents bring with them from provoking each other with uncertain consequences. Discordant retentions and preoccupations incite one another into unrecognizable shapes and diffuse spectral events.

Far from being withdrawn from the city, these megacomplexes end up functioning as massive arenas where sediments and sentiments of all kinds perturb one another. This perturbation is tempered and shaped by the relational and institutional thickness, forged by long histories of familiarity, economic practice, and social collaboration (real or not), that prevails in other parts of the city. This multiplicity of frictional retentions exerts a force, even if this force exists as a powerful myth about strange infrastructural occurrences.

In this way the megacomplex may operate not so much as the antagonist to the historical pluri-districts, or as their extension, but rather as some part-object, neither part of these districts nor apart from them—as a space in between. Perhaps it exists as some monstrous figure that the districts themselves had a hand in creating, something that takes on the work that is perhaps too dangerous for them to do but is ultimately part of the long tradition of speculation they have undertaken, which, like any speculation, threatens to get out of hand.

This, after all, may be the work of the near-South. It takes all of the models of efficiency, rightness, and supermodernity and twists them around, usually ever so slightly. In the process, it raises questions about what the city really is, how it really works, and reflects attention back to all those parts of the city that residents pieced together themselves, however problematic they may have been and continue to be.

] 2 [

THE URBAN MAJORITY
Improvised Livelihoods in Mixed-up Districts

Inventing a Majority

If I posit a provisional concept such as the near-South in order to explore a momentary in-between existence for the major metropolitan regions of the "non-West," the importance of this exercise rests partly in its also opening up exploration of urban relationality in general. What does it mean to be a collective, to operate within a collective relationship, in situations where the predominant terms of representation are inadequate to the local realities, but where emergent terms of self-representation are either too provisional or too marginalized to secure substantial traction or consensus? Given the variegated histories of specific regions and their articulations to national and global circuitries, the metropolitan areas I consider have always had to draw on a multiplicity of logics. They have done so in order to adjust to projects of development that have continuously concretized tensions and contradictions in the use of space and resources.

In many cities of the near-South, policy making and projects of development and the resourcefulness of resident livelihood formation have largely been elaborated as parallel, untranslatable worlds. It is self-evident that neither is sufficient without the other, although the terms of articulation are seldom apparent or consistent. The articulations and divides are full of complexities and deceptions: histories of apparent resourcefulness have often raised more problems than they have addressed (infusing cities with untenable degrees of complexity and dispersal). What often look like substantial assets of social capital, democratic practice, and social collaboration can be highly murky maneuvers of opportunism and trickery. Policy making is not always a reflection of capture to elite interests or an instrument of capital reformation. The categories I use to describe processes, actions, and decisions on the part of different social and institutional actors are usually too stark and deliberate, not reflective of the complicities, exchanges, and imitations that constantly take place among actors and sectors that seem essentially different.

At the same time, there have been protracted periods during which the intersection of officially private actors created a sense of public welfare that exceeded what the existing state was capable of. It is certainly possible to specify clear trajectories of systematic neglect, underdevelopment, and preferential treatment, as well as substantially divergent costs, rights, and opportunities. But these are processes that are mediated through mechanisms, alliances, financing, and practices that are not strictly public or private or always the privileges exerted by a clearly constituted class or regime. Distorted advantages, segregation, impoverishment, highly differentiated collective consumption, and democratic deficits may all appear, but the processes that enable them to have particular traction and form in a particular urban region may involve markedly different political and cultural arrangements.

If we are to try to reach for more inventive concepts and explorations of urban relationality, where should we begin? All of the cities I discuss here have demonstrated a capacity to generate pluralized urban formations, whether it be in particular histories of autoconstruction, capacities to enroll diverse ways of life or populations into loosely configured projects of political influence that slip through the crevices of bureaucracies and power brokers, or whether it be in particular constellations of seemingly unrelated economic activities capable of providing employment over time or in the mobilization of sentiment that protects specific cultural practices or ways of being in the city. These ways of being in the city often suggest interrelationships among bodies, things, infrastructures, materials, spaces, and languages that are radically different from those that are operative in the "normal" urban world. They point to a circulation, not necessarily of self-contained subjects and citizens moving through different dimensions and times of the city, but an intermeshing of different life-forms and materials that generates circuits of transaction and association that operate transversally across defined territories and sectors (Coward 2012). The existence of such urban formations raises what Foucault (2008) has called "the problem of multiplicities."

I propose that these domains and practices of resourcefulness can be considered under the heuristic figure of "the urban majority." As used here, *majority* does not refer to a social demographic group, a political statistic, a class in the making, or a community to come. It is not just a sociological figuration. To a certain extent, its use here is homologous to the notion of class elaborated by E. P Thompson (1968), as a structure of feeling used as a means of building relationships among people of distinct occupations, who attempt to find in each other a means of thinking through and responding to changing conditions in the societies in which they live. The notion also points to human actors who have participated, wittingly or unwittingly, in the constellation of urban environments whose intricacies depend on the densification of techniques—the intermixing of measures, angles, calculations, impulses, screens, surfaces, soundscapes, exposures, folds, circuitries, layers, tears, and inversions—as instruments for associating things, bringing things into association, where things get their "bearings" by having "bearing" on each other. As such, the density of the city is not just that of human bodies but also of the multiplicity of possible associations among bodies and various materials. While these associations have been subject to various political technologies of governance and control, there has always been in these cities something that slips through, leaks out, overflows, or generates long shadows.

Not dissimilarly to Rancière's (2010) notion of a people not subjected to any particular count, the urban majority does not make itself known or decipherable through specific modes of calculation. For example, if many residents have to largely assume the responsibility of supplementing their incomes, making their own livelihoods, or finding ways to insert themselves into economic and social activities of scale, they sometimes do this by reshaping their aspirations, skills, self-reflections, and social networks through the very ways in which they build, respond to, adapt to, and rearrange their material environments—in a kind of ongoing reciprocal feedback loop.

The identities and capacities of residents then are never fixed, or are fixed only under specific analytical gazes, in which images and impressions are not interoperable. Specific shared interests and vernaculars of recognition come to the fore that enable the articulation of particular demands and form an anchorage point or target for the application of particular policies, mobilization, and ideological engagement. But across most cities of the near-South, the concrescence of political subjectivity and the stabilization of constituencies over time ebb and flow—never entirely formed or dissipated, but porous and tentative (Berner and Korff 1995; Haber 2006; Konings, van Dijk, and Foeken 2006; Lovell 2006; McFarlane 2007; Bayat 2009; Lindell 2010).

The notion of "the urban majority" carries with it not only a sense of a provisional subject formation—a sense that is incumbent in operating outside or aside from the "official" contexts of building infrastructure, livelihood, and economic and political power. The designation also points to the capacity, across cities, for residents to carry with and among them a wide range of manifestations, outcomes, and vehicles through which to enact concepts and maneuvers at times antagonist, complicit, or supplemental to the predominant ways of doing things, as exhibited by government, private capital, or powerful families and clans. What the majority do is never "one thing"—never strictly compliant, complicit, or confrontational. As they take up a larger number of profiles, practices, opportunities, and spaces that otherwise are not available to the poor, the elite, or a growing middle class, they come to exude a connotation of "a majority"; they embody a "majority" of what the existent city could be at that moment in time, as well as what it could potentially become.

In some cities "the urban majority" is an actual majority, as it is in Jakarta. That is, residents who are neither strictly poor nor middle-class—who live within a highly differentiated "in-between"—make up the majority of inhabitants of the city. I do not offer this as some overarching justification for the use of this term, but simply to point to the ways in which the various kinds of resourcefulness that exist in different ways across cities have largely been occluded. At times, this occlusion would seem to leave out "most" of the city—that is, leave out the practices and logics most residents use to make the city work for them. Additionally, as cities are situated in the fulcrum of various contestations and unresolved tensions in relationships among popular beliefs, colonial pasts and postcolonial imaginaries, economic trajectories and the pragmatics of administration, there is a tendency to use the built environment as a means of intentionally forgetting these tensions, to defer them by undermining the spatial languages through which they had been recognized (Abbas 2000; Legg 2008).

Circumventing Territory

What is striking about the centrally located and nearby suburban heterogeneous districts of the near-South is the degree to which they are the homes of large numbers of nurses, transportation workers, civil servants, teachers, salespersons, police officers, security guards, office workers, and shopkeepers. Most are neither poor nor "solidly" middle-class—in the sense that they can derive economic security solely from a single job or that they are immune from any interruptions in their earning capacities. This does not mean that the majority cannot access sufficient funds for education, health, recreation, automobiles, or even limited investments. Many households live modestly yet have significant disposable incomes. These districts contain a great deal of purchasing power, a capacity that cannot easily be attributed solely to the occupations, livelihoods, or household histories of the residents. Opportunism, an increasingly important value, has long been a feature of these districts, and who plies such opportunism well is often more a matter of chance than of preparation or skill.

Most households have long depended on engagement with economic activities that supplement the income earned at ordinary jobs. Such activities include providing rental accommodations (most often to incoming migrants), running small businesses, selling services, and going in with others on schemes of various kinds and duration, from which proceeds are shared among the "investors." Many of these supplemental activities—as well as many full-time occupations—are "off the books," so their efficacy often depends on various forms of brokerage and intermediation. This dependency in turn fosters clientelism, but more often it produces local political arrangements that are open—with an emphasis on keeping various possibilities from being foreclosed. Residents rely on brokers to get officials to look the other way, not enforce regulations or bylaws, or put money into particular infrastructure or services. But it is also usually important for residents not to feel overly obligated to anyone. Already ensconced in

Tanah Sereal, a "majority" district.

hierarchies, associations, and ethnic or regional affiliations—which reinforce solidarity and obligation—they can easily get stuck in obligation and lose the sense of mobility they need to continuously access and revise informal economic activity (Abeyasekere 1987; Davis 1994; Grillo 2000; Dick et al. 2002; Perlman 2004, 2011; Secor 2004; Smart and Lin 2007; Telles and Hirata 2007; McFarlane 2008a, 2008b; Singerman 2009; Srinivas 2010; Bissell 2011).

Part of the issue regarding these occlusions in representation concerns the very notion of middle-class identity, associated as it is with individuation, self-sufficiency, privacy, and moral integrity. A middle-class household is supposed to assume the status of a corporate identity, styling itself with a sense of autonomous action, continuous improvement and attainment, and the moral capacity to make decisions predicated on what is best for the corporate unit (Rose 2000). The instantiation of the capacity for accumulation in any conceivable setting will lend itself to the organization of the corporate household unit. But to focus only on this dimension is to neglect the ways in which middle-class households, as integral parts of highly heterogeneous districts, seek not necessarily to integrate themselves with others but to establish a functional copresence.

The mechanics of such copresence have much to do with orientations toward notions of territory and the ways in which the urban majority historically has circumvented the institutionalization of its residential and commercial settings as "territory" in order to secure itself in the city. Territory is the creation of space as an instrument through which authority is exercised, an arena of command. Territory is a vehicle that occasions the application of various strategies, such as mapping, ordering, measuring, and demarcating, to establish terms of recognition and differentiation among inhabitants and spaces. It specifies the circulations and interchanges that are allowed and normalized through calculation—that is, what can take place and under what circumstances, and what value different activities and persons have in relationship to one another (Rolnik 1999; Elden 2010).

Political interests and actions certainly do emerge. Residents are often vociferous in their demands and in their identities. But the politics of everyday living are often opaque, reflecting a need to keep the playing field open. This attitude could be complicit with the murkiness and corruption of municipal administrations and may contribute to the long-term vulnerability of residents by not solidifying specific forms of accountability and decision making. Yet it also precludes the crystallization of power as the purview of particular kinds of local residents. Ethnic affiliations and other long-term histories of association often cross the apparent relational divides separating the middle class, the working class, and the poor. But this crossing also requires continuously improvised "venues" of collaboration.

Here, residents work out problems that arise as they undertake multiple initiatives to improve their situations or to seize opportunities when they can, often by coming up with new things they can do together—usually without it looking like they are doing these things together, since no contracts or accords are signed or officially deliberated. For example, if too many residents are getting involved in the same economic activity, and thus shrinking the numbers of customers for all, "scouts" are sent to look for areas outside the district where different "branches" of this activity might be inserted. This process relies on residents' ability to put together the different networks needed to establish the relevant contacts that make this branching possible. This practice might prove difficult if local politics were more formalized or normatively democratic (Cooper 1983; Eckstein 2001; Law 2002; Dikeç 2005; Haber 2006; Harriss 2006; Bayat 2007; Dill 2009; Hunt 2009; Khondker 2009; Kudva 2009; McFarlane 2009; Aksit 2010; Beasley-Murray 2010; Garmany 2010; Maricato 2010; Nielsen 2010; Pine 2010; Elyachar 2011; Marques 2011).

This is not a politics of identity; in fact, many residents of such districts are indifferent toward, even reluctant about, using democratic competition as a means to attain functional balances among different identities. However strongly residents may feel about the identities they carry with them, they do not activate these identities in daily life as if they were some format or program specifying what people should do or how they should think about what they do. Perhaps homologous to development systems theory, relations with the surrounds are part and parcel of the self-constitution of residents themselves in a process of systemic contingency. Individuals and their surrounds are cospecifying interactants embedded in expansive networks of relations among things—material, discursive, biological, ecological, and symbolic. The outcomes of interactions depend on contingent actions that derive from changes in the intensities of how various networks are linked. A sense of regularity is important; this is not a world where everything can be unpredictable (Oyama 2000).

But this regularity stems from reciprocal maneuvers on the parts of residents, pushing and prompting in crowded conditions to discover grounds of similarity—something recognized as sufficiently common to work with. The basis of similarity rests not in people's identities but in what people are trying to do. Control is not centralized and concentrated in a capacity to incorporate different actors as elements of some overarching program that assigns functions and responsibilities; rather, it is continuously transferred. In other words, every time relationships among actors are altered, prompting potential changes in individuals themselves, these changes bring a wider range of influences into play—ways in which individuals affect others and can be affected. In such a process, control is distributed throughout the system, with all of its concomitant blocks and unevenness.

A politics of representation leans toward a sense of stability based on the detailing of particular features. These features become the terms through which diverse experiences and individuals are subsumed. Those organized under a particular form of representation then seek to have it inserted in a particular arena of decisions and action. Those so organized seek to make themselves count—to make themselves significant through a process of establishing "how many" (residents) can be legitimately encompassed by a particular representation. This counting ensures that any deliberation takes into consideration the "core" of what constitutes a specific identity, excluding responsibilities, obligations, and participation based on conclusions that certain realities and matters are "not for us," not consonant to "our" values or ways of life. While representational politics has been an important device for facilitating the consolidation of individual and collective effort and for the translation of experiences and sensibilities across various social divides, in the urban districts of Jakarta it has often been perceived as limiting capacities for adaptation. It is also perceived as a way in which political actors at higher municipal levels play off identities against one another or justify their own actions or inaction because of the threats that one group may pose to another.

It is important for a locality to have some sense about "how many are we," but the importance does not lie in the consolidation of a count—of mobilizing the many into a more powerful "one." Rather, the question of "how many are we" concerns the possibility of distinct residents being able to reach each other, to have something to grasp—to be able to hold in place, however momentarily, the possibilities of mutual reachability as the tool that enables a sense of belief and conviction. As Latour (2005) indicates, the question of "how many" concerns the possibility of giving individuals "another turn"—another handle they can use to make space for themselves or, more precisely, to extend themselves through space, as selves that can feel and be affirmed through the dissipation of fixed boundaries.

Additionally, in urban settings representational politics is limited by the very changes affected within the built environment as an outcome of residents' efforts to both create spaces of maneuver for themselves and construct a working sense of stability. A district may have a specific genealogy. For example, it may have originated from a state-initiated project to allocate land to civil servants from a particular ministry, or it may have become the domain of workers in a particular industry or sector. Its economic or residential corridors may have developed along specific transportation routes, across public lands, or at the periphery of planned developments. A district's genealogy may account for how households gained access to basic residential opportunities, but it often does not tell us much about what the households eventually did with that access.

The Importance of the Incremental

The notion of the urban majority is also temporal; it is a particular sense of the timing of things, of when to move, decide, and implement. Across heterogeneous central-city and nearby suburban areas in many cities of the near-South, there has been an intensive focus on the incremental, on doing things in small stages and seeing how these efforts might relate to initiatives coming from neighbors, friends, and relatives (McFarlane 2011).

In urban development work, *incrementalism* usually refers to the development of residential areas one step at a time. In many so-called sites-and-services projects, states or developers plot out pieces of land and provide minimal basic infrastructure, and then residents construct homes and extensions on the land as their incomes permit. While in Jakarta *incrementalism* also refers to practices of self-construction a "little bit at a time," the term entails other strategic sensibilities as well.

First, there is the urgency on the part of many residents to do something, anything, to signal their willingness to work with others to help shape their neighborhoods. Whatever the individual intentions of a household might be, residents want to make it clear that they will try to adjust those intentions to the needs and aspirations of other residents. Changes such as the acquisition of plots, the construction of new thoroughfares, the extension of existing built structures, and the opening or remaking of commercial sites prompt discussions across the neighborhood. Residents undertake modest initiatives, without overly risky investments, as a means of eliciting feedback, to learn what others are thinking. Many times, reactions to these initiatives are not so much verbalized as "countered" or complemented by the initiatives of others. The proliferation of these "facts on the ground"—which sometimes do not fit well together, usurp common space, or violate protocols—then leads to adjustments, compensation, or repair. All of these are activities that bring people together, whether to work out conflicts (as when initiatives are withdrawn or ignored) or to join forces and find ways for the initiatives to work together.

Second, incremental initiatives serve as communicational devices indicating that residents recognize the uncertainties of their tenure. While many residents have sufficient documentation to lay claim to specific pieces of property, Indonesia's land laws make no provision for absolute freehold title. Faced with a government that is frequently erratic in its approach to urban development and an economy prone to marked fluctuations, residents are compelled to find ways of adding value to what they have. While finding specific ways to enhance available assets is largely a household matter, using these assets as means of enhancing security is also a collective endeavor, a matter of building practical solidarities that do not draw extensive attention to themselves or require too much time or effort to keep together. Here, incrementalism acts as a feedback loop of give-and-take, of residents working together in an atmosphere of muted visibility—signaling reciprocities and mutuality without necessarily giving overt voice to them.

Over time, residents' initiatives—incremental, individual, collaborative, short- and long-term—have exerted a substantial effect on the built environment. In some areas of Jakarta, for example, every street and lane is characterized by a hodgepodge assemblage of buildings old and new, single story and multistory, with all kinds of materials and design styles being put to use. While districts may contain mixtures of residences, single rooms for rent, commercial buildings, storage facilities, recreational spaces, and churches and mosques throughout, these mixtures take on variable forms and emphases block by block. Residents are thus embedded in a built environment that facilitates or constrains particular comings and goings, visibilities and vantage points, soundscapes, inputs and evacuations of raw materials and waste, and public exposure and private containment.

Within these environments specific kinds of witnessing and other social transactions are supported or restrained, as these environments outline possible trajectories of movement and proximity. Intensities of light, heat, circulation, volatility, tension, ease, amicability, and alarm are also modulated—so that no matter the backgrounds of residents, what they themselves have largely constituted in turn "puts them together" as particular kinds of persons, individual and collective. Close to what Gabriel Tarde's sociology indicates, simi-larities among them are attained through a mimesis of inclinations (Barry and Thrift 2007). In Jakarta, many neighborhoods specialize in particular economic activities, or in the use of particular designs, materials, ways of speaking, or spending available money. If you ask the residents of a neighborhood how its specialization came about, you may find a local historian who will render a seemingly convinc-ing account of the initial basis for the specialization. But as to how it spread, most residents will simply talk about how it just "took off," as if in a kind of contagion, without protracted planning, negotiation, or cost-benefit analysis. Here, the use of incremental initiatives does not usually aim for some definitive objective. Rather, the aim is to make something happen; the probable outcome is not clear, but it is likely to be "amenable" to being shaped by the common contributions of diverse residents.

In the Karanganyar and Kartini districts of central Jakarta, for example, specific ethnic backgrounds predominate: Javanese, Suda-nese, and Chinese Indonesian. The territorial consolidations of these groups are distributed in small segments, so that distinct ethnic groups are always living in close proximity to each other. Likewise, there are various concentrations of power, such as decentralized local authorities that sometimes operate extensive patronage games, as well as branches of the major Islamic organizations, including Muhammadiyah, Nahdlatul Ulama, Hizbut Tahrir, and Islam Lib-eral Network, covering the full spectrum of theological and political tendencies. Additionally, there are extrajudicial groups such as the Forum Betawi Rempug (FBR; Betawi Brotherhood Forum); these are nominally focused on ethnic interests but together act as a fulcrum for a wide range of agendas. All of the institutional elements partici-pate in shifting alliances and enmities. While they may dominate par-ticular neighborhoods or sectors, they act more as nodes in circuits of exchange across different territories, subject to ebbs and flows of influence, membership, and program.

With roughly seventy-five thousand residents, these are old dis-tricts just to the north of the Golden Triangle—the area of the city completely remade through superblock development and the elabora-tion of a new central business district. The districts are folded into a vast interior of old but still dynamic commercial and market areas,

A street in Karang Anyer, central Jakarta, with its dense intersections of materials and uses pieced together incrementally over time. This district is well-known for its small-scale economic dynamism as well as for the assertive practices its residents use in continually creating new schemes and new ways of being in the city.

with scores of small lanes of three- to ten-story houses. Overall, the districts seem dilapidated, despite widespread efforts to maintain well-tended and thoroughly greened lanes, but they are replete with residents of diverse economic backgrounds, occupations, and educational levels. For example, in our surveys we found similar percentages in categories of school leavers—from elementary, secondary, and tertiary stages—across the two districts.

Because the provision of rental accommodation is such a key element of many household incomes, a single property may include residents of very different social and work backgrounds. As sections of Kartini are the territories of long-term Chinese Indonesian entrepreneurs, some of whom have substantially regenerated their residential areas while others barely hold on, the density of these areas reproduces economic patronage networks. These networks generate a significant volume of jobs, even as they are often objects of resentment among non–Chinese Indonesian traders and entrepreneurs. Situated within the borders of an area containing the city's largest automobile and motorcycle parts and repair business, many residents participate in various facets of this trade—and it is indeed a trade with multiple facets and specializations.

Particularly significant are the practices through which related households or neighborhood networks cultivate niche activities within this trade, such as refurbishing used cars, panel beating, customizing parts for hybrid engines, converting automobile parts (metal, fabric, cables) into other applications, selling illicitly obtained parts, and leasing motorcycles—to name a few. Households often have various affiliates circulating through the different facets of this trade. So, for example, a family in the trade would not be inclined to consolidate a business that integrates within it multiple facets of the trade. Rather, the family would attempt to make its mark in one particular specialization and then have some family members access positions in numerous others. In this way, a family network maximizes its points of exposure to various relational networks and opportunities, preparing it to shift gears—invest different resources, change emphasis—when needed or opportune, as well as minimizing the risk of the family's putting all its eggs in one basket. These are strategic maneuvers that emphasize mobility through various networks, interfaces, vantage points, and exposures. The experience of mobility—that is, the sense that one is actually going from one place to another, marking a space that is traversed—then necessitates a highly differentiated social field. If all residents were basically doing the same thing and in the same situation, transactions among them would not easily generate an experience of movement.

Traders, motorcycle drivers (ojek), shop owners (ruko), carters, repairers, craftspeople, textile workers, and office workers all operate in an overcrowded field. They face declines in purchasing power or profit margins, and therefore must try to supplement their primary incomes with other activities. Alternatively, they link existent incomes to other accumulation scenarios. In part, this is facilitated through the management of everyday local relationships among neighbors and others who operate within a district. Such management entails a series of reiterated practices. For example, neighbors are likely to act as if wide-ranging transgressions of official social conventions are not taking place; they also tend to assume that all local households have basically equivalent social standing and capacity to tend to their own viability, and that domestic affairs, whatever they are, are the purview of individual households and, as such, are not to be the objects of speculation or interference.

Of course, in reality something very different is taking place. Managing local relations, then, is not simply a matter of navigating the different information and potential opportunities that a diverse field of occupations and network positions brings. It also entails engaging with the very different stories and trajectories of household accumulation and loss; of changing, lost, and new jobs; and of changing household affiliations and memberships. These are the very materials through which districts are able to reconfigure themselves and rearrange their overall relationships to the larger city. If a family faces a prolonged financial crisis and must sell their property, neighboring households may acquire it and rent it back to the family or redevelop it for an alternate use—such as a workshop or business. They may upscale its residential value and then find alternative accommodation within the immediate area for the family that sold the property. Here there is an incessant recalibration of accumulation and loss. Individuals may try to consolidate their economic and/or political standing within a district by pursuing new trajectories of accumulation, but this gain in stature is often reinvested into the development of economic opportunities outside the district for local neighbors and associates.

An examination of changes in the built environment in similar districts across the near-South over the past decades reveals that they are replete with diverse initiatives. These initiatives mirror one another, not so much in the content of the changes they register but in their embodiment of an incremental process. Households rarely stand still with what they initially acquire or have access to. Even at the level of the home, changes are made over time, and usually these changes are not exhaustive—in other words, households do not seek to reach particular goals or destinations all at once. Changes are piecemeal and informed by varying calculations and priorities.

Sometimes growing households need extra space to accommodate new members. Other times, households defer expanding their residential space in order to invest in small entrepreneurial activities, often converting available space or dedicating new expansions to those activities. Households initiate wide ranges of business, educational, and social projects, often with no clear end point in mind. The importance of this incremental activity lies in its usefulness for signaling to other households and individuals that a household is available for possible collaborations. A household must do something—maybe anything—within its means to indicate that its members are not going to stand still, that they are going to "put themselves out there," jockeying for opportunity, space, attention, and new possibility. Within this arena of contingency—where it is never clear what may ensue from the interactions of those participating—in addition to being able to shift gears and avoiding putting all their eggs in one basket, households need to be able to recognize the importance of the potential synergies of their initiatives with the initiatives of others.

Any initiative has to be steered through a complex environment of competing claims, skills, and aspirations. But more important, the impact of any single initiative may be exponentially increased if the initiative becomes an aspect or component of other initiatives. This happens not as the result of contractual relationships or implicit mutual obligations, but more from an approach to initiatives as mobile resources, things that households can use without precluding their usefulness to others. Collaboration here covers a wide array of possibilities, including residents simply paying attention to what others are doing in order to do something else, collective discussions about how to put different skill sets or contacts together to buttress largely individualized projects, implicit decisions on the part of residents not to interfere with each other's efforts, and residents running smoke screens for each other—pretending that certain conditions, events, or projects are under way when they are not in order to regulate the attention and (most likely deleterious) intervention of external actors. Of course, more formal agreements of cooperation may also be forged, but these tend to be rare, again because of the constraints they place on the mobility of efforts.

These notions are reflected in the comments of Bahwani, a long-term resident of the Menteng Dalam district in central Jakarta. In this district, according to Bahwani, collaboration is implicit, more a kind of underneath of things than an intentional practice. It is still something that enables a sense of dynamic change, but this change does not pose excessive threat to those who have lived and worked in the district for a long time. Neither does it deter outsiders from attempting to engage with these local sensibilities:

> We don't expect much from each other, but maybe that is why we can get along. I know people are going to do what they are going to do, but this way, I can at least hear them miles away; I can feel when a bad wind is coming, so I can step in another direction, let it pass; the thing here is that people have to keep their eyes and ears open, and this is not going to happen if people get too tied down expecting things or getting disappointed when they don't happen. I may not be as smart as the next person, but I can come up with the words or connections necessary to put a little extra on the table when I see something that others around me may not, and around here, as long as you don't interfere, a little curiosity and interest can go a long way. Everyone is putting himself on the line; it's not easy to have a project that probably won't succeed, so if you can offer a bridge to something that person had considered, well, that's like a line of credit at the bank. Maybe they'll offer something to you next time, but even if they don't, that's not important; this is not about obligations. All right, we're part of things, we're part of this place, but things sometimes go so fast in front of my eyes that I can't always say exactly what I am a part of, other than that this is my land, my house, and I am comfortable with it, and besides, where I am going to go? All this around this place, all of these big buildings, even if it is coming, even if it is going to get rid of us, for now, it keeps us from being too exposed; that's why some of these newcomers like this place; no one is paying too much attention, even though we spend most of our time looking at what goes on around us.

These opinions are echoed in other reflections as well. As Fendi, the twenty-nine-year-old head of a local village council in Kramat Sentiong, explains:

> If you look around here, it looks pretty messy and disorganized; people feel the need to always do something, and most of the time it doesn't really matter to them what it is, because the important thing is for you to show others that you are willing to do something, do something different. So people do what they can with

what they can afford, where they have connections to get hold
of the materials they need, and a lot of times the results are not
very pretty and don't work, so there are problems. But because
no matter how their efforts have worked or not, they have already let others know that they are willing to do things, and so
we, too, as a village council, can step in, see what's going on and
also ask others to get involved, either to fix things or help the
individual with a new project.

Ardhi, another member of the village council, added, "It's always a
matter of give-and-take; you look around and you can either see this
place as one big mess, a big construction site, or a place that is on its
way to becoming something really special; we don't know for sure
right now, but this situation where everyone seems to be going in a
million directions at once really keeps a lot of options open."

Residents continue to face many ethical struggles, none of which
are easily reconcilable. Threats of dispossession come from all sides,
as do possibilities of accumulation. Development agendas and practices at the metropolitan level can result in eviction, take-it-or-leave-it
formulas of compensation, revaluation of assets, or the introduction
of deleterious changes to the immediate environment. Unrestrained
incursions on both public and private space can emerge from a nebulous grass roots, and flexible livelihood practices can be manipulated
by an assortment of criminal organizations that exert monopolistic
control over local space and resources.

In part, these ethical dilemmas explain why mobility has become
a critical value for many residents of these heterogeneous "majority"
districts—mobility not so much in terms of physical movement or
moving up the social ladder, but in terms of an ability to circulate
through various vantage points, relationships, networks, sources of
information, and interpretations. This circulation brings new angles
to bear on decisions focused on balancing what are often experienced
as conflicting agendas, exigencies, and values. While many incremental efforts entail sunk costs and commitments to see certain projects
through to their conclusion, some residents try to avoid such efforts.
Their emphasis is more on configuring temporary arrangements—
perhaps sharing some resource or space, going in with other residents
to acquire discounted assets, or helping others concretize specific

building or entrepreneurial projects—so that participants can easily move away from them.

Residents enter into such arrangements as ways of testing the waters, expanding their personal or household networks, or creating incentive for others to help them with as-yet-unspecified future projects. Whatever the content of these arrangements, they operate as platforms from which to move, and so the participants try not to incur any long-term obligations, implicitly giving each other room to maneuver and not continuously consulting or attaining consensus over the work they do together.

The Reluctant Pursuit of Being Middle-Class

Let us assume for the moment that "being middle-class" is defined as participating in a predominantly individuated household strategy of livelihood and accumulation not dependent on collaborations with others in a shared residential space. This is in contrast to the usual definitions involving purchasing power and income levels, which multilateral institutions such as the World Bank and the Asian Development Bank stretch across a fairly wide range. Just to cite one example, the Asian Development Bank (2010) defines being middle-class as having a consumption level of two dollars to twenty dollars per day (in purchasing power parity terms). So if I am focusing here on residents who are neither strictly poor nor middle-class, then I am talking about the probable "majority" of residents of cities of the near-South. I am not concerned here with the majority as a statistical count or with the assumptions one would then make about how that majority shows up in democratic urban governance. Rather, I am interested in the majority as a way of thinking about how residents use and modulate their exposure to divergent processes of urbanization.

At times, residents have to make clear statements and claims about who they are, what they stand for, and what they are willing to do. At other times, they try to fashion their ways of doing things so as to maximize their points of contact with networks and experiences that they do not have easy access to or that they lack significant knowledge about. In doing so, they sometimes have to find ways of working with residents whom their values and identities would seem to rule out, because, in order to keep pace with the changes in the city, they need new sources of information and skill. All of these dimensions cannot be brought together into a ready-made composite. This does not mean that these divergences cannot be reconciled, modulated, or explained, but the forms of intersection that they take may themselves have to vary continuously, changing shape to work in given contexts and at particular times (Kusno 2010).

This is a process partially shaped through the intersection of urban modernization, coloniality, and other more transversal spatialization among variegated practices of rule, trade, cultural transmission, and the circulation of information, bodies, and power. In the interstices of these intersections, the majority live through entangled relations with others of different backgrounds and capacities. They consolidate territorial and social distinctions, while at the same time incorporating each other into differentiated understandings of what it takes to survive in the city. The commonality of those understandings is that any practice, idea, or agenda of inhabitation is never going to be sufficient for cities that themselves are largely perceived as projects that are continuously incomplete. Formal wages are never going to be enough in the long run; labor markets and workers' rights can never be adequately stabilized, so residents have to find ways to insert themselves in each other's lives. They do so through continuous appeals for cooperation, supplication, manipulation, and deal making of all kinds (Holston 1991; Askew 1994, 2002; Berner and Korff 1995; Jacobs 1996; Benjamin 2000; Hansen 2001; Bunnell 2002; Chatterjee 2004; Konings, van Dijk, and Foeken 2006; Lovell 2006; Fawaz 2008; Legg 2008).

The majority certainly aspire to many of the same things that have informed the residential and livelihood choices of residents throughout North America and Europe. They aspire to a more secure life, one that mitigates the need to engage in incessant improvisation or undue negotiations to attain a sense of stability. Most residents of São Paulo and Jakarta, for example, want to acquire the "good things" of life and often find themselves in debt because of their efforts to do so. "Being with the world" demands continuous acquisition, and the more things one acquires, the seemingly less need one has to participate in socially intensive engagements, particularly in one's area of residence.

At the same time, in conducting some four hundred household interviews in central Jakarta, I found that many residents are reluctant to pursue the trappings of middle-class success even when they have the income to do so. While they may worry about declining infrastructure, inflated land values, and a loss of neighborhood feeling, they hesitate to move away from their neighborhoods because they see that the available choices would leave them with far fewer opportunities. Social relations may be increasingly difficult and parasitical in their current neighborhoods, demographic changes may exceed the residents' ability to keep track of what is going on, and conflicts over how space and resources are to be used may grow messier. But together the materials of the built environment, the different histories of residence, the still-varied local economies, and the scores of different "players" and authorities provide what residents need to work with in terms of hedging, supplementing, and securing their livelihoods (Lora 2010; United Nations Human Settlements Programme 2010).

Housing markets across these cities try to draw residents into high-rise, lifestyle-promoting, all-amenities-provided housing developments. The relative ease of entry into these developments—which offer highly discounted prices, low-interest financing, and short-term leasing arrangements—and the comforts of anonymity are pulling people in, but those who have lived in the developments for some time report feeling increased anomie and disconnection from the larger city. Because everything they need, perhaps with the exception of work, is immediately present, their circulation through the city is limited. Although they may find it beneficial to avoid such circulation—which, especially in megacities, can be arduous and time-consuming—some megadevelopment residents describe having an increased sense of being cut off from others and limited in terms of their overall life options.

While developers have anticipated some of these reactions and have tried to mitigate them by infusing their complexes with social, recreational, civic, religious, and training opportunities, these sometimes serve only to reiterate the "leveling" of sociality in a heightened degree of sameness. Part of this sameness reflects the exigencies of consumer demand. As the 2012 Colliers International real estate market report for Jakarta indicates, present levels of development can add somewhere between fifty thousand and sixty thousand new residential units every year, but the potential demand exceeds two hundred thousand and is increasing yearly.

Speculations and Uncertain Futures

Even as historic districts persist with a highly differentiated temporal mix of middle-class stability, decline, renewal, new investment,
and construction, there is a persistent tendency to characterize these
mixed districts as districts of the poor. Repeatedly, popular representations indicate that the middle class has already left, moved to
new residential districts farther from the center or to the large apartment blocks. But any cursory overview of these districts reveals that
they include stable, even expanding, middle-class developments. While
such expansions may participate in the same speculative sentiment
that characterizes high-end developments and may be driven by a particular set of actors (such as Indonesian Chinese, with their long history of access to mortgage finance), that does not necessarily obviate
their integration into various circuits of local interchange. Additionally, many middle-class residents of historic districts have large sunk
costs—economic, social, and emotional—in particular sites. Even
if they could sell their property at high prices, they cannot afford
longer home-to-work commute times or diminished access to the networks of reliable labor and services they have built over the course of
their long-term residence. As escalating property taxes, particularly
in high-value areas, exert untenable pressures on certain households,
the great need for accommodation enables them to convert property
into multiple dwellings that then subsidize their continued residence.

No doubt, many of the historically heterogeneous districts are
in trouble. Physical environments are overtaxed. Infrastructures are
often no longer capable of responding to incessant local repair. Environmental irritants are increasingly noticeable, and residents are
losing their capacity to exert influence over each other so as to prevent
things from getting out of hand. The compulsion of households to do
something—to launch some new project, create some new earning
power—often comes with an intensified arrogance and disregard for
the feelings of others. So districts become implicitly more competitive
and more crowded—both with people and in terms of the agendas
and efforts residents make to get ahead. The local institutions—or,
more specifically, the particular assemblies of interests—that formerly exerted some influence in sorting all these out are hampered by
waning commitments and new generations convinced of the need to
maximize their mobility at any cost. In other words, groups that came

together originally to address particular concerns in ways that gave voice and consideration to a wide range of opinions and options—mosque committees, artisanal groupings, informal local security patrols, local government officials, ethnic associations, savings clubs, prayer groups, and women's and youth clubs—may continue to exist, but they have become increasingly particularized and pursue specific parochial interests. Thus the management of district affairs is implicitly outsourced to groups of "strongmen" or more powerful business interests that work hand in hand with local military and police officials to extract and manipulate local assets.

While speculation has always played a large part in the incremental efforts that residents undertake, such speculation is largely "domesticated" in its emplacement among many different individualized initiatives that have to find their way through, around, and with each other in order to be actualized. Initiatives are embedded in a context of multiple trials and errors that keep excessive claims and ambitions in check. But as the larger city changes and displays new forms of the spectacular and publicizes the abilities of some residents to get rich quickly, speculation across the city—from rich to poor—becomes more untamed. Shadow banking systems and unregulated loans at high interest rates fund projects with limited long-term viability. In one district where I work, Kemayoran—the site of one of the city's most vibrant informal night markets—a group of investors attempted to construct a small shopping mall for small retail outlets, basically replicating the night market but at much higher cost. The result has been a continuous 95 percent vacancy rate. In another example, an investor built a large building intended to house hundreds of small textile-related workshops in a district where hundreds of such outfits already exist in people's homes. Based on some fantasy of generating new interlinkages, the idea was to get textile workers to congregate in this center; what the investor failed to understand was that even in this home-based industry, many different forward-and-backward relationships already existed, and people saw little reason to pay rent to relocate their operations.

While speculation may too often focus on get-rich-quick schemes, it is also sometimes directed toward taking underutilized or degenerated infrastructure and making something work from it. There may not be any viable ideas that can convert these experiments into immediately profitable or sustainable enterprises, but in some way they do embody a needed effort to scale up initiatives so that local districts might play a bigger role in the city's economic and social life.

As multiple household initiatives are capable of adding economic and social depth—a thickness of interconnection and support—to local districts, the sustainability of such districts in today's globalized networks of implication is reliant on the residents' ability to find ways of exerting impact within and over their larger surrounds. The emphasis on incremental development reflected in local economies—initiatives affecting each other as they seek some way to implant themselves and then use that implanting as a platform to reach still other resources and opportunities—remains a vital element in this upscaling. The key issue is that as the assets to be attained grow more complex, visible, and far-reaching, notions of proprietorship, security, and value also become more complex.

In the past, these notions could be worked out informally or within the implicit understandings of localized associations, networks, or institutions. Today, however, new modalities of ownership, investment, and profit sharing may be required to adapt local infrastructures—both social and physical—to urban region economies increasingly staked to the rapid expansion of the middle class and the provision of premium services to a globalized economy. These may include designating areas for collective or cooperative tenure, converting decaying but still viable commercial infrastructure into cooperatively held work and living spaces, including zoning and tax abatement provisions for community-planned local economic development areas, and decentralizing the ownership and management of local traditional markets. As indicated earlier, much of what residents have been able to do incrementally with each other in terms of experimenting with new construction and commerce has been predicated on the ambiguities of land ownership and the impracticalities of enforcing zoning regulations. These practices have also been based on the ability of residents in lateral relationships among distinct economic practices to have the space to continuously observe each other and then work out specific collaboration projects that would come and go. These have been important conditions for the efforts of different kinds of residents, different aspects of the urban majority, to reach and familiarize themselves with each other, to concretize relationships of mutual feeling and perceived complementary interests.

As the urgency for official land registration, enforced spatial planning, high-rise density, and large commercial outlets intensifies—all with some aspects clearly promoting the public good—the historic districts will need new facilities and mechanisms that can connect residents from different walks of life to counter the individuating dimensions of these official changes.

Doing Things in Increments

Rafiq, one of the managers of Kalibata City, took me through one of the standard thirty-square-meter apartments that dominate this so-called superblock of nearly fourteen thousand residential units scattered across nineteen towers. The flat contained two windowless bedrooms no larger than small closets and a space that served as a combined kitchen and living area. The price had doubled in two years, from US$17,000 to US$34,000, and there were actually few units for sale, most having been sold prior to construction, then to be rented out to what Rafiq called the "majority of Jakartans looking for accommodation today, all of those who are neither poor nor middle-class, but somewhere in between. Places like this [Kalibata] are the future of the city, keeping those with limited but stable incomes close to their jobs and close to the center of city life."

Again, this "urban majority" is not a particular demographic, social, or political being but a heuristic placeholder, a means of talking about dynamic, continuously mutable collectivities of residents. The urban majority does not reveal itself all at once, nor does it act all at once, in some kind of unison. As I have attempted to show, such a majority acts through increments and "announces" itself a little bit at a time. Through a certain analytical lens, the components of these collectivities can be construed as stable particularities, with discernible identities, positions, histories, and inclinations. But, simultaneously, they can be construed as meaningful only through the intricate initiatives and adaptations they make in continuous interchanges with surrounds that are materially, economically, and socially heterogeneous. In other words, the components themselves must also be understood as trajectories of transience, of things continuously in the making,

Mass-produced housing for the lower middle class in Kalibata City in front of a traditional neighborhood cemetery. The border between them is occupied by small warung *(eating places) providing cheap food, in contrast to the restaurants inside the development.*

whose apparent stabilities of appearance take on new functions and meanings as they are continuously resituated in new constellations of relationships with other residents and the surrounding material and built environments.

This sense of the doubled—of the components as discernible both as entities with specific figuration and complexion and as plastic and malleable instruments of reworked constellations—is important, especially as the reality of a majority is being at last acknowledged by people like Rafiq and others across different sectors of government, business, and civil society. But if the majority is being addressed through built environments like Kalibata, rapidly constructed megawarehouses providing the barest necessities, this reflects the ways in which the conditions that have historically constituted and sustained such a majority may be eroded. If residential density becomes primarily a matter of affordable square footage on increasingly expensive central-city land, little thought is afforded to the kinds of relationships among residents that have prevailed across this central city for the past several decades. Here, through a continuous process of give-and-take and the interweaving of small and large initiatives that incrementally transformed built and social environments, residents elaborated spaces adept at keeping up with the changes under way in the larger city by generating new opportunities for accumulation, employment, and livelihood.

Responding to my incredulity that a family of five could dwell in such cramped quarters on the twenty-ninth floor, far removed from the streets that long served as the extension of living spaces for quarters that were always too small for growing households, Rafiq indicated that an apartment like this one was just the initial phase in an onward and upward trajectory. Young families, particularly, would save money and eventually afford more spacious surroundings. Besides, he said, residents in Asia's "most successful city" (Hong Kong) had long gotten used to living in such circumstances. Rafiq, too, had a certain idea of incrementalism in mind.

But the incremental in the history of Jakarta's urban majority usually encompasses a diverse range of practices. Instead of earnings, accumulation, and savings being directed toward a single developmental agenda or aspiration in an overarching maneuver of completion, the practice of the incremental is aimed at providing small supplements to whatever a household or individual has access to. These increments may be viewed as stages toward fulfillment of some larger goal, or they may be deployed as exploratory devices to see what opportunities or directions they might open up. Instead of committing resources and efforts to the realization of a "complete" project, these increments are instantiated to elicit particular kinds of attention and recognition.

Residences may be expanded or otherwise altered, small financial investments may be made in selling items in front of the house or in a wide range of other commercial ventures, and investments of time and effort may be made in running various social welfare or political programs as a means of testing waters, to show that residents are "on their way" somewhere or available for subsequent investments. The interest in eliciting attention and recognition is not so much to issue a signal that one has "arrived" at a particular status or destination. Rather, it is a way to make "something" happen without a clear notion about what exactly will happen as a result. The point is not to consolidate a position that then has to be defended, but to communicate that movement is under way, as well as to launch a ve-hicle through which an individual or household can move.

At times a household will initiate multiple increments as a means of covering a spectrum of needs, such as physical expansion of the family's living space and improvement of the household's livelihood. While the available resources, connections, and opportunities may be sufficient only to address one need at a given time, the household nevertheless spreads itself across multiple projects, knowing that only partial outcomes are possible. Here, the household is concerned with setting things in motion, creating trajectories of development that leave it little choice but to continue its efforts across multiple projects. At other times, multiple initiatives become ways of hedging bets. If one project—a small enterprise, a change in employment, involve-ment in a specific association or political party, the accommodation of additional family members, an attempt to elevate social status—does not work, then the household has already made investments in others that could potentially cover the losses or become steps along a concrete path to an alternate future.

In Jakarta, many districts founded with a certain commonality of population base, land certification, and economic development twenty to forty years ago have experienced marked internal differ-entiation. They are now replete with stories of accumulation and loss, of expansion and contraction. These stories are embodied in the shapes of land disposition and the built environment. Households that began with similar platforms of residency have pursued differ-ent forms of calculating and concretizing opportunity. For example, some have made investments in consolidating contiguous plots into facilities that combine residential and economic activities. Others have subdivided plots to accommodate expanding family size or sold off plots as residential expansion developed along a vertical trajec-tory. Some original pavilions have not been altered since their con-struction, while neighboring plots have seen owners, projects, and occupiers come and go. Single streets often display the inventories of discordant values embedded in the selection of materials used to sus-tain or remake built projects. The materials chosen for roofing, tiling, and frontage—ceramic, wood, tin, steel, cinder block, aluminum—reflect not only differences in affordability and assessment of environ-mental conditions but also social status and commitment.

Some residents aim for a "summation" of their living spaces—that is, they wait until they have the financial resources, certification, and permits to realize their projects all "at one go." Others "take their time," constructing things in stages, aiming to instantiate "facts on the ground"—that is, making additions that secure a fait accompli in terms of particular claims to land use or economic activity. They may not secure permission to build or operate but select ways of going ahead that convey the sense that erasing what they have done will be too complicated for everyone involved. If they are evicted, they do not incur debilitating financial loss or loss of prestige because they have not spent a great deal on the materials used. Still others may simply build slowly over time, adding some increments to a basic frame or multiplying the use of particular assets or spaces.

A Plurality of Surfaces, a Plurality of Stories

The differences in the surfaces of the built environment represent different stories, calculations, and ways of doing things. Yet, once concretized, these differences do not have to be used or apprehended in ways directly related to the histories these surfaces tell. While a given surface may have been produced from particular economic conditions and cultural practices, its existence as a surface is not dependent on them. The surface operates as its own series of relays, channels, and circuits that instantiate particular points of view, ways of doing things, and convictions among those who operate across this surface. It is a "de-signed" built environment, an act of fabrication in both senses of the word. It is something that is put together from available materials *and* something that need not tell the "truth" of a given situation, whether that situation refers to the process through which the built environment was constructed, what it was intended to be used for, or what use can be made of it.

Perhaps the easiest way to illustrate this point is through the example of Utan Panjang, a central-city district in Jakarta that is replete with differentiated surfaces. Utan Panjang was one of the first settled areas in the central eastern part of Jakarta and attracted large numbers of inhabitants of different backgrounds. A long-standing joke about the way the area was constructed is that the demarcations of plots and the designs of living spaces were so jumbled that residents kept waking up in the wrong bedrooms. Many different construction styles are seen in the district, and most plots have undergone successive rounds of remaking, readjusting, adding on, tearing down one house to completely remake another, and incessant division and consolidation. Again, all of these surfaces point to various stories about accumulation and loss, as well as multiple increments that have been elaborated, abandoned, or stalled. As is to be expected in an area of such intensely multiple histories, there is no easy fit among discrete components of this built environment. It is often difficult to discern where a particular construction or project begins or ends. Without room for horizontal expansion, residents often have to share spaces devoted to varying uses. Buildings that have an apparently lesser status because nothing has been done to them in decades suddenly become premium spaces for storing materials for workshops located in cramped upper-level apartment buildings or for accommodating local meetings.

The more recent consolidation of plots to build large single-family houses enclosed by high walls interrupts certain continuities in the built fabric. But these houses also constitute interstitial zones in the lanes and streets on which they are situated and on which certain economic ventures or local contestations are waged that might be too disruptive deeper into the crowded parts of the district. Accommodating new and temporary residents is a major economic activity across Jakarta. Residents often consolidate their living spaces into small portions of their homes in order to rent out rooms or parts of kitchens. In some instances, residents who share a lane will pool their money and buy a building in the local area and then either add on to the existing edifice or tear it down and construct a multistory dwelling; they then divide it up into rooms for rent, with each neighbor responsible for managing a particular portion of the building. At times neighborhoods do this to concentrate newcomers in intensive relationships with each other so that longtime residents can see what might occur in these dealings and how they might intersect with them. At other times, residents may insert a mosque into the residential fabric as a means of concentrating local interactions.

Residents continuously "play with" the textures of the surface; they connect wires and cables across different sites and kinds of ownership

Constructing a "complex" in Utan Panjang. This household space of many uses and styles has been made of materials available at different times.

and use; they fill in vacancies and recesses with provisional structures and activities; they "skip over" interruptions, blockages, and culs-de-sac to expand various projects. While the fabric can look—and indeed often is—chaotic, ill managed, and on the verge of collapse and overuse, it is also subject to incessant recalibrations, adjustments, and repair. In order to make discrepant uses and environments work together, residents need to engage in various negotiations and deals from which it is difficult to exclude particular inhabitants simply based on their backgrounds or identities. Identities, too, must be put into play; they become potential resources for the continuous process of working things out, of managing tensions and overloads. Spacing out the built environment requires that the facets of it remain available for repositioning. In other words, residents must set space aside so that they can enter into relationships beyond those delineated by official spatial plans, zoning, and land-use regulations, which—even if they apply—may not be functional for addressing local realities or getting residents to take them seriously.

Translation and Imaginary Crossings of the Divide

While the structural conditions of much of the near-South are well-known—the constraints of limited infrastructure, truncated governance systems, and insufficient scalar trajectories of economic activity—little research has examined how residents take what does exist and find ways of articulating it in order to assemble "machines of support" that generate income and opportunity. There is little understanding about processes of incremental effort or the calibration of expectations concerning what can work, what is viable, and when.

Thus processes of *translation* are important—translation not as a procedural rendering of something unfamiliar into the familiar, not the mechanics of equivalence, but more as a heuristic way of making connections across a divide. Take this example. Usually, individuals and households have particular ideas, norms, and cultural rules about how people and things are to be considered. Are they close to us, or are they far from us? Should we take them seriously or just not pay attention to them? There are people and groups with whom one can exchange things and to whom one can lend things, as well as forces and people that must be resisted. What I mean here by *translation* is a way of paying attention to what one's neighbors or associates, coworkers, friends, or acquaintances are doing, not with the familiar conceptualization of what a neighbor is or should be, but through creative conceptualizations that shift the conventional patterns of how distance, proximity, reciprocity, and resistance among people are orchestrated. Those who are familiar become something else. You are not quite sure what, and so you have to try different things on for size, or you have to not care so much what they think, or you hear them say the same old thing you've heard a million times before but now it makes a different kind of sense.

In the household surveys I conducted in three of Jakarta's central-city districts, I asked residents about how they perceived their neighbors and how well they knew them; I also asked about the content of their actual and potential transactions with neighbors. A common response was to report a limited knowledge of surrounding neighbors. "They are different from us" was a frequent refrain, with the difference at times attributed to a dissimilar job, ethnic background, or history of residence.

But just as important, this attribution of difference, this absence of substantial knowledge about the details of the surrounding residents' lives, did not necessarily foreclose a willingness to pay attention to each other, to discuss issues relevant to being a resident in the neighborhood, or even to spend substantial amounts of time with each other. "Even though our neighbors are different, doesn't mean we don't trust them; we don't need to know everything about them in order to appreciate them being here" was the reaction of Amina, the thirty-five-year-old owner of a small beauty salon.

What these responses point to is an important disjunction between the need to understand, or the need to compile a particular inventory of knowledge, and the ability of residents to make use of each other. Even when I inquired further into the nature of what perceived differences mean (What do the categories of difference, such as ethnicity or residential history, actually mean in terms of how neighbors lead their lives?), many residents were hard-pressed to substantiate specific areas of difference, such as the ways in which households might organize their domestic, financial, or larger social relationships. Instead, they at times insisted on difference regardless of what often appeared to be quite similar daily household practices.

Thus there appears to be a separation between understanding and association. In other words, residents did not feel the need to understand each other fully in order to consider collaborating with each other on a wide range of local projects. These projects might be neighborhood maintenance, programs for children and youth, income-generating projects such local gardening, the purchase of common items of consumption at wholesale prices, or the collation of neighborhood skills into neighborhood-run businesses.

When I asked residents about what the implications of knowing each other well might be, typical responses were similar to this one from Indri, a thirty-year-old high school teacher: "We would then always have to think about what we are doing and how we are doing it with the other people in mind; we would have a lot of obligations." Some respondents indicated that there would be a proliferation of misunderstandings and disputes. Rifki, the forty-three-year-old owner of a restaurant, stated: "If everybody sees themselves starting from the same starting point [being fundamentally linked and identified with each other], then we are going to have to look over our shoulder the whole time; we'll have little opportunity to make mistakes and to be free to do things differently than everyone else expects us to do." It appears that if a sense of basic difference is maintained, there is not only an attenuation of mutual obligations but also a sense of being able to use the act of paying attention to each other as a means to think about new opportunities and to gain access to new sources of information and impressions.

The Majority as Propositions

A key aspect of translation is the formulation of *propositions*. These propositions are not generated to represent what is really going on, or to make determinate judgments in a crowded field of representational possibility. They are not the best or most definitive renderings of what is taking place. Rather, as Alfred North Whitehead considered propositions, they are a form of definitiveness for actualities yet to be formed whose value is based on the correspondence between what is experienced as physically actual and what is conceptually felt as possible. Again, this is a matter of exploring ways in which the conditions people aspire to and struggle for are already evident, already operative in what it is they do. An urban majority may not have the concrete terms to represent and specify itself as a solid demographic fact or a political constituency in the making, yet it construes from its realities a sense of being able to act in concert even when the usual mechanisms for recognizing such action may not be available or even desired.

And so, without consistent recourse to class, ethnicity, or political affiliation through which to cohere a wide range of professions and histories, how do residents thrown together in cities, bringing together various walks of life and capacities, work out viable practices of interchange and collaboration? How do residents operate in larger world *together* in ways that do not assume a past solidity of affiliations, a specific destination, or an ultimate collective formation to come? If in each individual initiative of livelihood and mobility there is an implicit "proposition" for how spaces across a city could be articulated, how are these propositions amassed, how do they have traction with and imply each other? In light of these complexions, what does efficacy consist of? How do we make determinations about what works?

Cities too often become sites of *imposition* of particular agendas, styles, exigencies, and accumulations. Practices of imposing become generalized. For example, firefighters demand cash payment at the scene of a burning building before they will put the fire out; industries contaminate water basins. Imposition is a process of *not* taking relationship into consideration, and thus a refusal of relationship. If cities are a locus of making relations, even in the simple terms of dense physical proximities, then imposition is a refusal of a relationship with the city.

On the other hand, this does not mean that everything that takes place within a city has to be seen as relevant for any specific actor or position. Conversely, to see or feel connectedness and relevance to all that takes place within a city would be debilitating of the plurality of initiatives required for the city to function. Without certain impositions, there would be nothing for others to respond to, differentiate themselves from, or align with.

Throughout the major global meetings held to address urban issues during the past several decades, the mantra has been "Cities belong to their inhabitants." This worthy phrase is intended to promote greater inclusiveness in terms of urban planning and governance. It affirms that cities cannot work and are not sustainable if their resources, spaces, and opportunities are dominated by the few; that there is no urban future unless cities maximize the inclusion of their inhabitants in decision making and access to resources. The problem seems to be that our collective knowledge of these inhabitants is quite limited. Substantial attention has been placed, and thus knowledge garnered, on the urban poor—itself a highly murky and contested designation—and on those residents whose access to various media gives them opportunities to represent themselves. A transnational urban public sphere of educated cosmopolitans has provided reassurance that urban change is moving in similar trajectories across cities, no matter the cities' locations or macrostructural embedding. As pointed out earlier, the focus on the urban poor and a globally outward-looking elite provides the occasion for mutual recognition among cities across disparate national contexts (Roy and Ong 2011). When cities pay attention to each other, as the exigencies of economic growth require them to do, they can see in each other sufficient similarities that the critical economic actors and sectors have confidence that acting in these other places is like acting "at home."

In Jakarta large swaths of commonality undoubtedly exist among industrial and service workers, petty entrepreneurs and merchants, civil servants and bureaucrats, police officers, teachers, health care workers, and drivers. But mostly these lines of connection remain implicit. Aspirations to middle-class status and consumption patterns, including moves to suburban single-pavilion residences or apartment blocks, are just assumed to be the norm. There is of course substantial evidence of these trajectories. The labor-intensive management of urban residency in older, more central, highly dense parts of the city becomes increasingly expensive given the competition for land and services.

Yet, as I have emphasized, large portions of cities, particularly in the near-South, still are characterized and replenished by dense mixtures of residential histories, income groups, occupations, outlooks, and ways of doing things. My intent is not to proffer this continuity as some kind of counterevidence, for indeed the pressures of accessing safe, halfway decently serviced and affordable living spaces are intense across the global urban world. But this movement, as it is characterized by a more discernible spacing out of residential patterns, cadastral registrations, the taking on of mortgage debt, and an overall subjection to increasingly comprehensive mechanisms of accountability, does tend to "standardize" urban populations, making what is known about them conform to the application of a series of regularized data sets.

At the same time, in Jakarta sufficient numbers of inhabitants, as well as many new arrivals, continue to operate under very partial surveillance. Civil servants may continue to report to work and perform shrinking duties while entering into shifting collaborations with others on a wide range of income-earning projects. Many residents constantly circulate through various jobs, not to collect larger or more secure salaries but to have access to different social networks they hope will increase their opportunities. In other words, there are large numbers of urban residents—neither poor, middle-class, nor rich—who may on the surface look to be included in one of these categories but who put together livelihoods that remain "off the map." What kinds of propositions can bring them within a strategic visibility, if not necessarily into some kind of "account"?

Here, propositions are not necessarily discursive formations or focused understandings of what takes place or should take place. Rather, they are ways of acting as if certain realities exist when the terms of proof are not yet available but this indetermination can still be experienced and requires a way of keeping open the full range of concepts, interpretations, and translations that will eventually be associated with this experience. So in Jakarta, the "majority" is not only a particular kind of proposition, but it is also visualized and engaged through the particular propositions it enacts in various spaces and times. These are not principles or working procedures determined by consensus, nor are they a kind of collective unconscious where certain assumptions about the possibility of residents having to deal with each other in particular circumstances are better left unspoken. Sometimes propositions reveal themselves as orientations to events, as we will see in the following discussion of particular waves of violence. At other times they may be reflected in the specific forms of self-representation that residents insist upon, which do not in themselves embody the felt possibilities of systematicity or collective ethos. Rather, they leave open a space in which more experimental formulations come to the fore about who people are and what they can do together.

A TALE OF TWO DISTRICTS, PART 1: TANAH TINGGI

To illustrate this notion of propositions, both as a means to take up, point to, and talk about an urban majority in Jakarta and as a means to think about how that majority enacts itself as a collective force, I take the example of two contiguous inner-city districts in Jakarta, Tanah Tinggi and Kramat Sentiong. On the surface, these districts appear to be similar in many ways. But what I want to illustrate here is that the means through which they enact a collective presence—the ways in which residents deal with each other that ramify across the many different transactions they have on daily basis with neighbors and other associates—exhibit different propositions about the conditions the residents face and what can be done with them. These propositions act as instruments for a specific kind of operating in concert among residents.

Jakarta has a long history of highly localized and momentary explosions of violence that seem to appear out of nowhere and quickly fade away, even if within particular neighborhoods incidents of violence may be frequently repeated. Known as *tawuran*, these incidents tend to be largely precipitated by minimal triggers, such as competition over rights to a small parking lot, a dispute over a "stolen" girlfriend, or refusal to pay out winnings on a bet on a local football match. They are usually situated in the city's high-density districts, with their heterogeneous mixtures of ethnic groups, incomes, and residential histories, although they increasingly take place in the poorer sections of these districts. Analysts have frequently attributed them to the uncertainties infused into masculine and ethnic identities through the long decades of the stifling militarized politics of the New Order regime, and the way this regime capitalized on these uncertainties for its own legitimacy (Wieringa 2003; Boellstorff 2004; Sidel 2006; Tadie 2006; Brown and Wilson 2007).

Everyday violence has become part of normalized routine across many cities. It is an expression of the substantial undermining of conditions and practices that residents have relied on to make viable urban lives. But it is usually referred to in terms of local residents' inadequacy in fully adapting to the new realities of urban life by, for example, living in nuclear family households, pursuing education, engaging in formal wage employment, and supporting effective local governance. At the same time, as urban space is incorporated into logics of accumulation and use that are seldom attentive to past histories and valuation, the specificity of transformations under way also becomes occluded, in the sense that what takes place "here" takes place "everywhere," something beyond local collective understanding. There are then few mechanisms available to draw links among specificities. As the opening up of urban space to the maximization of speculative value erodes the social memory and resources required to imagine how a specific locality is positioned within a larger world of actual and potential connections, the etiology of such violence is something opaque, something that must be distanced and put "over there" as a kind of public secret (Taussig 1999). But perhaps this same violence also operates to keep attributions of culpability and ramification unsettled, and to defer certain apparently foregone conclusions.

Tanah Tinggi is one of Jakarta's densest districts. It is a place re-

Social housing in Tanah Tinggi.

nowned for family members taking shifts to sleep in overcrowded dwellings. It is also known for its extensive mixture of ethnicities and decaying infrastructure. It is popularly represented as one of the city's most dangerous and poorest neighborhoods, a reputation that available demographic and socioeconomic indicators show is not necessarily warranted. Having observed the entirety of the district, I am struck by the degree of heterogeneity in both its social and physical environments. The district is made up of a profusion of microterritories, even if the district as a whole is largely "summarized" in the oft-cited contrasts (and conflicts) between the contiguous neighborhoods of Kota Paris and Baladewa. In Kota Paris the plot size is just a little less divided than average, and the streets are just a little wider, permitting the passage of automobiles. This district reflects the slight advantages secured over four decades by its original Betawi residents in relationship to the surrounding neighborhoods. Such advantages have been subject to different explanations, from attributions to moneymaking in prostitution and gambling to capacities to resist incursions from outside gangsters to the Betawi being able to enforce a much more homogeneous ethnic composition. There has always been bad blood between Baladewa and Kota Paris, and the stories that attempt to account for this are constantly changing.

Likewise, accounts of the *tawuran* change all the time. Usually initiated and fought by youth, such incidents typically involve the throwing of stones and, more recently, Molotov cocktails; sometimes swords are brandished. Sometimes, depending on the time of day, as most *tawuran* occur late in the night, entire neighborhoods are mobilized to join the youth, and the fights persist until the police arrive. Even though the Jakarta provincial government has arranged for police posts to be widely established, particularly across historically difficult neighborhoods, the police wait until sufficient backup is assembled before they attempt to intervene. This is the case even when they know that trouble is brewing. A common sign of this is the scraping of electricity poles, which acts as a signal for opposing sides to mobilize their forces.

In a district where almost everyone knows pretty much what is going on, where word travels quickly about local events and personalities, almost everyone I talked with claimed to have little idea about what causes these outbreaks of violence. While they have been a feature of everyday district life for decades, there is also a nascent sense that these fights could become a serious problem. But when I asked residents why they should become any more of a problem now than they have been in the past—and whether there is something fundamentally different about these fights now—no one seemed to know.

The usual response was that Jakarta as a whole is becoming less tolerant of religious and class differences, and that these *tawuran* thus threaten to become more serious. But when I asked residents whether there is any evidence that current *tawuran* are reflecting religious, ethnic, or class divides, they firmly denied this possibility.

The residents' absence of confidence in making causative attributions does not reflect a reluctance to talk about these incidents in general. They are on people's minds, and everyone has many stories about them, particularly in terms of how superficial they may be in reflecting any deep-seated resentments or social differences. One local leader in a subdistrict just across the small river that divides Tanah Tinggi from neighboring Kampung Rawa, increasingly drawn into these local fights, said that his sons and sons-in-law live in different contiguous neighborhoods. "When fights break out they battle each other, but shortly after the fight is ended, they come back to the house, play cards and have a laugh as if nothing happened." Residents often offered such depictions to emphasize that these fights are not about specific personalities or issues per se. Rather, they are the characteristics of specific spaces, such as tightly compacted interfaces or *terroir vague,* where there is no clear possibility of mediating competing claims for use by different groups of youth. As one subdistrict head indicated: "There would be no problem with fights if youth were simply in their proper space. If they had somewhere to sleep during the night instead of having to take shifts with other household members this kind of trouble would not take place."

Tanah Tinggi has been one of Jakarta's most ethnically mixed districts, given its proximity to one of the city's oldest markets, Senen. This market has been used historically as a nexus for various ethnically based translocal commercial networks, such as the Makassar, the Padang, the Ambon, and the Batak. While most districts in the city have mixed ethnic populations, Tanah Tinggi tends to have a broader, more diverse mix than the surrounding areas, and with a larger non-Muslim population. As indicated earlier, Muslim–Christian conflict is becoming more pronounced in the city. This is in part because of the growth of Christian congregations and the increased difficulty they face trying to find suitable sites and facilities for worship, given the restrictive policies that require neighborhood consensus concerning the local insertion of religious buildings. But there is nothing to indicate that such splits have anything to do with the proliferation of fights in Tanah Tinggi.

Drug dealing has become a major feature of the local economy, especially in Baladewa. This has introduced large amounts of fluid money into areas where most people do not have a lot of money and work long hours for little; it has also brought to already nearly impassable neighborhoods a steady stream of outsiders looking to purchase drugs. The sudden accumulation of substantial amounts of money by youth has overturned generational hierarchies, and many households report an inability to exert any kind of control over their children. As one father, Aji, pointed out: "What can we tell our sons when they can buy us all out ten times over? If we try to keep them in line, they will just go to the police, give them a few thousand [rupiah], and tell them to come and beat us up. At the same time they disobey us, fight us, they continue to go out of their way to do everything for our needs." Households have increasingly become sites of domestic violence, particularly as elders lose their authority and then take out their frustrations on female family members. According to most local leaders, residents in their jurisdictions prefer to act as if drugs are simply not present, and even when there are residual benefits in terms of household accumulation, there is widespread resentment that the big profits are exported to police and military officials lurking on the sidelines and probably controlling much of the overall trade. Again, no link is made between drug trafficking and competition over markets and territory and the *tawuran*. In fact, those involved in the drug business express frustration with the frequency of these fights, as they must then lie low and pull in their operations in the face of more extensive police presence. As one professed dealer told us, "We are sick of this *tawuran*, especially because it gives an excuse for guys in all kinds of uniforms, we don't really know who, to come around and intimidate the officials we are already paying big money to."

Efforts are under way to substantiate the decentralization of municipal governance by making more development resources available to districts. The so-called original inhabitants and landowners of Jakarta, the Betawi, have largely divested their holdings in the face of their widespread inability to diversify from landowning to other economic activities. They have also had difficulty maintaining ownership because of rising costs and development pressures. They

A banner calling for an end to tawuran, *youth gang fighting, which occurs in Tanah Tinggi with great frequency. Because this is one of the most diverse and crowded districts in Jakarta, many explanations have been offered for why these fights occur; one is that they are responses to various shifts taking place in the district. Efforts to mobilize community involvement try to deal with the problem, but* tawuran *may be signaling other conflicts beneath the surface of everyday interactions.*

have increasingly attempted to compensate for this loss by seeking to dominate municipal politics through a wide variety of organizational forms, from *majlis t'alim* (informal religious gatherings that indirectly attempt to mobilize political sentiment) to extraparliamentary, quasi-military groups such as the Betawi Brotherhood Forum, which displays a highly visible defense of Betawi interests.

Local politics is also drawing upon a new generation of more educated residents who seek to bring more transparent and rational practices of administration to the running of local government. These residents usually possess full-time jobs and do not rely on the limited compensation offered to neighborhood and subdistrict political leaders. This change is a threat to an older generation of local leaders who used their positions as vehicles for a variety of informal accumulation largely centered on their roles in providing identity cards, registering local populations, and facilitating the processing of critical documents residents need to obtain health care and social services. While increased levels of fighting provide evidence that political challengers can use in pointing out the ineffectiveness of current local leaders, these local leaders also use the problem of the *tawuran* to cement ties across districts and consolidate resistance to these challenges.

Districts such as Tanah Tinggi are also subject to repeated waves of inward migration, often by individuals and households equipped with significant entrepreneurial skills. The demand for residential space has prompted most owners of homes and buildings to turn over at least parts of their dwellings for rental accommodation. In some neighborhoods this migration has tripled already dense populations.

The absorption process gives rise to many ambivalent feelings. Many migrants are young workers with jobs in the vicinity living temporarily in neighborhoods where many youth are unemployed, largely due to lack of education. Most youth in Tanah Tinggi never finish secondary school. Additionally, their Jakarta identity cards say that they reside in Tanah Tinggi, and employers often discriminate against them because of the district's reputation. Whereas new migrants may be required to register with local authorities, something that most single residents seldom do, their identity cards still reflect official residences elsewhere. Other new residents seek the locational advantages of Tanah Tinggi's proximity to key markets and transportation centers. Many could probably afford to live in better conditions, but they choose to live in the area to start businesses and also save money. Often they use this money to buy local properties and construct homes or commercial buildings that far exceed the prevailing conditions of the local built environment. These divergences prompt tensions and resentment on the part of households that have lived in the area for many years.

At the same time, the infusion of migrants opens up new fields of affective relations and wards off tendencies toward parochialism. New residents bring new vitality, and even if their enterprises rarely incorporate longtime local residents, there is widespread intermarriage and circulation of information. While the newcomers in one subdistrict may largely make up the force that fights youth coming from long-term resident households in a neighboring subdistrict, such clashes rarely take place within their neighborhood. In this way a doubled ambivalence may find expression—there is resentment, yes, but also most youth indicate that newcomers provide incentives for them to try on different kinds of attitudes and versions of themselves and to circulate through discrepant identities and affiliations. Iwan, a nineteen-year-old motorbike taxi driver, indicated that "with newcomers as customers they aren't always telling you what to do like the people around here you have known your whole life. They tell you things because they are worried about what other people think, and then I start thinking that there are different things I could do with my life. I like making them my customers because when I wait to pick them up or take them out, it gets me out of this place, because so many of the old-time people here, they never want to leave."

The difficulty of everyday life and the crowded conditions under which people live compel a certain sense of solidarity, such as a profession of family ties where everyone looks out for each other regardless of whether this indeed takes place or not. Still, under the rubric of such solidarity, everyone is expected to accede to the performance of this solidarity. No matter how essential or supportive, such a performance is also restrictive, reining space in rather than extending and differentiating it. The question becomes how such space can be elaborated, how individuals can act in ways for which they are not necessarily made accountable.

In some cities residents open up such space by extending the scope of actual mobility, going beyond the territory of residence to fan out across the city through the vehicle of popular culture. In Jakarta, this space tends to be opened up by youth circulating through various forms of affiliation and expression. For example, some youth involve themselves in a populist Islamic gathering on one night, participate in a theater troupe on another night, join in the activities of a local youth organization on another night, and so forth. The emphasis is less on finding coherence or ideological consistency in terms of associations and involvements, and more on using a plurality of opportunities as a means of creating space. This raises the possibility that the very same youth who are battling it out as residents of different neighborhoods may be collaborating as participants in the same Islamic youth group on another occasion.

During the time we were working in Tanah Tinggi many organized efforts were undertaken to address the purported intensification of *tawuran*. But the mobilization of a response almost always ensured that no adequate response would be forthcoming. District officials, appointed by the provincial government, usually notified elected subdistrict and neighborhood heads that some kind of organized response was necessary. Alternatively, certain local leaders called on district officials to facilitate or sanction such efforts. During a particularly acute period of *tawuran* in November 2010, there was broad recognition in Tanah Tinggi that something had to be done—or, more precisely, that the district had to demonstrate that attempts were under way to do something about these fights. A district-wide popular assembly was called for December 8.

In the days leading up to this event, I spoke with different subdistrict heads, residents, and religious and civic leaders about the shape of this assembly and what would come out of it. As with their attempts to explain the causes of the *tawuran,* they offered many different versions of this process of organizing a response, as if many assemblies, not just one, were to be held and many organizations, not one, would be formed to deal with the problem.

The organizers of the actual event turned out to have made little effort to draw in either youth or neighborhood heads, and the "popular assembly" was instead a gathering with strong traditional Muslim inflections, little representation from district administrators, and a somewhat odd announcement by the district head, the *camat,* that the major for Jakarta Pusat (Central) had been replaced by someone more in line with the sentiments of those gathered. The event turned out to be a stage where many actors were eager to perform. The district head was busy accepting interviews from local journalists. The FBR groups from different districts, with their distinct uniforms, came just to behave like paramilitary guards for the event, and the members of a local residents' group, in newly made T-shirts, acted as if they had helped to organize the event, their T-shirts proclaiming them as "community concerned with the neighborhood."

It seemed evident that this gathering was more a display of the way this particular configuration of actors, under the auspices of prolific religious symbolism, had persisted in the face of implicit—never mentioned or identified—challenges to this form of organized response. In other words, the threat being addressed seemed to be less the *tawuran* than an emerging managerial form trying to make district administration and politics more seamless and accountable.

On the day following the assembly, no one we spoke with seemed to take it seriously or had any conviction that it was actually organized to address the problem. Hirwarto, a local neighborhood leader who had told us he was going to be deeply involved in the meeting on December 8 but never showed up, said, "This is one of those things where the main purpose is for some of those who think of themselves as big leaders to try to put you in your place, make you stand to one side; there are no negotiations, no talk really, and you don't want people to watch this, especially if you have to deal with them every day."

Herein may be the "role" of the *tawuran* in local affairs. Tanah Tinggi is indeed subject to many strains and changes. Any urban district with this level of density, social mixture, struggles for space and opportunity, and demographic turnover is not going to persist without substantial volatility. Additionally, residents are largely aware of what the fault lines are and could be. They do not put excessive faith in local traditions of solidarity, even when such solidarity comes to rely on large measures of silence in the face of serious difficulties. Where drug markets, household conflicts, and complicities among police, criminals, and elites may be public secrets, everyone looks at and talks about the *tawuran,* while almost everyone claims to have no idea about where they are coming from. These fights cannot be included in the conventional ways of explaining local affairs. They indeed belong to Tanah Tinggi, and in such a way that people are more ready to talk about them than about any other feature of the district. But at the same time, they do not represent any specific conflict; they are not attributable to any specific condition, actor, or status, but they can be appropriated at will to point to the tensions they do not represent.

As Najar, a local businessman, stated, "They have always been with us, so, in some way, we are with them, even if we do not know what they are." This kind of intimacy, between historical prolongation and its inability to settle into any particular form of apprehension, goes beyond simply constituting an "alert" for the residents of this area, beyond being a problem that needs to be fixed. If *tawuran* do not belong to any contestation or group in particular, then they belong to everyone, can be used by everyone, despite whether a sociological instinct might relegate them to an existential condition of local youth. If they belong to everyone, then no one in particular is implicated in terms of transitions under way. This situation may defer any systematic way of dealing with a complex process of transition or of mobilizing resident involvement and support in local development activities. But it may also create the space necessary for residents to venture a wide range of initiatives without necessarily being implicated and measured by others. This does not mean that everyone gets along or simply does their thing without interference or contestation. Rather, the *tawuran* seem to indicate that the "real fight" is simultaneously very much in the moment in which it occurs and elsewhere. It is somewhere far removed from the fight itself, and something that permits these fights to have their own temporality, sometimes occurring in rapid serial succession persisting over months, and then nothing for long periods.

Their disappearance is then as much of a "mystery" as their presence, particularly as nothing really discernible changes and many of the apparent triggers remain on a daily basis. Seemingly unbounded to anything, *tawuran* occasion a multiplicity of responses. Each seems to embody a fundamental indifference to the fights themselves. They are about other things, other agendas. But since they link themselves to the *tawuran,* they come to the fore, are made visible in ways that buy them time, and do not necessarily link themselves to other issues of local politics and economy, even if these issues may be fundamentally about them.

A TALE OF TWO DISTRICTS, PART 2: KRAMAT SENTIONG

If an urban majority, as I have used the concept here, works and appears through incremental adjustments and shifting articulations, it does not avail itself of the usual institutional mechanisms that might secure its endurance through time. How, then, does such a majority keep itself together? How does it secure itself if it does not rely on a consistent and coherent image or repertoire of actions?

Notions that deal with securing the lives of individuals within a particular setting have usually centered on the willingness of those individuals to subsume their lives to an abstracted collective. This collective, in turn, becomes the object of protection (Weber 2009). That which acts as a sovereign power does so in the name of a people or citizenry that has no existence of its own except as the means through which that very power exempts itself, acts according to its own rules and decisions. Thus there is a fundamental gap at the heart of the predominant notions of security: that which is to be secured seems to be nowhere in sight. Without the specificity of a "target" and an object of concern, apparatuses of security become self-aggrandizing—that is, they attempt to tie together more and more aspects of daily life, implicate them in each other, and make them have something essential to do with each other. It is as if in the absence of something identifiable, the maneuver is simply to surround everything.

In many ways Kramat Sentiong upends these notions about security. In doing so it says something important about how an urban majority operates through time, how it manages to continue and endure. Kramat Sentiong is the district immediately to the west of Tanah Tinggi. It is an older district, perhaps not as dense, and its proximity to a major commercial thoroughfare, Jalan Raya, gives it the veneer of a more economically dynamic area. But in most respects, Kramat Sentiong is not that different from its neighbor, even though most local residents perceive a marked difference in terms of attitude and confidence. It is also a district full of talk; the streets are full of people engaged in animated conversation, something more than the perfunctory greetings and gossip of everyday routine.

Most of the original landowners are gone, and the area displays evidence of multiple generations of repair, rebuilding, and new construction. Because flooding is growing worse following even minor rainfall, efforts are always under way to improve drainage and circulation, and for this residents rely on reiterated solidarities. Even though the legal basis of their tenancy is secure, the signs of an encroaching larger world are everywhere, particularly in the spread of new office buildings and warehouses. The location of the district has opened up some of its areas to the infusion of new, more middle-class residents, who acquire contiguous plots on which to build spacious residences. *Tawuran* may be an occasional problem, but they seem to dissipate quickly.

Most of Kramat Sentiong's original residents were able to anchor themselves in the district through reliance on ethnic networks that

The border between Tanah Tinggi and Kramat Sentiong, two districts of similar social and demographic composition but with divergent approaches to everyday issues. Kramat Sentiong seems largely immune to the tawuran *problem, in contrast with Tanah Tinggi.*

elaborated specific trades and niches in the city. This does not mean that all residents, or even the majority, took part in the trades for which their ethnic groups were most well-known. Rather, these trades provided a kind of "coverage"—a base, an insurance policy—for members of their affiliated ethnic groups to undertake other educational, occupational, and political pursuits. If these ethnic affiliations were the way in which the majority of residents secured themselves in the city, given the hegemony a particular ethnic group could exert over a needed economic activity, they now act as a point of reference whose maintenance is precisely contingent on specific acts of risk. In the absence of new initiatives, business ventures, or attempts to network across discrete economic sectors or territories, ethnicity would seem to lose a great deal of meaning. Ethnicity now seems to operate as a vehicle for individuals to ensure "a piece of any action" instead of pointing to the solidarity of specific economic or social sectors. In other words, it provides a consolidation of residents that have to be taken into consideration by others.

Kramat Sentiong is made up not only of diverse ethnicities but also of a mixture of new and old residents. Most of the original Betawi residents have sold their land, and this land has been both subdivided and consolidated. These are processes that permit more inhabitants in dense conditions as well as investment by new middle-class residents in larger homes and businesses. Established ethnic ascriptions are crisscrossed by equally powerful notions of separating "stranger" from "local," "old money" from "new money," "resident" from "businessperson." Thus divisions can appear in many different forms, depending on where people are from, how long they have lived in the area, and whether their primary concern is residential, entrepreneurial, or speculative.

For example, the offspring of original inhabitants who spent their childhoods in the area, left for years of schooling elsewhere, and then returned to implant an upper-middle-class lifestyle may be considered "strangers." On the other hand, localities may actively "recruit" persons from underrepresented ethnic groups known for their skills at various businesses to locate in the area, where they may be fully embraced as having been "locals" all along.

Local government reform has introduced a new system of district management that attempts to strike a balance between the administrators appointed by the Jakarta provincial government and newly established and democratically elected district-wide village committees, *dekel*. These same committees, however, emphasize their reliance on quotidian informal consultations conducted in various configurations and sites. While local decision-making power across Jakarta is still centered in the *rukun tetangga* (RT), or neighborhood association, the ability to negotiate accords for the use of space and common resources, and to resolve actual and potential problems, largely rests with these informal consultations. As committee members point out, they take seriously the role of the *dekel* as a conduit between the district and larger administration venues and programs. They must demonstrate initiative and, increasingly, speed in working to reconcile limited budgets and widespread municipal needs. Still, this role is perceived as less important than the members' availability to circulate and "show up" in a wide variety of local contexts as a kind of hinge that opens any situation onto a broader range of considerations. And so this is what they spend most of their time doing: inserting themselves into different gatherings and conversations, not to appropriate them for local government business, but to do the work of local governance through them.

The role of the RT largely centers on keeping accounts: counting the number of people living in the association's small jurisdiction, counting the number of people who pay their taxes and the number who receive health benefits or supplementary income grants, and keeping track of just what kinds of support and favors the neighborhood may receive from the village, district, and provincial offices. But the real politics concerns practices that seem to defer keeping accounts. In the local vernacular, the process of everyday negotiation draws on but does not necessarily hold to account the kinds of problem solving and deals that have taken place before. As Rachman, a *dekel* member, put it: "In the administrative offices, people are supposed to come to them, and they exist as some kind of island in the middle of a big and often stormy sea. We go to where things are about to take a turn, for better or for worse, and use this as an opportunity for the people who live here to maybe see each other in a different way, to not take everyone for granted."

In a district where many different ethnic groups are present, and where ethnicity is reproduced in large part through economic specialization and commercial networking, it could be seen as reasonable to make each group accountable to the others, to ensure some kind of balance among how different groups use and live in the district. This would entail how they pursue economic livelihoods; use essential resources such as water, power, and sanitation; and perform their cultural and religious values. It would seem reasonable to elaborate some kind of common series of norms, some kind of practical behavioral shortcuts to minimize the time spent in dealing with regulatory transactions and misunderstandings.

But these are not the professed elements of day-to-day negotiations. Residents I spoke to in Kramat Sentiong prefer to shy away from social calibrations based on accounts of which group gets to do what, and under what circumstances. They do not want to be tied down to common rules or behavioral styles—after all, who would define them, what would have to be left out in terms of developing something recognizable and accessible for residents to get a hold of? Asma, who works at the local district council, stated, "We don't want to spend all of our time comparing each other, what one family has and what one doesn't; we like the fact that people prefer to do things in different ways; after all, how else are we going to learn how to live in this city, and besides, this way we don't always have to come up with new ideas just by ourselves."

In Kramat Sentiong, where everyone has to find a way to get along, the sheer plurality of actions and backgrounds is seen as a good thing. Residents do not worry if others are doing things that they cannot readily measure or understand. There is simply too much going on for residents to waste time feeling like their own lives are being judged, constrained, or made insecure by the diversities of their neighborhood. Everyone knows that ethnic groups have their own ways of doing things and that there is little anyone is going to say or do to change this. After all, these differences often come in handy in a district where incomes, residents, and opportunities come and go.

At the same time, as individuals conduct daily informal negotiations, they are cognizant of the ethnic backgrounds of the participants. Residents try to find ways of accomplishing tasks, disseminating information, testing out interpretations about what is going on, and solving problems by virtue of their being simultaneously neighbors, perhaps relatives, workers in particular trades or enterprises, and members of particular religious organizations, civic groups, or political parties. In such an economy of transactions, there will always be those who get more and those who get less. But these dispositions are in turn themselves rapidly recalibrated in different settings, at different times, and for different tasks. A household runs out of materials for raising their home's ground floor several meters to keep out floodwaters; the sudden illness of a breadwinner seriously strains a household budget; the death of a local imam necessitates funeral preparations and new recruitment; a raid on informal sellers forces schoolchildren to travel outside their regular routine for after-school lunch; a household wants to hold a daughter's wedding on the street in front of their house, which will close down through traffic for several hours; a household wants to construct two extra levels on their home, which means that the new spaces will overlook the roofs of several neighbors who use those roofs as occasional bedrooms—this is just a small sampling of the kinds of issues that prompt negotiations.

Participation in negotiations as individuals is important not in the sense that these are transactions among autonomous, individuated citizens responsible for managing their own lives. Rather, individuality is important here as a sign that everyone is eligible to negotiate. If everyone is eligible, then the concept of "eligibility" has limited use in terms of specifying the rights and responsibilities of those who deal with each other on a daily basis. Again, this does not mean that there are not authorities and hierarchies at work in sorting out social and political arrangements. Rather, it means that in the contexts that are viewed as the most significant in terms of working out the governance of the district, residents can make their views known and make recommendations without necessarily having to consider whether they are eligible to do so. In this position, the transaction exists as a potential singularity. In other words, it need not be tied to what has happened before; it need not participate in a particular calculus of balanced interests or compensations. Instead, it is a possibility of keeping people on their toes, deferring any reified notion of what an ethnic group can or cannot do, or what it has had an opportunity to do in the past. Ethnic affiliation, then, is something that can participate in what is to come, not only in the characteristics, practices, or occupations of the past. It becomes a resource to be put to work for the future as a point of orientation and stability that can now risk undertaking new perspectives and tasks that may be too difficult or risky to contemplate for individuals without such affiliation.

What is particularly significant here is that the vast majority of the residents taking part in these negotiations continue to see themselves as "newcomers" even when many have resided in the area for decades. Even residents of a younger generation born and bred in this district tend to view as their primary residences and affiliations the towns from which their grandparents or parents came—places like Kunigan, Yogyakarta, Pekalongan, Cirebon, Padang, Makassar, and Malang. Every Eid al-Fitr, at the end of the Muslim fasting month of Ramadan, more than one-third of Jakarta's population undertakes an exodus to hometowns and home regions, obligated to return with gifts and displays of well-being from their time in the nation's capital.

Money remitted from Jakarta continues to constitute an important share of household expenditures and budgets in these areas. While a small number of Jakarta residents continue to profess their intention to return to live in their "places of origin," few do, and now the largely youthful population of Kramat Sentiong has only a cursory familiarity with these places. On top of this, those considered the original inhabitants, those who belong to the district, are largely gone, leaving almost the entirety of the district to so-called strangers.

Kramat Sentiong is a district where the proficiency of daily negotiations is still valued as the key aspect of local politics and decision making. These negotiations are conducted on the basis of individuals who simultaneously embody many different positions and roles for each other. If this is the case, why the persistence of ethnic identification, which would seem to impede the cultivation of a full sense of residents being citizens of Jakarta? Continuing to emphasize residents' status as migrants or strangers even when they have spent most or the entirety of their lives in Jakarta would seem to limit these residents' ability to exert effective power over the decisions and directions of the city. As long as they defer fully identifying with the city and retain significant affective ties elsewhere, it seems that their supposed temporariness could be used to legitimate the actions of more powerful forces capable of appropriating land and resources. Reiteration of the salience of ethnic identity over citizenship would also seem to mean that individuals are more implicated by the dynamics of their corporate belongings than by their own attainments and aspirations.

Not only is urban citizenship deferred through these more primordial affiliations, but also these affiliations increasingly gain credence, not in terms of what they actually perform or remember but in their sheer capacity to defer citizenship. They thus become a kind of negative, shell identity that steers politics at a metropolitan level into being increasingly a patchwork of balkanized accords that hinder the kinds of spatial and transportation planning that need to be coordinated at a regional level.

Yet this persistence of being strangers potentially raises important questions about what citizenship actually does. This is reflected in a somewhat oblique comment by Roy, a twenty-nine-year-old musician and mechanic: "They say Indonesia is one of the most populated countries in the world. As this neighborhood is full of people from all over Indonesia, we are a really big neighborhood."

What does it mean to be a citizen of Jakarta? Local sustainability and livelihoods in Kramat Sentiong are matters of how the fragments of various institutions, practices, and backgrounds are interwoven, and they are interwoven so as to maximize the inclusion of all that occurs within a particular place. It is not that the residents do not take the specification of rights seriously or dismiss wanting a sense of being "covered" by a municipal framework of administration and services. Rather, as Ardhi, one *dekel* member, emphasized, "not every situation demands the same cast of characters. We all know each other fairly well when we stick to a day-to-day routine, but this is a really busy part of the city, with many things going on, and so it is also important that we constantly try new approaches to working things out, and we can only do this if different kinds of people are involved at different times, and this is only possible as long as the rules are not written too tight and as long as people don't think they only have one kind of job to do, one kind of responsibility."

The ability of the district to stay in tune with the larger city—to anticipate what changes need to be made and what interactions are needed to engage the multiple networks that run through the district and beyond—does require a sense of stability. But, critically, the bulk of local attention is not placed on maintaining that stability, but rather on maintaining individuals' freedom to pursue a wide range of livelihoods and engagements with larger metropolitan spaces. This freedom can exist only as long as residents are not overly tied down to having to calibrate their actions toward each other, as long as they do not feel that they must assess everything they do in terms of its implications for their neighbors. As Wanda, another *dekel* member, pointed out, "We all respect our neighbors, or at least pretend to, but this is mostly only what they want anyway, just this gesture. It is not like we expect to live with people just like us, this is a big city after all; many of us may have come from small villages but now we have to become smart enough to live in a thousand different villages at the same time, and we can't expect that the way we behave or others behave is going to be anywhere near the same in each of those villages."

Because this is not a district of atomized households but one where everyone knows and deals with each other on some kind of basis, residents can work out tensions and misunderstandings through the very density of interactions in which they have no choice but to participate, day in and day out. Just how ethnicity is taken into consideration in the day-to-day informal negotiations among individuals, not impeded by specific forms of eligibility, is an open-ended question. These negotiations do not ask individuals to "perform their ethnicity," but they are the venues through which interethnic deliberations take place. Within them, ethnicities are stretched, regarded in different ways, compelled to do things outside their stereotypical purview, but also remain points of anchorage.

The ability of an urban majority to continue its work over time entails the oscillation between stability and risk, between reiterating what one is known for and deploying it in new arrangements with other residents. Because ethnicity retains its power, when it no longer necessarily needs to do so, either as a locus of economic accumulation, social security, or as a matrix of affective ties, it remains something to be engaged in everyday district life, something that warrants negotiation. But, again, as I have pointed out several times, everyday negotiations seem to "forget" ethnicity as soon as they begin. What is important are the negotiations themselves as a context in which residents can continuously realign their efforts and break open new potentials for accessing information, support, and resources.

In this way, the work of the nation, of which Jakarta is the capital, is performed on this day-to-day basis. Rather than national belonging being the protection racket to which individual residents subsume their possibilities and maneuvering, the work of nationhood instead takes place in a wide range of settings among individuals who are simultaneously many different things to each other, who work out temporary arrangements knowing that there is always a "drawing board" to go back to.

This does not mean that an overarching framework of rights and responsibilities usually associated with citizenship is not salient. The ability of the residents of Kramat Sentiong to secure the opportunity for them to keep going is closely wrapped up with the possibility of being able to make urban life in ways that keep open a wide range of aspirations and potentials. For many residents their best bet for securing a place in the city rests in the density of heterogeneous public transactions that life in districts such as Kramat Sentiong engenders on a daily basis.

The Ghosts of Tebet

Once again, I will end a chapter by talking about ghosts. It is not that I am obsessed with ghosts, but rather that ghosts seem to promise a sense of nearness even when the body of a thing is gone. Ghosts seem to indicate that what is seen as distant is always in some way near. The conclusions that particular ways of life are over, then, are perhaps premature. In chapter 1, I discussed the spectral dimensions of life in the megacomplex. Here I return to spectral matters, but this time as reflections of the concerns residents have about the prospective disappearance of the ways in which they have managed to secure their lives.

I live in Tebet, a lower-middle-class area in the center of Jakarta. Tebet is a warren of small streets with mostly single-family pavilions tightly packed together. It was originally developed some fifty years ago as neighborhoods in Senayan, to the west, were displaced to make room for a new sporting complex and governmental district. The area is popularly known as a seasoned, streetwise "combatant" in the struggle for attention and autonomy. The eastern section of Tebet has in recent years become a center for teen culture, full of clothing boutiques, night markets, and cheap coffee shops and restaurants. Music and film studios, fashion and design businesses, and art collectives have also gravitated to this area. Somehow a wide variety of actors and activities manage to coexist without the difficulties that increasingly plague other districts. This is partly due to the urbanized ethos of the Muhammadiyah, one of the main organizational branches of Indonesian Islam, whose institutions are well spread throughout the area.

The strategic location of Tebet, right at the center of Jakarta, also exerts great pressures. Some areas of the district are subject to severe flooding during the rainy season; its dense population and the concentration of economic activities across an overtaxed infrastructure have left much of the district in acute need of substantial repair. The infusion of businesses has taken place largely without any sense of strategic planning. Illicit economies have swept through some parts of the district, bringing in people from various parts of the city that have little interest in their sustainability. Their presence depresses land values and thus opens the door for large-scale residential developments that are often poorly located in terms of the major transportation axes.

Still, much of the area is eminently livable, replete with new residential projects that do not substantially alter the existing scale but add new capital to the area and signal its capacity for renewal. Compared with much of the city, the area is clean and well maintained, as the existing residential base seems geared to remain for the long haul. But there are anxieties that accompany this determination.

Throughout Tebet, motley local "security" crews put many road barriers in place every night, well before people fall asleep. Many of these barriers are manned throughout the night. Residents who are known to the security personnel may pass through the barriers as they wish, but the majority of residents are not, so they have to learn which circuitous routes, avoiding the barriers, will take them closest to their destinations. The ostensible reason for the barriers is to limit the number of car thefts. Because most households have more than one vehicle but are equipped to park only a single car, and most do not have space in front of their houses to park the overflow, cars are often parked out of sight of their owners' homes. (This is the case even though any available space can become a car park overseen by yet another security person.) The barriers are supposedly erected to cut off the possible escape routes of car thieves.

Car theft is a reality in Jakarta, but not excessively so—not to the extent that it warrants a profusion of barriers and men attired in various uniforms. The layout of the district already creates the sense of a place full of deep interiors, and the barriers accentuate this sense. The very diversity that is the trademark of Tebet and a factor contributing to the growth of local small- and medium-scale enterprise is the thing that people do not want to pay too much attention to during the night. The willingness to let things happen is something that can be monitored during the day, but it poses implications for the night that are more difficult to detect and control.

This is perhaps why rumors spread about various spectral events, of teenagers who disappear while making out in the park, of sudden and gigantic bursts of growth in local vegetation, of houses engulfed in flames that somehow do not suffer any damage. "There are some things you can keep out, but for others the only thing you can do is to push them into corners where they have to show themselves," said one security guard doubling as a local gangster doubling as a security guard. No one talks about ghosts directly, even though once again this year Jakarta is preoccupied with them. One example of this pre-occupation was the rush in 2012 to complete a whole slew of new ghost movies, popular novels, and television shows.

It is obvious that barriers such as these are not going to keep ghosts out, let alone a crew of criminals determined to go after some big prize, which really does not exist in this neighborhood anyway. Then again, the road barriers become a sanctioned occasion for certain groups of men to occupy the night with gambling and narcotics, as well as impromptu sing-alongs and the occasional party.

The same security guard told me, "We welcome outsiders here, and you are certainly welcome here, as long as you don't make your presence too clear." When I asked him what he had in mind with this, he said that people need to know just enough in order to have something to keep them interested in talking about you on occasion, to keep them guessing. But, at the same time, it is not good if they have to be worried about what you might do or have to end up counting on you for something you have no intention or capacity to deliver. When I tried to turn the topic back to that of ghosts, his response was that if you do not want them to be around, then you have to find a way to be more complicated than they are. Ghosts already have a lot of complications to deal with. After all, they are ghosts, with at least the theoretical capacity to go anywhere without physical or temporal constraints, but they find themselves stuck in associations to particular lives and places that will not give them up or whose familiarity is the very thing that the ghosts rely on to organize their schedules.

When I tried to argue that it seemed that the neighborhood shut down prematurely at night for no apparent good reason, and thus seemed to shout out its simplicity rather than complication, the group of guards insisted that people these days increasingly have to retreat to their dreams to come up with new ways of doing things. With its constant traffic jams, overwhelming pollution, and alarming levels of subsidence, Jakarta has already become more complicated than its residents could ever hope to be. Even though the barriers will not keep the ghosts out and even though most local spectral events are considered harmless, there is still a need to keep an eye out for them. That means signaling some kind of respect for them, or letting them be, as my neighbor puts it, the itch in the hands.

It is no wonder that ghosts, far from being objects of fear and anxiety, have become almost hoped-for presences in the daily life of Tebet and other neighborhoods across the city. Big developments are eating up the city, its land, water, and former ways of life. The complications of everyday living prompt many residents to opt out of neighborhoods like Tebet in favor of the large housing complexes. As I have mentioned several times, these not only promise convenience and ready access to consumption but also seem to guarantee a future that allows individuals to improve themselves, make as much money as they can, and be safely removed from the exigencies of the street. Inhabitation in Jakarta continues to demand an astute ability to deal with the streets. This is hard work, but it is largely worth it in the sense that individuals can not only carve out niches for themselves but also have their niches connected to others. The connections are not static but continuously improvised and replenished. There is competition for space and resources, but the overarching practice is focused on the synergistic potentials of different kinds of things and activities existing in close proximity to each other.

But these kinds of complementarities and complex local systems need their space—or, more precisely, need the care, time, and resources to create space—and it is this capacity that is being choked off. It is being choked off in the substantial curtailment of functional circulation of nearly everything, from water to bodies to sensibilities. While Jakarta has one of the world's highest user rates for social media such as Twitter and Facebook, physical circulation across the city is declining (Coordinating Ministry of Economic Affairs and Japan International Cooperation Agency 2012), and the capacity of different facets of the city to be continuously articulated and the sites of continuous interchange is shrinking. As the circulation of populations stutters, these facets of the city become fragmented and particularized. This situation has impacts downward even to the household level, where "solutions" to daily problems become more individualized. For example, because of inadequate investment and poor service, the declining use of public transportation shifts the majority of "rides" to private vehicles. Given the problems of circulation, it becomes difficult for a household to use a single vehicle to distribute household members to their daily destinations; this problem is compensated for by the acquisition of more vehicles, which simply adds to the traffic.

The overproduction of shopping malls pushes prices downward, opening up consumption opportunities for people who never had them, offering products such as cheap motorcycles, electronics, and knockoff fashion goods. This, coupled with the profusion of images of success and well-being disseminated through local and global media, redirects affective energies toward the acquisition of things and experiences as the primary markers of individual efficacy. Why spend so much time attempting to negotiate intricate local collaborations with others when the entire city, even the entire world, is the more appropriate arena? In this arena, individuals are basically on their own, trying to be as connectable as they can to anything that happens in order to gain enhanced opportunities for self-aggrandizement and accumulation.

After all, in Jakarta, what is it that most inhabitants can realistically hope for? They see the massive construction of residential and commercial towers all around them, and while they may know about the long-run deleterious impacts of these megadevelopments, they feel powerless to stop them. Some may plan to reconstruct approximations of their present lives at the periphery of the city, where things are cheaper and not so crowded. But most have to implicitly prepare themselves for much more privatized, individuated existences, disentangled from the complex sociospatial arrangements that have acted as devices through which they could improvise and improve their lives. As these arrangements fade, the criteria for efficacy are much more standardized and idiosyncratic. In other words, there are more rules and assumptions to adhere to, but even if one does this diligently, this is no guarantee for success, as chance seems to play an equally powerful role. Relations, connections, and configurations of places, persons, events, and things may produce substantial possibilities at one moment, but the significance and force derived from these may fade at any time.

As I sought to illustrate earlier, the draw of superblock housing is

A view of the encroachment of megadevelopments on the dynamic popular district of Tebet.

that it posits its own explanation of things. It provides easy entry—a small down payment and a protracted period of installments—as well as access to the same stores, restaurants, and cinemas that one would find anywhere else. As a result, nothing is really missed.

Still, the self-containment is illusory in that the city is literally bursting at the "semes." It is increasingly difficult for individuals to even provisionally secure a vantage point from which they can draw viable narratives about factors and sequences that have impacts on their lives. It is difficult to know what happens first, what is most important to know, and what is possible.

Thus the preoccupation with ghosts is a reflection of this concern about the future. It is a future that promises security through disappearance, where individuals are enfolded into a world where everything seems to be there but does so only because it sets itself apart from a larger city that finds it more difficult to enact a productive circulation of things. Such circulation would enable things to be both intact and mutable. Relations would give rise to specific entities and identities that would then use this momentary coherence as a device to steer relations in unexpected directions. Here there is a play of invisibility and visibility, of person and network, of built and social environments that prompts the continued exertion of effort and striving. The future that is held out for most Jakartans is one in which they disappear from view, where they can be anything but in doing so are nothing, and thus are more ill equipped to deal with growing disparities in wealth and opportunity. This is a situation in which inhabitants find themselves turned into ghosts for each other.

Tebet is not afraid of being articulated to the larger world. After all, its advantages and well-being are largely derived from the way in which it is linked to the rest of Jakarta. It also knows what happens when districts find themselves increasingly cut off. The residents of Tebet have only to look at Menteng Atas, for example, just next door to the north, where megaprojects on all sides are chipping away at the dynamism of the area, leaving it increasingly squalid and rapidly heading for oblivion.

Areas like Tebet hang in a knife's-edge balancing act. There is plenty of evidence of decline and vitality, making confident predictions difficult, as many dynamic prospects could be anticipated, at least in the medium term. As the vitality stems largely from what Tebet avails the larger city, the local economy is not very local. Rather, many residents grow anxious over the ways in which articulations with the rest of the city are hammered into a limited number of forms. For the big developers and entrepreneurs Tebet exists as something eventually available for purposes that have little to do with what Tebet is now. Thus ghosts inhabit the imaginations of residents not so much as a submission to the supernatural, but rather as a provisional placeholder, something that reminds residents that certain possibilities and experiences are not yet finished, nor are they now translatable into easily recognizable forms. Instead, they have to be lived through a medium that is for now neither alive nor dead, something that cannot be bought off, endangered, terrorized, or easily sated. Ghosts become model citizens. Perhaps they will become another urban majority.

The Contributions of an Urban Majority to Urban Thought

Despite the challenges embodied by Tebet, such districts of the near-South have much to offer critical urban thought. We are currently surrounded with a plethora of models for sustainability and best practices, which fits into the ethos of redemption and salvation that has long been associated with urban life. As a locus of aspiration, the city was to be the place where people could change their lives, leave behind the strictures of claustrophobic accountability and obligations. The haunting of guilt and ancestors, the pull of the land, and the anchorage of individuals within ecologies of seasons, crops, and spirits could be dispensed with in favor of a more systematic, rational formula of self-design and the shared benefits of public life and urban citizenship.

As there were perhaps few real instantiations of such an ideal, the imagery of citizenship was to be more a matter of accords and deals. The city had to be made sufficiently livable—in terms of the salubrious, the industrious, the moral, and the consent to be governed—in order for its profitability to work (Harvey 2006). In opting for a more "civilized" existence, those inhabiting the city were more inclined to leave "civilization" behind as well, as the capacity to fight and disrupt could also be intense. The irony here is that the evidence for the scope of such transformations of human possibility inherent in the modern ideal of the city may largely come from that section of the urban population that we know little about—a kind of phantom majority. The task is not to know precisely who this majority is. Nevertheless, it has left behind a broad range of messy, entangled "works," and it is not easy to know what to make of them.

We may not know who this majority is in any way other than through the traces, built environments, and assembled and dissembled projects of livelihood and social affinity that can be read in many different directions. Behind the emphasis on transparency, accountability, and effective performance that thoroughly pervades contemporary discourses of urban governance lurks the long-term obsession of the city with cleanliness, with open corridors through which everything can circulate clearly and quickly, and where light can be shed on any murkiness. Reluctance to work, failure to manage households according to increasing efficiency, and hanging out on the streets while indulging in irresponsible talk or inclinations have long been construed as incipient forms of insurrection. Life has to be made useful, and this requires objectives and outcomes.

Yet cities are full of indiscipline, of those who simply take what they have or have access to and connect it with something else. There are fixers, brokers, go-betweens, and mediators working the gaps, turning memories, past conversations, and observations into work and money. The impression that many are left with is that there are a lot of people sitting around not doing very much or, conversely, always on the go with no particular method or objective in mind. It would be best, then, to put these people to work, get them regular jobs—even if "regular jobs" increasingly entail proficiencies in the very same "social skills" that are at the core of "irregular work."

Take my friend Abaye, a forty-nine-year-old father of two of the best heavy metal musicians in Indonesia and a guy who largely grew up on the streets cajoling and hustling for every little opportunity. The big payoff would come in his organizing the defense of a local market, Pasar Nangka, with its highly strategic location straddling five different kinds of neighborhoods. He expelled gangsters who were using the market to gamble and sell drugs. While the struggle was protracted, his key decision was to keep the market open around the clock, organize clear thoroughfares, and generally make it a place where everyone could safely come at all hours. To keep the market open through the night, Abaye trained and organized a "night staff" made up of some the most marginal "losers" in the area, giving them a chance for steady employment, even if at a cut-rate wage. Widespread use of underinvoicing and direct contacts with farmers—avoiding the use of middlemen—ensured that prices at Pasar Nangka were lower than at any other market in the region, thus guaranteeing a high volume of turnover, a percentage of which Abaye and his staff extracted for various services, such as cleaning and security.

Instead of pocketing all of the proceeds, Abaye bought up property in the surrounding area for a variety of ancillary businesses. These sought to take advantage of proximity to the market and developed opportunities for the wholesaling of rice in a partially successful effort to break the hold of long-established monopolies. Parts of these new expansions were used to house traders in the market, as well as the market's staff. Abaye also lobbied for the placement of an official police post at the entrance of the market, literally subcontracting out security to those who otherwise should be legally responsible for enforcing it. All of these efforts cemented a great deal of loyalty, and loyalty in turn generated financial rewards.

During the entirety of this process, Abaye had no formally sanctioned role in the market, which officially falls under the purview of a municipal association of small enterprises and, as such, is not even registered as a market. This maneuver keeps the official market authority, Pasar Jaya, out of administrative control, and thus prevents it from extracting service fees and taxes. The maneuver has entailed some dissimulation on the part of both Abaye and the traders. Because the requisite infrastructure and building codes associated with official markets have to be kept in abeyance, Pasar Nangka has a largely ramshackle appearance, even as its trading and transportation are highly organized. The market looks like a mess, with lots of people wandering around seeming to do nothing. But there is a lot going on, not all of it immediately useful or apparent. This excess acts as a reserve—it is something that can be put into play when the time is right. And the time will be right only if there are people paying attention, finding a lot of different ways to see what is going on.

So the majority here exists as a particular mode of witnessing, or, as Isabelle Stengers (2010) would have it, a practice of hesitating in the face of aligning one's life with the predominant rules, expectations, norms, or commands. If we consider Stengers's notion of "hesitation" more in the sense of "waiting" or "watching," it becomes a means of seeing what others are doing, of paying attention to a multiplicity of "movements all around" without knowing exactly what they mean or where they are going, and in this process of hesitation, configuring collective practices—practices that require hesitation, caution, and witnessing to find ways of making use of what "comes their way."

Witnessing here is not a form of recuperation, not a means of bringing back the truth of a situation. Instead, it is a constructive and constructed process of imagining what takes place, a process always already too late to do anything about the reality witnessed. As such, the witness technically has no obligation to prove anything, for if testimony were only proof, information, certainty, or archive, it would lose its function as testimony. As Derrida (2000, 29–30) indicates: "In order to remain testimony, it must therefore allow itself to be haunted . . . parasited by precisely what it excludes from its inner depths, the possibility, at least, of literature. . . . there is not testimony that does not structurally in itself bear the possibility of fiction, simulacra, simulation, dissimulation, lie, perjury—that is to say the possibility of literature."

So the majority I talk about here is not a people to be saved or preserved. Rather, it is the work of continuously reimagining the city as something else, no matter how adept particular residents are at trying to exceed their knowledge, their sense of themselves and others, and risk what they have to reach beyond what is familiar. Thus the thrust of practice, politics, and policy is not to preserve, sustain, and readapt these districts to new contingencies and visions. Rather, the task is to use them to discover the city that they were "reaching" for, that they had "in mind and body" when they continuously and incrementally tried to use their realities as a launching pad to go somewhere else, to bring something else into existence.

] 3 [

DEVISING RELATIONS
Markets, Streets, Households, and Workshops

Making Things Relate

Cities are contexts for the dense proximity of living and nonliving things, materials, and abstractions of all kinds. Proximity does not guarantee relation. While the intensities exerted by things and bodies may generate attractions and repulsions, draw things near or push them away, there are no predetermined reasons why things or events should necessarily connect, be in relationships with each other. The subsequent relationships may retrospectively reveal properties that explain how things are attuned to each other, how they complement or engender new capacities, but these characteristics or properties of the relationships cannot fully account for how the relationships were operationalized.

Inhabitants have their bodies, identities, life stories, and aspirations. Devices exist that subject them to certain counts—that tell us how to count them, how to take them into account. From this we can ascertain relationships, the comparability, compatibility, and functional coexistence of things. Yet people and things are what they are not simply because of some preexistent plan that has unfolded according to plan or with a few minor adjustments along the way. Rather, they enact efforts that have ramifications across their surrounds in complex ways and that materialize specific domains of action. These domains enable or foreclose particular intensities of witnessing and their effects, and certain effects get screened out, modified, or concentrated in forceful vectors (Connolly 2002; Protevi 2009).

The density of the emplacement of bodies, materials, objects, experiences, and affects does not necessarily mean that they will inevitably have something to do with one another. Their compact juxtaposition may generate frictions that prompt diverse operating systems to grind to a halt, overcompensate, or attempt to immunize themselves against the effects of such proximity. So getting around the risk of implosion requires different devices that attempt to figure productive accommodations of potential frictions. These devices may include a range of territorializing mechanisms that measure, calculate, anticipate, constrain, and enable particular kinds of functions from what is brought into relationships. A panoply of urban planning techniques—from the cadastral to zoning regulations, sector organization, and the reticulation networks of infrastructure, transport, and services—have long constituted technologies for devising relations.

But here I also want to consider how things are put into relationship with each other so as to make contingent the use to which they have been put in the past, to open up spaces of contestation and experimentation (Brighenti 2010). I want to consider how the process of devising emerges from the intersection of diverse materials, actors, and conditions. Certain forms of individuating specific relational forms may be immanent within the unfolding of specific realities. But such virtual configurations are less specific maps of instruction than they are the capacities of differentiated operating systems, such as residential ecologies, built environments, and social economies, to develop what Simondon (2009a) has called an associated milieu. In other words, the milieu consists of conduits through which these operating systems work on each other to develop a broader range of functions and domains, where each component attains concreteness and stability through the very process of a heightened openness to various possibilities.

As Elizabeth Grosz (2012) points out, sense already inheres in things and relations, as the very materialization of their existence is their capacity to be otherwise. They are already on their way somewhere else, and the material instantiations of inhabitation—of things coexisting with each other—rest in the distribution of sense across it. There is a subsidence of the incorporeal in all materials that becomes the "lining of things in their connection with other things that allows them to change, to reorient and reorder themselves" (8). This preindividuated sense, however, is actualized only in the efforts a collective of things makes to particularize its functioning and contributions in relation to each other so that the dynamics of relationship precede the specification of components. The individuality of the components emerges from relationships among the potential "sense of things" that has not been exhausted or fixed.

Rather than relationships being a feature of the particular character of preexistent things, things come into being as a multifaceted concrescence of capacities and features actualized in their association with other things. The modality of association is not specified by the identity of the components but is itself a product of materials, bodies, and things working through those aspects of themselves, which are not of the order of their particularity or identity but are the sense that precedes them.

From Jakarta, then, I want to explore various ways in which built and economic environments depend on the devising of relations in order to maximize the capacities of people, materials, and places that already exist. In this way, any given district, institution, household, or economic activity continuously repositions and readapts itself to the multiple environments to which it is associated. These environments then constitute the arenas through which residents, materials, things, designs, and discourses take on various capacities, with those capacities in turn reshaping the environments so as to further generate new potentials and events. Particularly important in this regard is the need to continuously enable the capacity for work—that is, for the exertion of effort that enables individuals both to ascertain the efficacy of their operations in the city and to provide the means to reproduce their ongoing existence within it.

On Lures

Alfred North Whitehead employs the notion of the lure as a means of accounting for why people and things are drawn to exude particular feelings or qualities; for him the lure is a kind of overarching motivation of the ways in which things grow or take place in relationship to each other. I want to stretch his use of the term in order to point to a broad range of devices for thinking through how different domains, matters, and forces connect; these can include affect, forms of calculation, practices of decision making, and spatial behaviors and designs, such as folds, curvatures, knots, and twists. These devices include modes of seeing and saying, screens, speculations, aesthetic forms, temporal intervals, information processing systems, media, measures, forms of attunement, and institutions.

A key aspect of the use of lures as ways for devising relations, then, is to understand how the components of relational constellations contribute to the formation of built and human environments but, at the same time, view these components as alternate formations of each other—in other words, where spatial aesthetics are those of time, institutions as particular forms of attunement or witnessing, calculations as impetuous decisions, and so forth. For it is indeed these "switch-ups" and "reversals" that do the "luring." In this way it is possible to at least provisionally see many of the conventional divides to which we assign distinct experiences and phenomena as complicit in creating indeterminate, uncoded gaps and in-between spaces. These gaps and spaces give rise to various twists and turns, hybrid objects and even inversions in the relationships among things otherwise not easily relatable.

In Jakarta, the making of these relationships among the discordant, the not easily relatable, becomes a form of work, opens up possibilities of employment where there would seem to be none, in part because work is not simply a matter of doing specific tasks that are mapped out in advance. Work is also a matter of instigating unexpected convergences that link up different domains and networks that eventually come to depend on one another but never quite get used to one another and require constant attention, smoothing over, and readjustment.

Let us start with an example from Jakarta. The night street produce and meat market at Kebayoran Lama is one of the world's largest, with more than one thousand stalls scattered across the streets and lanes that run from the "official" market. This site, perhaps more than any other, embodies the capacity of the poor, the working-class, and the "barely" middle-class—still the majority of the fourteen million people who live in Jakarta and its immediate suburbs—to viably reside there. This is a city that exists on small margins and incremental accumulations, always with the need to keep costs down. This is a city where hundreds of thousands of residents exist by preparing and selling food.

As such, Kebayoran Lama is a site of various temporalities. Premium produce is delivered to local markets through just-in-time cir-

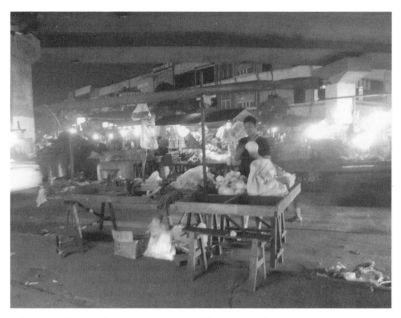

Street seller in the night market at Kebayoran Lama.

cuits, and various gradations of freshness and quality assume different positions downstream. Thousands of truckers, porters, cleaners, sellers, and brokers have long rehearsed the intricate choreographies and financial transactions necessary to convert this four-square-kilometer area into a vast nocturnal trading floor, with its array of locational advantages, costs, spatial arrangements, word-of-mouth consumption, and networks of supply and distribution. Few mistakes and contestations, few grand maneuvers for competitive advantage, can be tolerated, as vast numbers of livelihoods rely on the market's seemingly seamless performances.

At six in the morning, there are very few traces that this trading floor ever existed. As such, it is one the few major operations that works in a city that otherwise appears enmeshed in congestion, confounding rules and regulations, and widening class segregation. It is a city desperately in need of efficiencies, planning, and rational land disposition, but also a city where the confusions and the mess become important guarantees of its plurality.

Kebayoran Lama is important because it is an expanding opportunity for work in a city where work is increasingly hard to come by. But it is not only a place of work. In addition to the work—of selling, transporting, and managing relationships; of parking incoming trucks, unloading them, carrying the produce to designated spots and sellers, and territorializing the types and qualities of particular goods; of servicing the needs of the sellers who work through the night; of distributing, storing, or disposing of unsold goods; of repacking carts and cleaning the area so as to leave few traces of the market's nocturnal existence—it is also a place of affective reverberations and attractions.

Many of the sellers working on the periphery of the market, who usually sell produce of lesser quality or gear their retail to traffic skirting the more crowded core areas, either have other jobs or have given them up for the allure of life in the atmosphere of the night trade. They indicate that they feel joined to something larger than themselves, but without too many rules and obligations, without needing to know precisely all that is taking place around them, and they enjoy the easy conversations with fellow traders and passersby. At the core of the market, where the pace is more frenzied and carnival-like, traders cite the constant swirling of tricks and dissimulation performed with exaggeration and flair. Few are trying to hide anything in a game that suspends the usual Indonesian caution. The constant display of bravado in the gestures applied to setting up shop, cutting meat, displaying vegetables, reciting prices, measuring volume, and bargaining for access to customers and other opportunities spurs vibrations that keep the actors in the market circling each other in ways that spin out across the city through the distributed products infused with different stories and supplementary value.

Before the major buyers arrive in the hours before dawn, the market's main customers make small purchases. It is not unusual to see families piled onto motorbikes, all dressed in pajamas, coming to the market to buy a few cuts of meat or a few pieces of fruit. Despite the advantageous prices, these can hardly be their sole motivation, given that some have spent whatever savings they could accrue on gasoline to make the trip. Rather, many of these customers talk about being beckoned to the market, of needing to pass through only momentarily to soak up its energy, to feel connected with it, to take up its allure.

Clearly, Kebayoran Lama survives because of the efficacy of its role as a major distribution hub for supplying local produce markets across the city in a way that almost completely circumvents formal distribution mechanisms and provides a more resilient skein of inclusiveness for different kinds of labor with different kinds of capacities. But it also persists because it acts as a lure for both traders and buyers that goes beyond this more narrowly drawn sense of efficacy. In the case of Kebayoran Lama, the lure is a multifaceted operation that employs particular devices to generate reverberations among different actors, settings, and actions, which also themselves become lures, particularly in the way in which the dispersal of goods is widely believed to be accompanied by the "story" of the market itself. One of the reasons a pajama-clad household makes a special trip at midnight to buy a pineapple is to capture something of these reverberations at their source, to draw them into their own aspirations and routines. Part of the allure of the market is the way in which the area surrounding the official market facility is so suddenly and completely transformed into a massive trading floor, which has over the years drawn parts of the official facility into an ancillary extension of its operations in a kind of inversion. At the northern periphery of the area, a special market was opened by presidential decree in order to "join" the proceedings and find a particular niche within it. This conversion of space entails the use of existing infrastructure, such as road dividers, as places of display, the distribution of lights unofficially connected to the grid, the acrobatic movements of carters who quickly parcel out large volumes of products for sale, the near-instantaneous loading and reloading of vehicles, the intricate choreographies of butchering, the makeshift construction of micro fish farms, and the incessant banter of "market authorities" who collect fees but, more important, take the pulse of the market's mood, coaxing it along, infusing it with revelry at moments of exhaustion. These are just some of the devices acting as lures, lures that effect a sense of intimacy among things, articulate disparate considerations—economic, affective, political, spatial—into a way of acting in concert that is never fully stabilized through the allocation of clear-cut roles or the implementation of unyielding rules.

Despite appearances and the almost wondrous way in which the market goes about its business, this does not mean that the actors, events, and materials lured into all kinds of relationships with one another in this market intersect in seamless fashion. Those determined to make the hard sell at any cost interact uneasily with those who use the performance of the sale to accomplish other things—whether it be a spirit of conviviality, access to information, or insertion into other kinds of work. Traders trying to temper either their eagerness or their indifference to making a sale at a particular moment, transporters trying to unload their goods as quickly as possible without stepping on anyone's toes, all of the unofficial and official figures trying to impose their authority over their zones of interest without ruling each other out or layering on too many demands—all of these make for unwieldy balances. The excessiveness of the stylized arrangements and performances of selling seen at Kebayoran Lama exist so that the market can reach deep across the city, penetrating as many local markets and households as possible. It intentionally tries to spill over into many different worlds, knowing full well that this makes the "interior" of the market harder to manage, opening it up to a nearly ungovernable number of variables. Yet, while there may be a series of unwritten but well-understood rules governing what is allowed to take place in the market, these rules must leave room for continuous adjustments and shifts, since the market succeeds largely in its capacity to surprise: the best deals, the best stories, and the best opportunities will not be found in the places where traders and customers expect to find them.

The Limits of Maps

Throughout the pluri-districts of Jakarta, the application of available demographic maps by municipal authorities can never keep up with the speed of changes in neighborhood composition. This prompted the "outsourcing" of information gathering to specific local authorities or specially constituted surveillance agents who would continuously feed information back to the "center." But worries about the tendency for these local surveillance groups to operate with excessive autonomy or to be folded into local agendas and economies that would then manage impressions to their own advantage led to a proliferation of competing policing agents. These agents would often provide different viewpoints, attributing power and responsibility to those who had none, in the process giving those persons opportunities to do things that the surveillance was meant to impede.

All of this work of "mapping" was situated in contexts where the distribution of urban services was organized around varying levels of eligibility, in terms of formal proprietorship and organization of residence. Districts were made up of "formal residents" equipped with proper identification cards and "informal residents" whose apparently problematic status could often be converted into many advantages—that is, they could do things that formal residents could not do because to a large extent they simply did not "exist" on the official books. The distribution logics of basic urban services were continuously reassembled as water and power supplies were constantly rejiggered to accommodate a mixture of residency, production, business, and cultural life.

This continuous enfolding of different agendas, settings, and practices put to work many different ways of doing things, of generating and disseminating information. In the built environment, there was a mixture of purchased, scavenged, recycled, and hybridized material inputs. Plots of land were divided and consolidated, often with those consolidated divided again and those divided pieced together into alternate arrangements. In some areas of a district, large-scale interventions could take place quite suddenly but also coexist with small incremental changes made over time. In the local economy, a move toward intensive specialization and upscale, multidimensional production occurred at the same time as the proliferation of small diversified businesses owned by related family and social networks and the aggrandizement of economic activities under the corporate ownership of previously unrelated entrepreneurs. Different municipal institutions tried to graft an array of policies—zoning, cadastral— onto these developments that were simultaneously going in different directions. While usually ineffectual in terms of steering behavior and events in clear-cut directions, these policies nevertheless became important pieces of information and interchange that were put to work for outcomes that the policies did not or could not specify. For example, a rule limiting how much space a formally registered building could take up on a plot opened up opportunities for some settlers to insert themselves "invisibly" into the vacant spaces implicitly created by such a rule. These are just some of the procedural frictions that precipitate the continuous reorientation of residents and environments to each other.

As noted earlier, while the intensities exerted by things and bodies may generate attractions and repulsions, draw things near or push them away, there are no predetermined reasons why things or events should necessarily connect, be in relationships with each other. The subsequent relationships may retrospectively reveal properties that explain how things are attuned to each other, how they complement or engender new capacities, but these characteristics or properties of the relationships cannot fully account for how the relationships were operationalized. Things are lured into proximity, and then are held together as constellations, through affective interchange, probabilistic modeling, remote sensing, signaling, coding, random selection, or algorithmic operations. Such constellations individuate ensembles of things, make them hold or endure across different times and situations, while at the same time they are capable of endless variation (Simondon 2009b; Halkort 2012). Instead of taking notions of who people and things are or what they claim to be or what they have been through as a starting point, it is important to consider the kinds of calculations, procedures, anticipations, and contingencies that bring different groups and materials to take note of each other and enter into some form of exchange, collaboration, or even contractual relation.

At the same time, no single element in this process of putting together constellations has just one function or task. Each element always operates simultaneously as input and output value of the exchange process and the formal expression it engenders. As Deleuze (1995) indicates, the virtualities of what any "whole" can do are irreducible to the parts, as the virtualities of the parts exceed whatever the whole might be, even as parts and whole constrain each other in terms of how they exert their capacities. The inherent instability of constellations thus requires thinking of matter as fundamentally unstable and fluid, as an *emergent property* of the very process of constellations' coming-into-formation (Deleuze and Guattari 1980; Colebrook 2010).

In Simondon's (2009a) notion of transduction, things have no proper mode of existence that could determine their function, properties, or impact, neither as a prognostics nor as a diagnostics applied retrospectively. Transduction rather thinks in terms of *absolute contingencies* (Meillassoux 2008), where things do not exist in possible states but are what they are, precisely because they also could be otherwise. Yet this *otherwise* is not a function of the passage of time, but a fundamental principle of the inner constitution of things. It is a function of their *ontogenesis*.

In this way, the urban residents of the districts I have been talking about in the near-South put together and are themselves put together through a continuous interchange of materials and the expressions these interchanges make possible. These are expressions of physical exertion, visible arrays, and symbolic arrangements, all of which constitute possibilities and constraints for what can be done. Infrastructure exerts a force not simply in the materials and energies it avails but also in the way it attracts people, draws them in, coalesces and expends their capacities. In the process, infrastructure takes on different capacities, stabilizes itself in the very open-ended activities it helps make possible. Thus the distinction between infrastructure and sociality is fluid and pragmatic rather than definitive (Woodward, Jones, and Marston 2012). People work on things to work on each other, as these things work on them.

The Hinge

It is easy to slip into a sense of the city made up by clearly defined components, units, scales, sectors, identities, and structures. Each exists in a relationship with everything else, nested in hierarchies of power, reach, and relevance. Everything is exposed to everything else through structured relationships, where the impacts of these relationships are clear and measured. But everything that exists within a city has shifting exposures. What looks to be of overarching importance may not be. Attention is usually drawn to that which appears to be the product of substantial investment and effort, as well as to facets of life that are easily recognizable and translatable across urban contexts. But what happens if the exposures and the attention are altered, if the aspects of urban life that seem to be the most crucial are intentionally "underplayed," allowing other things to be seen? What happens if the connections among places, economies, institutions, and walks of life are not specified but are instead allowed to waver, to take on different hues and complexions depending on how they are exposed to each other through particular devices that shift the angles through which they view each other?

In this book I want to explore various devices for putting things into relation with each other in shifting angles. As part of this exploration, I want the book itself to function as a kind of hinge that emphasizes counterintuitive facets of urban life—aspects that are not expected, that may exist only momentarily yet register an impact. Part of this process is to consider how cities of the near-South themselves function as some kind of hinge.

Recall the previous discussion on the near-South, in which I offered a provisional formulation that pointed to an interstitial space, neither of the North nor of the South, that challenges the solidity of both designations yet is nevertheless proximate to them. The notion is intended to act as an instrument of translation among distinctions that do not really exist but still have purchase on our ways of knowing about the urban world.

I want to pursue this notion now by emphasizing a relational device, a particular means for devising the relations between urban realities that seem to veer all over the place—that cross the divides of economy, fiction, politics, and spirit. A hinge is a device that connects two objects and allows specific angles of rotation between them. On one level, the objects remain the same; they consist of the same materials and retain their distinction. The hinge is a connection that exists to ensure their continuous proximity, but proximity based on movement across a circumscribed plane of mutual existence. Depending on the light source, the hinged relationship casts divides of shadows and light. It mobilizes spaces of interiority and exteriority, allowing particular openings, perspectives both for those who operate the hinge and for those subject to particular manipulations of it. The simple opening and closing of a door is thoroughly reliant on the hinge. It allows operators to control what a particular space is exposed to and structures an angle to a view from that space to the outside. In the manipulations of the hinge, the definitiveness of inside and outside is blurred, so no definitive statement can be made about the character of the threshold—that boundary between "in" and "out."

The hinge is the mechanism of a fold bringing distinct spaces— made distinct only by the operation of the materials that are connected—to each other, as a conveyance, a mixture. With these notions about the hinge in mind, it is possible to think of certain cities as hinges. They act on multiple forces and flows to construct particular thresholds of intersection and possibilities of perspective. They create specific spaces whereby discrete histories, capacities, and practices are "led into" contact and interchange with others. While they can be said to structure the composition of those interactions by maneuvering to allow specific angles of exposure, they cannot assume complete control over the subsequent volatility of the mixtures. As hinges are neither parts of the objects they connect—as they can conceivably be dismantled and attached to other materials—nor necessarily concerned with the events prompted by those that manipulate them, they have a degree of autonomy. They have a sense of "standing back" or "away" from the ensuing dynamics.

Angling for New Perspectives amid Structured Connections

Cities such as São Paulo, Jakarta, Taipei, Manila, Karachi, Cairo, and Mexico City—to name a few—operate like hinges. Each connects the multifarious commodity chains, processes of production, environmental shifts, political actions, and financial and cultural flows making up planetary urbanization with the expanse of quotidian arrangements, associations, volatilities, tactics, practices, and modalities of inhabitation and economy of a city's "inside." The hinge permits certain degrees of mutual exposure and thus mutual constitution. We cannot really say that these things—planetary urbanization and a local city reality—are two different things. We cannot say that there is something about these cities in particular that make them hinges where others are not. Rather, what I have in mind is that cities of the near-South exist as the "crossroads" of conflicting trajectories of urbanization that exist simultaneously but without an overarching framework that would accommodate them to each other or integrate them (Mehrotra 2002; Baviskar 2003; Bishop, Phillips, and Yeo 2003; Mongin 2004; Boucher et al. 2008; Elsheshtawy 2008; King 2008; Robinson 2008; Abramson 2011; Harms 2011; Kusno 2011). This is then, in part, a function of these cities acting as hinges.

What are to be "hinged" are themselves increasingly complicated series of uncertainties. Cities and the larger regions in which they are situated grow more closely linked and further apart. Certain urban trends may be intensely global, but there is renewed emphasis on the particularities of specific locations, potentials, and problems. What are to be hinged are not simply any clear distinctions between urban development in the "North" and urban development in the "South," but the diverging trajectories of priorities everywhere, and the sense that the cities themselves no longer possess much of any kind of coherence (if they ever did).

Much of urban analysis in the past two decades has centered on the increasing privatization of resources and processes critical to the making of urban life and urban space. The rendering of both space and life to various calculations of efficacy, profitability, normative use, and eligibility in making a market of everything considerably narrows how cities, and all that is within them, can be engaged. Policies and practices grouped under the rubric of neoliberalism emphasize the overarching value of enrolling space and life to projects for maximizing capital accumulation. Urban government, rather than being a mediator among distinctive class, economic, and political interests or a guarantor of access to the possibilities of a viable life embodying a wide range of aspirations, becomes a mechanism to promote the potential for economic growth.

Instead of growth being defined as the process whereby the potential contributions of all residents to a productive life are recognized and facilitated, it is calculated by a total output to be largely defined by a highly circumscribed part of a city's space and population. Maximization of ground rent, inward financial investment, contraction of public budgets and collective consumption, privatization of urban services, and flexible production and work are all components of a process that territorializes urban economic growth as primarily a function of ever more concentrated wealth in the upper tiers of a city's social hierarchy (Shatkin 2008; Peck, Theodore, and Brenner 2010; Swyngedouw, Moulaert, and Rodriguez 2010; Dixon 2011).

No city anywhere has been immune from being affected. One of the primary effects of neoliberalism has been a radical respatialization of cities. Residency and commerce have become more dispersed and homogenized. Provisioning systems are particularized through the privatization of once-public assets, leading to a highly skewed distribution of basic urban services, investments, and thus capacities. The centers of cities are remade to mirror those of others in the constitution of a plane of similarity. This becomes a new "urban commons" established to facilitate a sense of seamless, instantaneous communication—a coexistence where each city recognizes in others participation in the same space. Homogenization raises risks of expendability, so each city must also amplify its own sense of distinctiveness, whether it is a particular economic or cultural asset, a locational advantage, or simply sheer size. Meanwhile, large numbers of residents are pushed to peripheries where spatial contiguities are at times excessively balkanized (Zhang 2001; Caldeira and Holston 2005; Portes and Roberts 2005; Kooy and Bakker 2008; Banerjee-Guha 2010; Daniels 2010; Shih 2010; Soja 2010).

The trajectories of central-city development are often clearly legible. They are legible in the formatting of the built environment, the use of eviction and dispossession as a way to gain control over space, and the overreliance on foreign investor capital. They are legible in the development of the "all-in-one," the megacomplex, where work, leisure, residence, schooling, and nearly everything else are combined and used as an instrument to consolidate links between emerging and historic elites. At the periphery, clarity is usually hard to attain. Cheaper land is used for warehousing the poor, but also for relocating a wide range of manufacturing and back-office services. The periphery is also the site of elite gated communities, as well as a wide range of old and new projects in various stages of ascendancy and decline, mixed in with agriculture and wasteland.

This has left urban regions with large amounts of uncertainty as to how to establish regulatory frameworks and governance practices capable of managing both the fallout and the potential of urban globalization policies. Cities find themselves situated in expanding urban regions where what takes place in the core of the central city diverges from what takes place in the rest of the region. Sometimes growing municipalities at the peripheries of such regions try themselves to become new urban cores, setting up competition for resources and attention. Individual cities increasingly find their hands tied in regard to decisions about water, power, transport, and other services as regional agencies take over these responsibilities. This has led municipal and national policy makers to concentrate on generating multiplier effects in an increasing array of forward-and-backward linkages within specific regions themselves, rather than thinking only about how an urban economy is linked to the larger world (Parr 2008; Torrance 2008; Goldfrank and Schrank 2009; Hodson and Marvin

2009; Moss 2009; Hesse 2010; Sassen 2010; Storper 2010; Vind and Fold 2010;Young and Keil 2010).

Planetary urbanization—the way in which the entire world has been urbanized in the relationships among spaces and territories of all kinds—fragments the administration of urban regions and simultaneously compels larger territorial arrangements to operate as coherent entities (Brenner 2004; Cochrane 2012). Discourses of globalization and the accompanying "modules" that supposedly integrate cities into more substantial circuits of flow and interchange are waning as cities and urban regions try to come to grips with complex topologies of governance and economy no longer accountable within the terms of clearly identifiable scales, sectors, or functions (Allen 2011). These are increasingly inward-looking moments, with the emphasis placed on getting interior articulations right and helping cities to be more "well versed" across a wider range of functions (Keil 2011).

At the same time, the notion of the hinge is important here because São Paulo, Jakarta, Bangkok, Manila, Lagos, Karachi, Cairo, and Mexico City—neither definitively of a so-called Global South or developing world nor fully integrated into the most advanced circuits of capital accumulation and transmission—may be viewed as occupying their own space. But this is a space constructed only through a hinging device. In other words, they have not necessary "won" their own mode of existence in relationship to the remaking of capital through planetary urbanization or to the multiplicity of livelihood practices, accommodations, tactics, and locally generated powers—or *potentia*—constituted by the interactions of agendas, histories, and affect swirling through any given city. The city remains both within and outside these only apparently discrete phenomena—whose discreteness is again a function of the operations of the hinge. The city is tied to these phenomena as it ties them together.

Yet the operation of this hinge manages to eke out a working sense that whatever its hegemonic status, the neoliberal has not thoroughly "captured" the city. Rather, the notion of the hinge becomes important in its capacity to affect different angles of rotation and interaction between the trajectories of planetary urbanization through neoliberal mechanics and the particular powers of *cityness* generated by the volatile intersections of those who live and operate in a given city. The hinge can thus produce a space of *captivation*.

Undercurrents of Change

I use the term *captivation* here in the sense of a momentary holding in place of different practices and sensibilities, lured into some kind of proximity to each other. This momentary holding in place then creates provisional subject positions in the encounters of different kinds of actors—institutional, local residential, associational, and so forth. It is both a space and a time when different kinds of actors take notice of each other, find a way to pay attention to each other, outside the conventional ways the nature of their identities would usually mandate. It emphasizes all of those moments when city planners equipped with their plans, residents with their interests and needs, politicians with their schemes and powers, and business interests with their smell of profit and financial tools intersect in ways that make all actors put aside what they are equipped with, at least for the moment, as all involved sense different constraints, possibilities, cautions, or adventures applicable to them and outside their usual way of operating. It entails the use of the city as a means of inciting the imagination to the existence of certain possibilities. Here, no one knows for sure how to act; there is a moment of hesitation, a process in which different actors and spaces "check each other out," without moving definitively. In more general terms, captivation opens up an encounter between the inhabitants of a city and a larger world that is not fixed, that has no consistent account or form of legibility, as the hinge modulates different angles of view of what the assumed realities are.

If there is to be something that can be considered as existing within the trajectories of planetary urbanization not as alternative or resistance but as an undercurrent, then this something must be exposed to such larger forces in ways that are fluctuating and partial (Thrift 2012). Such undercurrents are produced by the confluence and divergence of many different facets: a wide range of urban practices are holdovers from times past or reinvented compensations that attempt either to circumvent the dominant logics of resource accumulation or to fix problems concerning access to important resources. The proliferation of smart technologies that monitor and regulate different transactions across urban environments exerts impacts that are not completely discerned or controlled (Parisi 2012).

The profusion of provisional alliances among different sectoral actors that come together to anticipate and sometimes implement particular projects produces a range of highly visible developments but often results in collaborations and side projects whose content and scope are not clearly established for any party. The sheer excess of intersecting networks, life trajectories, occupational mobility, and knowledge transfers generates spillover effects whose composition and implications may not yet be clear. There are also many different planning processes that never reach fruition, but the efforts and impacts of which are never fully discarded—particular ideas and ways of doing things leak out into the wider environment. All of these constitute entangled undercurrents whose effects are never fully subsumable within specific ideological parameters.

The result, then, of such captivation is the persistence of spaces within the cities that remain largely heterogeneous in terms of their social composition and use. While there has been substantial contraction of such spaces in these cities, a mode of urban existence continues to survive—within various stages of vulnerability, acceleration of decline and precarity, and forms of regeneration—that depends on circumvention, refraction, and incorporation of the neoliberal. Here there is space for the productivity of the frictions among operating systems mentioned earlier (Yeoh 2001; Elyachar 2005; Chattopadhyay 2006; Whitson 2007; Benjamin 2008; Gibson-Graham 2008; Holston 2008, 2009; Wilson 2008; Guarneros-Meza 2009; Hansen and Verkaaik 2009; Kamete 2009; Perera 2009; Turner 2009; Bayat 2010; Fernandes 2010; Heller and Evans 2010; Melly 2010; Pløger 2010; Sundaram 2010; McFarlane 2011; Raco, Imrie, and Lin 2011).

Working against Uncertainty and Uncertainty as an Incentive for Work

Of course it can be argued that it is primarily a matter of time; that these areas of the cities are simply residues in an urban game whose outcome has largely been determined. It could be argued that as cities undergo the process of transformation from industrial to entrepreneurial economies, as the once vast public sectors responsible for managing populations give way to more complex and diversified apparatuses of control, as relied-upon forms of sovereignty are increasingly particularized in terms of religious belief, lifestyle, and technical interventions into life itself, and as domestic markets are flooded with commodities from elsewhere, the very underpinnings of these districts—whatever their management of local political processes—will crumble.

The densities of interchange that provided thick networks of support and innovation will be circumvented by the demands of individuated efficacy and security—that is, the game of "you must do everything for yourself and only have yourself to blame." This becomes a motivation for situating oneself in one of the megacomplexes. As labor markets expand in only certain technical sectors, a premium is placed on exposure to communicational proficiency and the concomitant staying up-to-date with the latest devices. Increasingly social media and instantaneous documentation of nearly everything become the means of creating a sense of shared responsibility among people living in a highly individuated world—even if this sense of responsibility is reduced to the need to share every little piece of ordinary life with a large number of others.

If urban residency takes place in increasingly formatted and programmed environments, then the very incentive for substantiating relational knowledge—the knowledge about how to act within and make use of varying kinds of relations—is undermined. However messy and untenable certain heterogeneous urban environments may have been, they were a context for training residents in the skills needed to conduct relations. These relations may not have been consistently generous, tolerant, or wide-ranging, but they were diversified. The mixture of sentiments and practices that coexisted in these environments—often uneasily and sometimes destructively—generated in residents the capacity to apply resourcefulness to what they lived with. Now, exposed to the same images, the same mediated experiences, individuals come to experience themselves in an intensely synchronized way; thus the role of urban life as a locus for desiring social change is diminished (Purcell 2006; Heller and Harilal 2007; Huchzermeyer 2007; Raco, Henderson, and Bowlby 2008; Bhan 2009; Duke 2009; Logan, Fang, and Zhang 2009; Peters 2009; Shatkin 2009; Turok 2009; Wang, Wang, and Wu 2009; Zaki and Amin 2009; Bunnell and Maringanti 2010; Lyons and Msoka 2010; Silver, Scott, and Kazepov 2010; Berney 2011; Hogan et al. 2012).

Yet, with millions of city inhabitants unemployed or barely employed, the creation of work remains a matter of pressing concern.

In cities like Jakarta, many service jobs that would be parceled out to more marginal residents in the United States and Europe require college educations and the ability to speak English. These are valued jobs. For the vast majority of youth in Jakarta, who have no university degrees, access to work is diminished; they face lives stuck as food hawkers, motorbike taxi drivers, or waste collectors. In part, the continued existence of large sections of Jakarta as highly mixed districts of various histories, income levels, and ways of life is dependent on the extent to which this very heterogeneity creates work. The mix of different backgrounds, skills, and income levels provides spaces of complementarity, where the costs of inhabitation for everyone are adjusted in terms of the very availability of their interaction. The poor supply cut-rate services for the middle-class, lowering their costs of consumption and keeping money in circulation locally. Diverse sets of skills in close proximity give rise to different "styles" of aggregation, so that niche enterprises emerge to address the increasingly diverse interests of an expanding urban population.

While entrepreneurial activities of all kinds emerge to consolidate a space between large-scale manufacturing and service provision and highly localized economic forms—sometimes displacing both—these "meso-level" enterprises have many different and changing forms of composition. Sometimes they are the work of big businessmen simply mobilizing the cut-rate and undercompensated work of scores of small producers whom they articulate in various configurations of mutual dependency and specialization. At other times, these meso-level aggregates are the products of inhabitants themselves, varying from formal corporations to more informal accords of collaboration—all of which aim to expand market niches and thus income for local actors. The focus on entrepreneurialism in these districts may mirror the enthusiasm of neoliberal economists who overvalorize the initiative of the lower classes. It may even attempt to convert various long-honed practices of economic collaboration into calculable social capital. But it is, at the same time, something perhaps different as it manages to keep in place—at least for the time being—modalities of urban inhabitation that, on the surface, operate against the grain of neoliberalism.

In variegated neoliberal urban conditions, probabilities, accountancy, and the stochastic modeling of risk are the things that really matter. They matter not only because they are the instruments that work with large assemblages of data and uncertainty to specify the positions, the hedges, and the arbitrage that are critical for any urban economy but also because they are the seemingly proficient instruments of dissimulation. They cover up for the fact that no one knows quite what is going on. They derive this efficacy from the way they make everything count, everything accountable, the ways in which they scrutinize large volumes of raw data in order to establish the visibilities, the patterns that are worthy of being discerned, that will constitute the locus of intervention. Everything else that falls outside such modeling does not seem to matter (Callon, Millo, and Muniesa 2007; Foucault 2008; Cooper 2010). For large numbers of residents in cities of the near-South, then, the dilemma is how to demonstrate that where they live and what they do matter when the possibilities of translation, visibility, and value become more problematic.

On the other hand, it is important to stay outside the count, to not get sucked into the game of who and what is or is not eligible (Gooptu 2001; Roitman 2005; De Boeck and Plissart 2006; Whitson 2007; Ndjio 2008; Bayat 2009). One way to avoid getting sucked into the game is to act as if one is very much involved in it, in a kind of mirroring process. The idea here is for particular communities, populations, or networks—otherwise considered to be divergent or incapable—to show back to hegemonic actors aspects of the practices that are acknowledged as playing a critical role in the reproduction of that hegemony. This constitutes an implicit acknowledgment by the weak of the capacities of the strong, but it also inevitably signals that the weak can never implement these practices in ways sufficient to challenge the strong. The very same kinds of practices that in the hands of those with power are construed as calculating, daring, and innovative are seen as impetuous and self-destructive in other hands. These are the very behaviors, then, that would seem to disqualify "ordinary residents" from being eligible to participate fully in a wide range of managerial decision-making processes.

Yet if the hinge is moved slightly, in this process of mirroring, limited spaces of maneuverability are opened, and for many of the very same reasons they are opened for those supposedly much more well versed in using them (de Certeau 1998; Taussig 1999; Williams 2002; Goldstein 2004). In this process, other, "weaker" collective actors appropriate the devices associated with global capital—such as speculative finance, cut-and-paste modularization of spatial products, translocal configurations of production mechanisms, and the privileging of surface maneuvers emptied of historical reference—as a means to create space and opportunities that ensue from different logics and aspirations. For example, under certain urban conditions, residents of lesser means and subject to the arbitrary constrictions on anticipating the future associated with race, ethnicity, or other attributes have often used the very bodies of their households and kin to hedge against uncertainty. Family members all take on very different roles in life and positions in society as a way to hedge against being hemmed in by the character of their exposure to any one domain or facet of the city. They spread out across different locations, institutions, careers, and exposures and extend themselves across different sources of opportunity. Household life thus becomes a kind of hinge—altering points of view of and exposures to the city (Smith 2000; Roitman 2005; Mohan 2006; Cross and Morales 2007; Kothari 2008; Meagher 2010a; Roberts 2010).

The Hodgepodge of the Urban Landscape

One way of thinking about bringing together things that do not seem to belong together is to look at the material environment of Jakarta. Across much of Jakarta, it looks as though a huge container full of stuff of all sorts, textures, and sizes has been tipped over and the contents strewn across the landscape. While this hodgepodge can to a large extent be traced back to scores of particular decisions and accommodations, the surface arrangements have no rhyme or reason. Varying materials are emplaced in contiguities that make little apparent sense or at least would seem difficult to manage on a day-to-day basis. Different dimensions of space coexist with accompanying uses that defy conventional expectations. A household will make great efforts to beautify a building, yard, wall, or path, only to find the surrounds packed tightly with as much stuff as possible, full of objects that retain some use and others that are useless. Large plots are endowed with the smallest of built structures while neighboring ones cram in layer upon layer of extensions that erode the sense of any boundary.

Describing a place as made up of defined objects of diverse com-

A courtyard in Pasar Senen, one of Jakarta's oldest and most important markets. From surveys of people managing the stalls that surround this courtyard, it is clear that the space belongs to no one in particular but is claimed by different sets of people who use it for various functions throughout the day and night.

position and character that are strewn about is problematic in that it presumes the design and fabrication of already existent and intact things. A container that spills its contents across a landscape would not disrupt the integrity of the character of the objects, either in the loading or in the spilling. Someone and some process made these things with certain concepts in mind and with some intent to differentiate them from other objects in existence. The subsequent appearance of disparities and jumbling as these objects are "laid out" would then seem to come from the inability of these objects to arrange themselves in some ordered, even seamless, fit.

The problems of such hodgepodge landscapes would then seem to derive from a plurality of initiatives that are not sufficiently planned out, from a lack of consensus among neighbors, or from a regulatory framework that fails to specify how different actors and objects should relate to each other. But in the genealogy of these landscapes,

A place next to Pasar Tambora to store the "tools of the trade" necessary to run the market, such as carts, bikes, baskets, and selling tables, as well as a small "headquarters" for those who manage the daily rental of these tools.

this is not the case. The shaping of what appears is not predominantly an outgrowth of the mechanisms that would seem to individuate actors and spaces. It is not a matter of dividing the space into territories and zones and then seeing what takes place within each of them and the subsequent patterns they collectively give rise to. It is true that spaces in the city are plotted and distributed. The acquisition of a plot gives the owner or user certain authority to do what he or she wants with it and on it. There are also other arrangements that provide for various forms of collective ownership, trust or use rights that do not fall under the rubric of private property. Individual plots officially registered as such are frequently subdivided in ways that adhere to different rules of use. Still, all of these mechanisms individuate spaces and assume that what ensues in terms of built structure or activity reflects the capacities and interests of the occupants, no matter how defined or assembled.

Using roofs to dry krupuk, *a snack of prawn or fish cracker that residents sell in a nearby market.*

Conversely, however, the seeming hodgepodge composition of these landscapes is the product of reciprocal adjustments, where the unfolding efforts of one project constitute a series of constraints and opportunities for other projects. A plurality of efforts is always under way. These efforts may come from different places. They may represent the consolidated aspirations of a single household or a formulation that attempts to take competing agendas or needs of household members into consideration in such a way as to show each of them a certain respect. Many different efforts are generated from single individuals in terms of shaping performances suited to the various networks and activities they must negotiate. All efforts also represent responses to other efforts; they never exist in and of themselves as emanations of unmediated ideas or aspirations.

Thus efforts are situated in complex surrounds. Efforts are manifested through the shaping of materials, the arrangement of things, and the various devices of signaling where meanings are constructed, conveyed, and translated. Buildings are built, materials are assembled, scenarios are enacted, things are put to work and sometimes transformed, and speech and gestures circulate, as do objects. The materialization of effort generates a wide range of effects. It enfolds or opens up spaces to include and exclude. It casts shadows and funnels transmissions, and it lays out vectors of movement, imitation, and contagion. Vistas and vantage points are constructed that enable or foreclose particular kinds of visibilities that in turn shape what gets considered as an event. As certain things are kept from view, out of the "picture" that is framed by the intersection of materialized efforts, each event comes with its own uncertainty. This is uncertainty about who and what might have been involved and for which it is difficult to make any clear attribution of culpability. These events steer attention toward particular elements and possibilities while occluding others. As a result, this economy of visibility also provides a context for how subsequent effort will operate. Some actors and things will come under great scrutiny while others remain under the radar.

Putting things in motion and getting something out of the effort that has been materialized can provoke conflict. Some efforts are not easily translatable, and some actors are not even interested in having their efforts understood, as they try to dominate space and cut off the need to respond to what others are doing. But the way in which the majority of residential areas in Jakarta have been developed over the past fifty years has necessitated mutual adaptations. Such adaptations may not be formally or intentionally negotiated; rather, they entail residents' efforts to respond to the efforts of others by trying to step around rather than on one another.

These adaptations also entail varying concentrations of function: some spaces are focused on absorbing intensifications of energy produced by the heterogeneous composition of a population or the activities that take place there. For example, mosques continue to be built all over Jakarta. There never seems to be enough of them. This may not just be an outgrowth of the particular faithfulness or status of actors, or of a particular approach to Islamic practice; it may also reflect the need for places that conjoin disparate energies in a focused and concentrated activity, such as prayer.

Some spaces, such as local eating places, absorb the disparate schedules, personalities, and confusions of household life by providing "escapes" that become extensions of households. Others, such as

The accretion of temporalities in Karang Anyer, the material manifestations of incremental efforts of renovation and adjustment over time, as the old and new work around each other. Longtime residents and recent arrivals mix and take advantage of their respective efforts and networks as they adjust to one another in the materiality of the space.

large residences constructed within overcrowded quarters, absorb collective anxieties about uncertain futures. Such construction may displace some local residents, but it can also signal the possibility of some form of future success for all.

These examples are somewhat overgeneralized, representing rather large chunks of the many different "basins" of concentration that exist, as most exist at a more micro and diffuse level. The ways in which constructions and roads snake around each other, avoiding straight lines; the ways in which sleep, sociability, entrepreneurship, domesticity, entertainment, and authority entangle themselves in spaces that are not clearly public or private; the ways in which the profusion of intentionally planted vegetation in neighborhoods counters the escalating levels of carbon emissions; the incessant arrangements and sorting out of various ways in which people move from here to there, whether it be in cars, on motorcycles, through cell phone communication, or through television—all open up various possibilities for the concentration of particular energies, effort, attention, and collection.

Everything that takes place is in an ongoing give-and-take with its surrounds, and thus the built environment, including the various pipes, conduits, drains, wires, fibers, antennas, roads, and flows, are continuously affecting each other in ways that are not always directly traceable to clear causes or origins. A plurality of materialized efforts is a plurality of effects dissociated from any clear connection to something we can definitively identify as "the cause" of what happens. Each neighborhood or district may have its name and authorities, its history of settlement, its collection of practices and dispositions. But whatever seems to be the "story" of the place, its reasons for being as it is, remains a partial line of articulation drawn through this plurality. Instead of wrapping everything up, the story is a way into the thickness of things, an inducement to enter the fray rather than a summation of it.

People's efforts may be steered in certain directions. They may pursue popular styles of improving living spaces or try to accommodate economic activities within their living quarters (or vice versa). The speeds at which these efforts are enacted also vary. Some residents proceed full speed ahead, while others do what they can as their means allow or adopt a wait-and-see attitude. Even in the pursuit of similar objectives, the gaps in acceleration become both constraints and opportunities for various adjustments, deviations, improvisations, and reversals. Actors change their minds, or set off in new directions, especially as these directions are suggested by changes in the surrounds, and especially since certain opportunities are time limited.

Here, as indicated earlier, I find analytical antecedents in developmental systems theory, which suggests that organisms do not adapt to one or more fixed environments. Rather, in paying attention to its material surroundings an organism abstracts a range of different features to put together its own context of inhabitation and operation. This niche acts as an interpretation of the "larger world," which in turn operates on those material surroundings as well as on the plurality of feedback loops generated by other organisms and environments. All organisms then exist in dynamic relationship with their surrounds in such a way that many different domains, reflecting many different abstractions about what nature may be, all have impacts on each other, and where there is no natural imperative, there is no sense of certain things having to take place (Taylor 2001).

The Dynamics of Heterogeneity

Inhabitants have their bodies, identities, life stories, and aspirations. Devices exist that subject them to certain counts—that tell us how to count them, how to take them into account. From this we can ascertain relationships, comparability, compatibility, and functional coexistence. Yet people and things are what they are not simply because of some preexistent plan that has unfolded as designed, or with a few minor adjustments along the way. Rather, they enact efforts that have ramifications across their surrounds in complex ways that materialize specific domains, which enable or foreclose particular intensities of witnessing, effect, and where certain effects get screened out, modified, or concentrated in forceful vectors. The heterogeneity of the population that still makes up most of the residential areas of Jakarta is a function of the particular materialization of efforts of the inhabitants as they work themselves around and through and with each other. In doing so, they enact a particular built environment that in turn sets up particular pathways of movement, exposure, interchange, and isolation that recursively generate their own multiple implications, especially on the capacities of actors and things to operate in particular ways.

The heterogeneity of districts is not so much a matter of flexibility and openness, not so much a matter of a tolerance to difference that in turn is fast fading. Rather, this heterogeneity is the materialization of a plurality of efforts that have had to contend with a wide range of conditions, from a rapidly expanding population to the availability of land at particular prices to constraints on accumulation through formal employment to highly prescriptive and narrowly drawn regimens intended to generate national economic growth—to name a few. During the long three-decade rule of the New Order regime, which largely focused on controlling Jakarta's population rather than on attempting to develop a viable city, whatever sense of development that was going to happen was largely the purview of the inhabitants themselves. If they were to make something happen, regardless of the place or the capacity from which they started, they were mostly going to have to find ways to contend with each other, use each other, and, at the same time, not overburden each other with plans that were too definitive or that risked too much.

Urban planning and governance of course must work with and through the identifiable pieces of the composition of spaces, built environments, and populations. This is what they understand and can deal with. But there must also be recognition of devices that enable us to see the ways in which the relationships among a plurality of materialized efforts constitute the very things that are counted, classified, measured, and, most important, attributed with the authority to have generated their own plans, projects, and capacities.

The historic popular built environments that remain in Jakarta are not simply reflections of different sequences of a narrow range of developments that have proceeded toward their goals at different times, thus leaving a diversity of forms in their wake—a diversity that is expected to end as each space reaches its completion. As mentioned earlier, such sequencing does exist, but it poses its own unanticipated openings and effects. Rather, the diversity is also a starting point from which initiatives create space for realizations of various kinds, sometimes according to "plan," but mostly as a means of making something happen for actors who exist in an increasingly crowded and complicated field of efforts.

In some ways the very strength of these neighborhoods is also their weakness. Given the ways in which their existences are wrapped around each other, what we see as discrete places, economies, households, and actors may, when disentangled, find it difficult to compensate for the disruption in the ways in which they were held together. At times, a history of continuous adjustments provides the experience to make up for the loss of complementarity offered by the dissociated element. At other times, the disturbance has impacts across the neighborhood, mobilizing all the compositional elements into defensive maneuvers, which detract from the other things that they do. In Jakarta, big developers have often manipulated the situation in this way in order to obtain large blocks of land without having to pay market prices in compensation. In homogeneous neighborhoods laid out on a grid or in regulations that specify uniformity in a building's appearance or management, the removal of one or a few components does not really have any deleterious effect on the local system. But in these heterogeneous districts, interventions that actively delink particular spaces, economic practices, or constellations of actors from these neighborhoods may have effects that are difficult to compensate for. This is why it is important to understand the relational systems of urban local built and social environments and the ways that various materialities shape each other according to intensity, resource use, and temporality. Such relational systems then also provide the basis on which to identify potential synergies that might generate new value in terms of the provision of work opportunities and the management of local ecologies.

Spreading Work Around

As indicated earlier, providing work is an ongoing challenge for cities of the near-South, as it is for cities everywhere. One of the accomplishments of the so-called urban majority has been its capacity to stretch and provide work. This work may not be well paid or lead to ongoing and diverse careers; much of it comes simply from the provision of services to the members of a young workforce who need to be physically close to their workplaces. Providing accommodation for the members of this frequently mobile, casual workforce allows some households to supplement their incomes without much initial investment. For this to be possible, however, there must be a steady stream of young people continuing to have confidence in finding employment. Jakarta's current official unemployment rate of almost 8 percent barely exceeds the average growth rate of 7 percent. Jakarta is fortunate in the sense that it has a large domestic market to produce for.

Whatever strategic opacity may be at the heart of this majority's capabilities, cities are exceedingly visual worlds. They are full of things to be witnessed, experienced, and compared. That residents with incomes sufficient to take care of basic necessities but not much more have been able to create social interchanges, built environments, and economic operations that maximize collective consumption and household accumulation is largely the result of local effort. This effort takes place in a larger environment that has at times been excessively intrusive or indifferent.

While municipal governments may not ever have effectively provided adequate housing, water, schooling, electricity, or enabling environments for continuously improving lives in systematic and sustained fashion, they have engaged in bursts of activity that have been critical to providing residents with infrastructure to work with. Local governments' may have largely failed to act in the general public interest in most cities, but at various times they have demonstrated the ability to stop massive land grabs and prevent the monopolization of economic activity. If these governments' bureaucratic procedures have been arduous and arcane, ultimately deflating initiative, they at least have slowed things down so that big players with big money might have to take other things into consideration in addition to their own avarice.

Cities are driven by their inhabitants' desire to work at something. This something might not be measured in terms of income or other material acquisitions; it may be enough for residents to have some sense of being able to get by and an understanding that their prospects of thriving are not completely foreclosed. It is important for cities not only to have adequate supplies of work but also to possess a wide range of conduits through which individuals may see themselves on the way to having work. Cities need a sufficient range of contacts, territories, and experiences that an individual can "pass through" in order to be available to a wide range of possible employment opportunities.

The irony is that this volume of opportunity to a large extent stems from all the ways in which a city itself does not seem to do a very good job of working. For example, in Jakarta, tens of thousands of jobs are linked to steering vehicular traffic along roads that are too narrow and too clogged with traffic and through overcrowded lots where vehicles are forced to park at difficult angles. Restaurants and stores retain staff levels that on average double those in New York. This is not only because of prevailing assumptions concerning individual job productivity or as a hedge against unanticipated spikes in absenteeism. More important is the anticipation that problems will arise that will need to be compensated for. Although a wide range of expedited services have been vastly improved through online communication and coordination, the expectation remains that difficulties in the management of work tasks will necessitate the efforts of several workers instead of one, even for what seem to be the most minimal of tasks. Additionally, there is often a reluctance to manage entrepreneurial activities at scale. While this proffers certain advantages of circulating work through shifting networks of individuals with different skills and contacts, it can escalate transaction costs due to the exigencies of negotiating different "buy-ins" and production schedules. Subcontracting down has long been a common feature of Jakarta's entrepreneurial psychology, particularly where it is cheaper to outsource the work and retain the price differential as the basic source of profit, rather than the quality of the work itself.

Although this passing of things downward opens up a large number of low-level jobs, it also encourages the passing on of implications and responsibilities. From the working poor on up, almost every Jakartan household employs at least one housemaid who works exceedingly long hours for little money and basically takes care of the bulk of domestic and child-care responsibilities. Security guards not only watch premises but are also supposed to be available to run errands of all kinds. The estimated one million food hawkers in Jakarta dish out just-in-time meals at almost all conceivable locations. Many times, one gets the feeling that coresidents, divided by these subcontractual processes, do not share the same world. Those above talk to those below with little sense of commonality and attribute to them the responsibility of things working or not. As long as tasks can be passed along, and value accumulated through this passing, then one need not take responsibility to pay attention to the overall conditions, or to which forms of work and agendas are reasonable or not.

This is work in parts and parcels. While in some sectors this kind of work opens up possibilities for agglomeration, particularly in printing and textile production, it is generally not work that exerts multiplier effects. These effects come from the proximity of diverse activities whose intersection is seen as enabling capacities and markets not otherwise available to them. Such multipliers usually are by-products of expansionary maneuvers as work attempts to take on new lines, territories, and production capabilities, instead of the process of breaking down tasks into component units and procedures.

The Jakarta region now encompasses 6,580 square kilometers, yet the potential of job expansion based on the thickening of interrelationships among sectors remains almost exclusively within the urban core and not in the enlarged periphery. Jobs may be added on, but they have limited interrelationships with other forms of work; thus specific territories may be residually agricultural, or more dominated by manufacturing and growing residential areas, but these activities remain largely insulated, with limited lines of connection among them (Hakim and Parolin 2009).

This does not obviate the need for national economies to create conditions for industrial investment and other projects that are able to absorb large numbers of people in need of work. Rather, it points to the importance of thinking about *relational economies* as processes where specific needs and opportunities are produced. Let's take one example of what I mean by relational economies from Jakarta's thriving textile sector.

Intermeshing Logics and Styles of Production

The Pademangan district of North Jakarta is one of the city's most mixed and densely populated areas. Parts of the district are a bastion of Chinese Indonesians who developed one of the first middle-class areas of the city and continue to earn significant incomes from their dominance of the electronics trade in nearby Glodok, along with small factories producing textiles and hardware and an extensive service economy. These areas are surrounded by large working-class and working-poor areas, which have historically provided labor for the industrial plants of North Jakarta as well as the large retail centers of Manga Dua. Like veins on a leaf, the poor are insinuated in various pockets of these areas, along train tracks, underpasses, creeks, service roads, and gulches between warehouses and industrial plants. The predominant economic activity for much of Pademangan remains centered on small-scale and artisanal textile production, particularly since large-scale clothing manufacturing shrank significantly following the economic crisis of the late 1990s. As manufacturing largely shifted to domestic production and distribution systems that had been oriented toward export attempted to regroup to claim increased local market shares, a growing diversification of production practices, plant size, and labor organization also ensued.

The bulk of local production is centered on providing for the city's main "traditional" market at Tanah Abang, with its ten thousand

Tanah Abang, one of the world's largest textile markets and a key contributor to Jakarta's economy. Nearly half of all merchandise sold in the market is fabricated within the city.

stalls mostly oriented toward clothing, fabric, and accessories. An intricate system of circulation exists in the market's retailing operations, where different volumes of goods are put into play—into various baskets of goods, such as jeans, headwear, shirts, and Islamic dress, that aim to provide advantageous prices for family-wide household consumption. Given that traders in rural villages and urban neighborhoods often pool money to gain lower wholesale prices but also feel obligated to maintain individuated connections to particular retailers, at Tanah Abang individual retailers are constantly contributing available goods to be repackaged for singular consumption needs. On the other hand, new styles are being generated to appeal to youth markets and emergent middle-class buyers who cannot afford to purchase from shopping malls but wish to signal their changing status. Consumption volumes also fluctuate according to season and religious holidays, such as Eid al-Fitr, when the purchase of new clothing is at its highest.

All of these marketing practices require flexibly configured supply systems, which means piecing together different kinds of relationships among different kinds of producers, suppliers, and transporters. As such, household textile production may specialize in innovating new forms of embroidery and design, which, if they prove popular, can be produced in larger volume by a medium-size production plant, usually averaging twenty full-time and thirty part-time employees, down the street. Slight but discernible differentiations in the quality of materials and the styles of cuts correspond to different levels of affordability. Some operations are completely legitimate, with proper licensing and wage policies, whereas others are completely illicit, operating behind closed doors and drawing in pools of short-term, underpaid labor to quickly generate large volumes of knockoffs of higher-priced goods that may be in sudden and short-lasting demand. Both skilled and unskilled labor circulates among different kinds of operations, in part because of seasonality and in part because workers seek to forge relationships with different kinds of production centers. These relationships are critical in terms of regulating costs, so that some operations have enough of a cushion to experiment with new designs and others have a sufficient amount of volume from different smaller workshops in order to maintain their specialization in turning out sizable volume in short amounts of time.

There is also a wide range of workers who perform ancillary activities related to the actual production of goods, such as repairers, labor brokers, transporters who know how to get goods through the gridlock of Tanah Abang's overcrowded streets, carters who load and unload goods at both ends, and investors who use their connections at the market and with various local power brokers to insulate producers from intrusions and shakedowns. The volatile complexity of Tanah Abang, and other local markets, means that entrepreneurial relationships are continuously reworked, as few aspects of the overall trade function with clear-cut, long-lasting contracts. Opportunistic attempts to control market shares, niche markets, popular designs, and advantageous retailing locations require an openness of various production units onto each. There must be not only a circulation of information but also ways of assessing the value and implications of such information from diverse vantage points. This is not simply a matter of cultivating trust in affiliations. One can trust in a source of information, but it is important also to understand what that information may mean from different perspectives and in different contexts. There must be flexibility in the capacity to convert available labor and resources into different uses when need be, and such capacity derives only from a social field that is itself able to move across different identities, statuses, backgrounds, networks, and positions.

Relational Economies

In conventional economic calculations, individuals are viewed as largely autonomous entities maximizing self-interest through the acquisition of resources and positions, which in turn allow them to obtain other goods and services that fulfill specific needs and desires. The price relationship is the device through which these transactions are made optimal given the volume of things to be transacted and the relative demand for them. Actors and the things they deal with, then, are simply considered according to a limited set of uses. But when people and things come in contact with each other, a wide range of unanticipated results and opportunities can be opened up. Here, things and people may be used according to the normative concepts through which they are framed, but different mutations can also occur.

The objects transacted index a particular relationship between actors that is always in transition, as the implications of any transaction may have ramifications across different aspects of the actors' lives, enabling or constraining them as they do and think certain things as a function of the transaction itself. Buying a car or a house, investing in education and training, spending money on travel, investing in business or in the market, bartering possessions—all have ramifications that cannot be fully anticipated, specified, or costed.

Motorcycles play a major role in Jakarta's transportation system. In 2002, nearly one-third of all households possessed at least one motorbike. Ten years later that figure had increased to more than 70 percent, with a majority of households now owning at least two motorbikes. Nearly nine million motorbikes are registered in Jakarta, a number just short of that of the city's total population, and an estimated two million new bikes are sold every year. Half of all commutes are conducted by motorbike (Coordinating Ministry of Economic Affairs and Japan International Development Agency 2012).

Although licensing and vehicular regulations are officially in effect, the actual use of motorbikes, particularly within residential districts, reflects few age limits, and 67 percent of citations for traffic violations are issued to motorbike drivers. Although recently instituted financial regulations mandate that a down payment on a motorbike be at least 20 percent of the purchase price, the expansion of the industry had been driven by average down payments of as little as 5 percent of the purchase price.

Given the volume of motorbikes in circulation, retail sales of parts and bike repair make up a major sector of the urban economy. In the massive motorcycle parts and repair district of Taman Sari in central Jakarta, there are continuously oscillating relationships among individual retailers, who are often grouped through joint ownership or family relationships. For example, I came across Hikmat, whose family owns and operates a string of motorcycle repair shops in Taman Sari, where hundreds of such shops are clustered together. I asked him why the family operates several shops rather than just one large one, where they could save on rent and labor—what value could having several of them basically in the same place provide? Hikmat told me that although his family's different shops operate as distinct entities, with each responsible for its own costs and profits, they are all basically the "same" shop. They are the same not in terms of the products sold or the ways in which they are run, but in how the different ways they are situated in the district complement each other. "All the different shops in the end succeed or fail together." The differences are those of what Hikmat called "perspective," or vantage points, not just to capture different kinds of customers but to build on the different relationships that the immediately surrounding shops have with each other and the relationships of these shops to a larger world.

For example, for those outfits situated at the poles of the district and along the major thoroughfare entrances, the priority may be the quick capture of particular kinds of needs, such as the rapid acquisition of small parts and accessories. In addition, transactions may be geared to making assessments about the largest volume of flow-through traffic as possible so that the retailers have some idea about what aggregates of demand look like: how many customers are looking for repairs, and how many are seeking new or used parts; how many seem to know the nature of what needs to be fixed, and how many are less certain. Outlets also have to anticipate how potential customers think about the different reputations that have been made and lost among them, and where to situate themselves in relationship to each other.

While each outlet exists as a distinct entity, all are continuously being reassembled into various chains of cooperation. Such cooperation may entail pooling money to buy from specific wholesalers, sharing skilled labor, and investing in particular kinds of engagements with customers to glean information about their backgrounds that can then be passed on to other outlets that might be better prepared to capitalize on it. In this way, information about the district and groups of outlets within it is more easily amassed and spread across a larger territory. Even if the workers at a given outlet are capable of fixing a particular problem, they may know that the outlet across the street has better mechanical capacity. If they find out, for example, that a motorcycle and driver come from a pool in a specific company, they may attempt to capture some of that larger pool for sales of parts or accessories. They make this attempt by steering the customer in front of them now to the best possible deal. Outlets do not want only to grab on to traffic passing through, looking for specific goods or services. They also want to use these moments as opportunities to reach out into and tap the larger collective dynamics of hundreds of outlets, with their different suppliers, skills, networks, and reputations, as well as the larger city itself.

Here, the objects and actors are engaged in what look to be fairly straightforward and simple transactions, where customers are looking for the best price and outlets are looking to make the best sale. But what also takes place is a more oscillating cascade of relationships where a wider range of outcomes is possible. Specific ends are addressed—making outlets profitable, paying workers, and putting bread on the table. But the performative characteristics of transactions also are devices to facilitate greater maneuverability in the relationships that exist among people and things within and outside the district. This maneuverability constitutes a kind of momentum that can solidify a particular bringing together of action, understandings, and components but also rearrange the operations of a larger field of transactions in which this bringing together is situated—thus altering its meaning and the scope of what it brings about. As William James (1976, 8) indicates:

> The relations that connect experience must themselves be experienced relations, and any kind of relation experienced must be accounted as "real" as anything else in the system. The parts of experience hold together from next to next by relations that are themselves part of experience. The directly apprehended universe needs, in short, no extraneous trans-empirical connective support, but possesses in its own right a concatenated or continuous structure.

As in any large city, in Jakarta the increasing bulk of work takes place inside large offices, and workers are assigned particular tasks and operational spaces, most of which are well defined. While some similar specificity is replicated on the street, in the production of furniture, textiles, electrical parts, foodstuffs, and clothing, as well as in services and repair, at this level there is also an emphasis on situating whatever transaction ensues within multiple intersections of vantage points, sectors, and customer specifications and origins. While shop owners and entrepreneurs make the gestures necessary to ensure the "integrity" of their own operations, their decisions about where to locate, whom to hire, how visible to make the insides of their production practices, how much to subcontract tasks to other businesses, and to what extent to share orders or appeal to particular customer bases reflect their need to concretize more "public" ways of performing entrepreneurship.

For them, it is important to visualize concretely how one things leads to another, how transactions in businesses related to theirs turn out, how the relationships between businesses different from theirs but on which they depend are conducted. In general, it is important for them to gain some sense about who is buying what from where and in what conditions and volumes. It is important that they have concrete opportunities to anticipate the possible ramifications of changes in the ways they conduct transactions, even though they will never have definitive proof of specific cause-and-effect connections. This is particularly important in Jakarta, where the use of customer surveys and interactive media is barely developed in small business. All of this helps sellers and service providers to gain a collective "sense" of things that, in turn, enables them to make decisions about whether to intensify particular behaviors or slow them down, whether to make certain impressions and information widely available or keep them out of view. In the economies at the level of the street, people are always passing through different transactions and opportunities even if they have specific targets in mind; their trajectories can always be interrupted or resteered.

Emerging from the Midst of Things

This story rings true across the highly dense residential districts of the urban core, from Pasar Melayu to Kemayoran to Galur to Jembatan Lima to Penjaringan to Tanjung Priok to Manggarai to Kampung Rawa. In these districts, almost everything a household does has to pass through the events and transactions of, at the very least, several other households. Each may have its specific agenda and way of doing things, but these are enacted in the midst of a wide range of others. Even when households ignore others, they still take those others into consideration in order to get away with ignoring them. These enactments in the midst of things act as both constraint and potential. But an individual does not know exactly how things are going to turn out. This is because any given transaction takes place in the midst of multiple transactions whose course cannot be determined definitively in separation from all of the transactions it is possible for participants to witness, remember, visualize, or otherwise be convinced are taking place regardless of whether they can be seen or not.

Districts are full of tough guys and tough women, shrewd operators who know how to make a buck out of anything, diligent civil servants who show up for work on time every day, studious children determined to get ahead and get out into the wider world, manipulative housewives with nothing better to do than spread malicious rumors, dedicated civil activists always pushing for collective responsibility to keep the neighborhood clean and safe, reticent retirees who are simply content to watch the ebb and flow of daily life, self-righteous clergy who make a mountain out of every molehill of moral dilemma, and gregarious tricksters who know little about holding down full-time jobs but manage to cajole their way into people's hearts and pockets. These are not predetermined personalities but modes of enactment congealed into shape in relationship to intricate surrounds, into a readiness to be eventfully folded into each other. This is the sense of the "whatever" that William James saw as the condition of all relationships. As these everyday performances intersect, particular needs and opportunities are created.

The needs that arise from the production and intersection of the diligence, trickery, rumors, activism, passivity, and initiatives performed by civil servants, clergy, tricksters, civil servants, students—to cite a few of the many different kinds of characters residents deal with every day—can be tended to through the provisioning of certain services, assistance, and even products. This tending remains an important form of work. It may not be directly monetized or motivated by monetary incentives, but it may lead to heightened access to the possibility of some form of remuneration, even if not directly in the form of a wage, profit, or other monetary reward.

Such efforts at tending and taking care constitute work, however, only if these intersections remain in view and are directly experienced as immediate features of surrounds shared with others. In other words, the intersections of individuated performances, which themselves reflect various potential trajectories of collective life in a district—particular ways of doing things that push and pull discrete performances, skills, and actions in various directions—have to be witnessed. They have to be commented upon, and the impressions drawn from this witnessing must be put into circulation to be available to those not always immediately present.

One of the reasons for the enduring popularity of social housing developments constructed in the 1960s and 1970s, albeit now for largely middle-class residents, was that they were built around semienclosed public squares full of small shops and workshops, makeshift offices, eating and drinking places, and street businesses, as well as notice boards and repair services. These squares were connected to the surrounding neighborhoods through multiple pathways, so that there was always a sense of being both folded in from the neighborhoods and joined to them through different vantage points. While living quarters were small, the overall environments of the developments conveyed a sense of spaciousness capable of absorbing the crisscrossing of different daily trajectories and improvised encounters. The design facilitated a sense of mutual witnessing. The developments were large enough to accommodate a wide range of activities that never felt intrusive on personalized spaces. They encouraged all kinds of mediations that promoted different kinds of connections among residents, as well as between residents and the surrounding areas.

Warding Off Relations

In contrast, when people live in large apartment superblocks, they theoretically have equal unmediated access to the larger world. They come and go via elevators that whisk them to and from their living quarters to awaiting private cars in the garages underneath, or to public transportation or taxis that queue by the front entrance. Residents need not say anything to each other or acknowledge each other's existence, and they can construe very little about each other from their minimal public encounters. For many urban inhabitants this anonymity is a liberating experience, a relief from the labor-intensive conditions of negotiating daily life in "thickly" social neighborhoods. Others who have grown up in such conditions may consider the surrounds of the megacomplex to be largely of their own making, shaped through volitional choices or contingent on what they have been able to accomplish or afford.

But there are large swaths of urban populations everywhere who are disadvantaged by such removal from access to a larger world. The wide world may be there, available for them, but it remains largely an abstraction, without concrete entry points and linkages. Even when such linkages exist, they may be quite limited in scope and content, or fraught with potentially dangerous interference from more desperate and marginal coresidents.

In large housing estates or projects, the volume of collective space exceeds the total square footage of the individual flats. Even though the buildings may simply consist of large numbers of discrete, individually occupied and administered living quarters, there is something about the space in its entirety that exceeds this. Part of this excess can be attributed to the plurality of transactions that could ensue from potential relationships between residents. In other words, given the numbers of different residents who exist in close proximity to one another, on the verge of having something to do with one another that goes beyond simply existing as relatively anonymous neighbors, many different associations among residents could open up, not only in more multiple uses of available space within the designated confines of individual apartments but in the larger world as well, where each resident supposedly has an open-ended possibility of engaging. Buying clubs, religious associations, sports leagues, parent–teacher associations, joint business ventures, mutual investment funds, intracommunal marriages, and voting blocs are just some of concrete examples of what could be seen as enlargements of space.

But this collective sense goes beyond the adding up of the potential engagements of coresidents; it also includes all of the ways inhabitants make sure that these potential associations *do not* come about. As indicated before, the fact that people live in close proximity does not guarantee that they will have anything of substance to do with one another. But, at the same time, the fact that large numbers of people who live in close proximity are expected to keep their appropriate distance does not guarantee that they will automatically resist any inclinations, desires, or propulsions to cross those lines of propriety. Even though the design and management of the built environment may not be conducive of such associations, the very performance of people having to reside in the midst of others at close proximity— and where interactions among coresidents are not necessary—still requires that residents actively *not* pay attention to one another. It requires a habitual keeping away of the concretization of any persistent desires to substantiate and multiply intersections.

So a kind of void is created by the combination of the virtual space of potentiated associations and the space formed by the efforts to make those associations improbable. This void is an undomesticated no-man's-land potentially subject to arbitrary actions and displays of power. If the spaces between residents are shaped through the warding off of the possibility of heterogeneous and unpredictable associations and come to be marked by the absence of potential transactions, then these are spaces that remain largely unoccupied.

The collective interstices that exist as this void are maintained through an implicit violence. This violence does not inflict bodily harm, but it eliminates any but the most minimal encounters and ensures the persistence of practices in which neighbors have little to do with one another. There may be instances where such violence flares up explicitly. Here, the minimal scope of everyday encounters and the void created is seized opportunistically as a means of positing direct threats or used as a way of immobilizing the reactions of residents in response to potentially unwelcome activities. Such explicit violence may become the occasion for concerted efforts by residents to make their living conditions more secure, which then by default brings residents into closer association with each other. But without larger supports that take these associations into various beneficial directions, they themselves become overly complicit with the very threat of violence in order to continue.

At times, of course, the lines are not drawn so starkly. In *Made in Hong Kong* (1997), director Fruit Chan's first film, the story centers on a group of youth who share an existence of fractured domestic life in a massive housing block whose inhabitants are permanently in debt and thus prey to the economies of lending, extortion, and extraction that make it difficult for household units to maintain any sense of coherence and mutual trust. Nevertheless, there is a surfeit of generosity that cuts across both parasitic and defensive maneuvering. For youth seemingly immobilized by depression, illness, the rampant availability of criminal work, or other kinds of incapacity, the housing blocks become a backdrop and orientation point to a "joining of forces" that takes them across Hong Kong's dense fabric of interruptions and constraints in a solidarity of spirit. Sometimes this spirit haunts their dreams and, with the film's main character, Autumn Moon, compels unwanted ejaculations in the middle of the night, indicating the ways in which such solidarity can literally drain life's vitality. But the film reflects a constant fidelity to the possibility of creating new kinds of urban sociality even when these youth know, without cynicism, that the "real" opportunities for this are almost nonexistent.

Likewise, the more thickly mediated residential districts in Jakarta are not immune from violence. Such immunity would hardly be the case in areas characterized by a common and intensive impoverishment or an inability to provide residents with a variety of external linkages to the larger city. When competition for scarce resources diminishes the viability of complementarities and divisions of labor, neighborhoods implode. Residents avoid each other for fear of incurring untenable obligations, and then purveyors of extortion step into the gaps.

In addition, the dynamism of local district economies often depends on the mixtures of work anchored in different forms of production, remuneration, and longevity. In the districts of Jakarta, residents are situated across different kinds of labor—they are wage laborers, artisans, entrepreneurs, hawkers, salaried office workers, and small- and medium-scale entrepreneurs. As trade liberalization has opened up urban markets nearly everywhere to the influx of goods and services drawn from multiple circuits and states have withdrawn subsidization for many aspects of domestic production, the distinctions between formal and informal work have become increasingly blurred. This is especially the case as many formal goods producers subcontract facets of production to informal enterprises to cut expenses, especially labor costs.

The criteria for being able to capture these processes of "blurred" production also become murky. In Jakarta, the complicities among military and police officials, bankers, property owners, transporters, public ministers, and politicians that have for decades captured a large amount of capital and opportunities for developing enterprises are expanding in scope as the "thickness" of other local economic relationships at neighborhood and district levels dissipates under pressure from escalating land values and land redevelopment. As others have noted in regard to work in urban India, the scope and composition of criminality within urban economies go beyond the parasitical extortions of rackets and strongmen or the control of particular illicit sectors. Rather, criminality entails complex relationships among the politicians, bureaucrats, and financiers who increasingly dominate the murky interstices between formal and informal work and production (Sanchez 2012).

In the past, the functionality of thickly mediated districts depended on the residents' capacity to fold the heterogeneity of their styles, positions, networks, and practices into various connections to the larger city to produce "baskets" of goods and opportunities available to the larger community. This was a situation, then, where residents did not face a wide-open external world, but rather existed within a highly textured environment where there were different mechanisms and conduits for reaching specific resources, services, institutions, and authorities. All of them may not have been available simultaneously; some may have opened up as others shut down.

This continuous give-and-take would then often curtail the efforts of various kinds of power brokers who would try to put their stamps on as much as possible. The charting and availing of a replenishment of pathways of access became the very stuff of interactions among residents, as they coaxed, cajoled, challenged, and incited each other into demonstrating what they knew and whom they knew. The viability of the collective atmosphere lay in how it was able to push a district into more intensive engagements with the larger world, not in its ability to multiply opportunities for internal parasitism.

Relating the Now and the Then, the Here and the There

In all instances, the viability of economies and work based on investing in thickly configured local relationships depends on scale. As such, it depends on the ability of residents to experience the different transitions under way as they move from one facet of a district into another. It is the sense of things being under way: how things, conditions, buildings, styles, and uses change and, more important, how these changes are suggested by what one experiences in a particular location. Instead of a homogeneous modularity or an optimum concretization of diverse needs and habits, the built and social environment in one locale not only posits its own suggested resolution of problems and desires for now but also suggests the possibilities of transition that are evidenced "around the corner" or "down the street." These are not necessarily logical or developmental outgrowths of what existed before, but an opening up of those temporary "resolutions" to other designs and layouts. The intensive contiguity of these different configurations, then, concretizes a collective sense of permutation—of how things open up, consolidate, and stabilize themselves again in different forms. But these are forms that, through their coexistence with multiple others, do not rule anything out, do not advertise themselves as the best way of doing things.

Certainly, these transitions require an infrastructure. But the infrastructure need not be seamless; it need not overwhelm the capacity of different transitions to take place in close proximity to each other by requiring either perfectly efficient reticulation or a clean and smooth surface. Initiatives to make economic and residential spaces that derive from different readings of conditions and possibilities will

Ruined spaces in the center of the city often become convenient storage places (in this case for cooking oil) and workshops. Sometimes these spaces are the results of land disputes that have remained unresolved for decades.

not easily fit together or coincide with each other. The experience of shifts can be jarring and even threatening to some. Some places will be left vacant and untended, either because they are seen as not being in the purview of residents or because those who control them want to keep them out of potential disputes. Individual initiatives may pile up fast and generate results that seem to overwhelm one another. But this is the very stuff of repair and adaptation that has historically brought together different actors in these Jakarta neighborhoods to figure out how to articulate things and conditions that have gotten out of joint.

The messiness of environments that ensues from conditions that do not prescribe specific trajectories for making things happen or enumerate fixed sets of values for the results is the very condition that propels new relations, however provisional, to work coexistence into seemingly disjunctive states of being. Instead of coherence being the product of prescribed connections, discrepancies and discordance are hinged into mobile intersections where they can work their way

Tanah Sereal in North Jakarta, with its mixtures of housing types and conditions, reflects the intense social heterogeneity of the neighborhood.

around each other without being hampered by the recognition of stark differences. For the poor and the well-off to have lived so many years together in much of Jakarta, mutual accommodation among substantially unequal statuses has necessitated not so much a practice of give-and-take as a practice of working around, and sometimes through, each other.

Such coexistence has been greatly facilitated by a vast in-between, where elements of both the haves and the have-nots have been folded into large swaths of the built environment. For example, remarkably stylish homes are sometimes situated right next to small ramshackle dwellings. This is an important facet of diversified local economies that absorb the investments of the better-off and the labor of the lesser.

Adequate water supplies and electricity are important facets of these economies, as are efficient drainage, sewage systems, and thoroughfares. Higher efficiencies could probably be attained if people did not

Neighborhood in Pejaten. Continuous efforts to improve the material conditions of residency are under way no matter where households are located.

have to spend as much time as they do working around widespread infrastructure deficiencies. But the jumbled nature of much of the present urban core—its discontinuities and interruptions, breakages, and discrepant speeds—is not an entirely negative condition, for it does compel different kinds of actors and materials to stitch themselves together in various ways to assure continuities that may have few guarantees except for the memory that people were once able to deal with almost anything that came their way. Efficiencies in service provisioning systems do require forms of harmonization, but too often the language or coding systems through which harmonization is recognized as operative require excessive homogenization of the visual landscape. There is often limited appreciation as well for the ways in which very different-looking built projects manage to adjust themselves to the lines of basic standards.

Now it can be reasonably argued that a great deal of effort is required in order for these adjustments to work. Why should residents spend so much time and effort trying to make many different kinds of constructions, adaptations, and activities functionally connect to each other in ways that ensure a generally equitable distribution of critical urban inputs and supplies? After all, isn't that what public institutions, with their overview and oversight functions, as well as their authority to generate and apply financial resources, should be doing? While I would fundamentally agree with such an argument, I would also assert that it too often presumes that there is just one correct way of doing things. With an existent landscape that reflects different residential histories, capacities, and practices, it is also important to find ways of concretely demonstrating the provisioning of equitable opportunities and resources based on residents' ability to take these differences into consideration. Public institutions must find ways of working with residents, understanding the processes of give-and-take among them as well as the constraints they impose on each other, in order to maintain their histories and future potentials of working together.

As I have pointed out in describing Tebet, intensive mixtures of commercial and residential opportunities introduce many tensions into the daily lives of districts. Physical and noise pollution, traffic, safety concerns, availability of recreational space for children, and divergent tax bases, property values, and costs all place strains on the capacities of residents to have comfortable places to live and dynamic, efficient places to work. Conventional planning solutions tend to separate these functions spatially as a means to regulate them more efficiently and minimize deleterious impacts. But these solutions rarely take into consideration the ramifications of such separation for residents whose work, domestic, and other responsibilities do not fit easily into strict time schedules. At certain points, tensions go beyond residents' ability to deal with them effectively. Municipal interventions should take some cognizance of just how these capacities are being exhausted and what kinds of adjustments have been made so far.

Stories as Relational Devices

Again, the sense of manageable scale—the sense that people can see and feel how things work—is critical. An important aspect of such scaling involves the kinds of stories people tell about their experiences, what takes place in a given district, and what they think is possible.

Scaling concerns not only the sense of what spatial parameters are taken into consideration but also matters of time. Stories modulate time; they call attention to certain things in order to concentrate action, to steer things in one direction and not another. Stories also buy time. They speed things up or slow them down, particularly in the way they can influence feelings about things. They can put people at ease or rile their passions.

If stories constitute a particular way in which people connect to each other, then what kinds of stories buy people time to attain some level of confidence in what they are doing? When do particular stories come to dominate collective imaginations in ways that seem to foreclose the possibilities of people doing different things with each other, of taking charge of their lives in new ways? Do certain stories come to the fore that attribute histories and capacities to particular actors, presenting functional abbreviations of complex events but also leaving many things out? Are the capacities and events left out—seemingly marginalized—by these stories then disadvantaged in terms of what they are actually able to do? Or, for the time being, is such occlusion a beneficial tactical maneuver? In other words, does everything that happens in a locality, whether a neighborhood, an economic sector, or a network of institutions, attain a wider range of possibilities by being included in the stories that come to represent that locality?

In the locality of Bungur in the Senen district of central Jakarta, the accelerated growth of the printing industry during the past ten years has substantially changed the character of the area. The industry has enfolded former residential areas as extensions of commerce and drawn in local households to the lowest level of subcontracting. While artisanal printing has existed in this area for a long time, in part because of the area's proximity to one of the city's major transportation hubs, the extensive agglomeration of designers, lithographers, cutters, finishers, maquette producers, platemakers, and digital operators is a more recent phenomenon. The consolidation of all facets of the printing industry, as well as the ability to service almost any customized order in a short period of time—given the wide range of artisanal production centers that coexist with larger-scale but more standardized operations—enables the district to dominate the printing market across the country. This domination is also supported by the district's ability to peg pricing to its management of a broad range of transshipment opportunities, so that quick turnarounds can be actualized through linkage to various airfreight services. Economic efficiency is evidenced by the fact that yearly growth of the sector in the district has tripled the previous year's expansion in each of the past five years.

Still, local officials and residents widely bemoan the loss of their district. Perhaps more important, they feel that there is little they can do either to secure some benefit from the industry or to engage it as a mechanism for pursuing their own development agendas in Bungur. To a large extent these concerns are legitimate. Few environmental controls are in place to deal with increased volumes of toxic wastes, and local authorities have few jurisdictional powers to enforce specific regulations dealing with commercial and employment practices. Local employment opportunities are largely limited to positions managing parking or performing low-end tasks such as page compilation and binding. Most of those who populate the sector are designated as having come from the outside. Many of the artisans indeed apprenticed with firms that were once located elsewhere, and the sector has folded in those with skills, which in most cases have not included local residents whose primary economic activities were in other sectors.

But the key story told over and over again about changes in the district centers on the almost absolute dominance of the printing industry by Indonesians of Chinese decent. Ten Indo-Chinese firms are seen as controlling almost every aspect of the industry, to the extent that their supposed control of market access, information, and orders gives them the capability to define how the hundreds of differentially scaled workshops and factories in the district are articulated. So even though the vast majority of actual producers may come from a broad range of Indonesian ethnic backgrounds, the ways in which they are connected in a series of forward and backward linkages—who gets orders in terms of volume, specialization, and frequency—are represented as the purview of these ten firms.

It is true that the capital investments required in the technology that prepares photographic plates are usually available only to Chinese entrepreneurs. Thus their control of this essential aspect of the industry automatically propels them into a commanding position. This often translates into an ability to function as the key intermediaries steering the sequence of the production process through artisans specializing in one or more aspects of it.

Still, anyone, no matter how big or small, along the chain of the production process can serve as an intermediary. A customer can take a job to the smallest of artisans with the guarantee that he or she will steer the job through the system. Each artisan maintains his or her own relationships across a wide network of others, although the need to call on that network may be infrequent. Individual artisans know what others are capable of doing, and they know that they have considerable latitude in negotiating a final price or delivering reciprocal favors so as to broaden their access to a potential market. While they may largely depend on the capabilities of the Chinese firms to secure a steady market share for themselves, this does not foreclose their own abilities to map out and negotiate their own pathways through the production process. Unlike the Chinese firms, with their large sunk costs and their tendency to transfer significant profit shares to larger ethnic-based entrepreneurial groupings, these artisans are not obligated to act as intermediaries and sometimes use their positions as means of experimenting with different ways of articulating themselves to other actors in the printing sector.

While local residents rather than artisans are usually the ones responsible for the attributions of Chinese dominance, small artisans have little interest in making any countervailing evidence visible. They may not doubt their potential ability to pool resources and organize to circumvent the power of the Chinese, as reflected in their control of essential yet expensive machinery. Yet they also know that the risks incumbent in such a move would be great. Their willingness to accede to these popular stories about the Chinese can thus act as a screen—a place to project the concerns and worries of a community in transition and also a means for staying "off the radar." In other words, they have the space to experiment as intermediaries in a highly competitive business where success at the top requires the ability to include a broad range of small artisan producers within a company's orbit and to find ways of setting them against each other so as to keep costs as low as possible.

When small artisans offer to act as intermediaries they usually have a different motivation in mind: to explore relationships that can find their own pace, that need not be reproduced time and time again as a means of protecting a high-risk investment, and that potentially can lead to other things having little to do with the printing business per se and its schedules and exigencies. These efforts are not to be construed as a business challenge or a means of consolidating greater sectoral control. This is why the majority of such artisans tend to leave the Chinese alone and let them play the part of some essential overseer.

What is troubling in the use of this story line, however, is the apparent inability of the local residential community to see through it, to see a way of getting through this story in order to take some greater advantage of the presence of this growing economic sector. Too often the residents seem to absolve themselves of their responsibility by turning themselves into victims. But given the dissatisfaction of many residents with conditions in the district separate from the growth of the printing business, even this performance of being victims may, as one imam at a local mosque told us, function as a kind of ruse. According to the imam, residents have been looking for ways out of the community for some time, but they have been reluctant to make final decisions given the way land values have been rising, feeling that they should hold on a little longer. With this story line of Chinese dominance and their own inability to do anything about it, residents can disentangle themselves from this dilemma and finally feel free to decide to leave; with the increasing demand for commercial space, they can sell their property for a good price and move on.

The problem with their moving on, however, is that this potentially undermines the highly textured forward and backward linkages and ancillary economic activities that have made such sector-specific districts viable in the first place. It also skews the defense of specific neighborhoods, in the face of the encroachment of mega-developments, against the practice of "building large"—of heightening land values through expanding the size of individual household residential units. Even a cursory survey of urban core districts reveals that increasing numbers of plots are being consolidated to build such large residential edifices. In part, building large is a declaration of status and an exaggerated affirmation of some residents' intent to stay put in the central city. In some instances, as mentioned before, building large is a hedge against debilitating family disputes over inherited property—it is a statement that everyone in the family will potentially get something, if nothing more than space to reside in. But this excessive enlargement of the residential built environment may have deleterious effects in the long run, as the consumption of land and services acts against the larger collective interests of housing residents in close proximity to employment and of intensifying the long-standing synergies that result when different kinds of residents live close together.

Bringing Jakarta Together

As I have tried to show, forging a sense of the common in Jakarta, a sense of people being brought together from different walks of life, has depended on a wide range of devices. Much of the capacity and actuality of people being able to operate in concert is implicit in everyday relations of negotiating space and resources, of putting together individuated and particular spaces of maneuver in the midst of intensely heterogeneous histories, aspirations, and practices. Proximity is no guarantee of interaction, so the city is replete with various "machines"—markets, local production zones, and religious institutions, to name a few—that act as lures to concentrate attention and effort, to intensify synergistic effects that aim to have impacts across wider spaces. Not everything connects or should connect. An important facet of people's ability to live in conditions of high density is the option not to pay attention to everything, or to pay attention to certain things from a distance, gleaning information and impressions from them without having to be necessarily implicated in their stories and outcomes.

Bringing together what on the surface exist as discordant or incommensurable variables or domains has been an important process through which work is created in Jakarta. Not only do subsequent frictions have to be tended to, and relations coaxed from initial resistances, but also the ramifications of bringing things together that have little familiarity or history with each other may spill out in all kinds of directions or may need to be steered in ways that people can anticipate or at least continuously adjust. Residents have to be able to see what is occurring, to place their own concerns and practices within a larger series of intersections with others, and so the ability to see, to witness the surrounds, is important. But since the cognitive constraints of individual viewers and the fundamental instability of any particular view on the surrounds make any event of witnessing always partial, it is important to alter the angles, the vantage points from which the surrounds are observed.

Much of this process of hinging is embedded in the built environment, in the ways that buildings and spaces are constructed and in the materials deployed. While residents are compelled to sustain notions of individual and integrated personhood, and are largely responsible for managing their own lives, part of what they are and do is also distributed across ever-shifting constellations of human and nonhuman assemblages, crisscrossing circulations of materiality, design, infrastructure, metabolism, and subjectivity.

So there are times when the built environment speaks for its inhabitants, conveying a capacity of assembled action of which the residents are a part but of which they are not directly aware. There are no forms of conveyance, representation, or consciousness that would identify them as the purveyors of a strategy. This is just one example of the ways in which a sense of collectivity emerges in the ground of everyday urban life, not as the outgrowths of striving bodies but as collisions of materials and processes that generate impacts far from their initial sites and "steady states." They have ramifications across diverging tendencies. The operations of things in tandem, in high-density proximities, whereby they attract and repel each other, as well as leave each other alone, are not tools grounded simply in the intentions of human inhabitants, aiding and abetting their survival and other aspirations.

Just as traders and customers in Kebayoran Lama seem to infuse the market's products with stories and traces of a seemingly magical sense of efficacy and transformation embodied by the nightly setting up of the market, a wide range of sites and materials are imbued with particular energetic potentials that exceed any symbolic meaning, that act as lures and provide possibilities for people to witness their surrounds in multiple ways. People do live out daily routines largely in quiet separation from others, but they do so in environments of their own making, and they make these environments so as to ensure an implicit sense of intimacy, of touching, of affecting and being affected, even when more explicit political mobilizations are not possible or people find it difficult to envision and concretize particular strategies and actions to make Jakarta a better city for all.

] 4 [

ENDURANCE
Risking the Familiar

Look Both Ways before You Cross the Street

How do the residents of a city like Jakarta keep going? How do they endure the volatility of the city, its massive growth, and extensive fragmentations? How do they persist as familiar sources of anchorage slip away? I begin this chapter not with a story from Jakarta but with a description of the daily practice of a friend of mine living in Kinshasa, the capital of the Democratic Republic of the Congo. I do so because Kinshasa is a city that has few formal instruments to hold on to, few unyielding frameworks that residents can use to track their lives from here to there. As such, it can serve as an important backdrop for a discussion of what it takes to endure. Kinshasa is city renowned for lacking almost everything. Yet it sustains, however barely, nearly ten million inhabitants. My friend, Joaquim, is a twenty-eight-year-old metalworker who has lived his entire life in the *parcele* (compound) of his parents, Tunda and Josephine, not far from Ronde Point Victoire in the KasaVubu district of Kinshasa. Over time, the household has subdivided the *parcele* into rental accommodation for temporary residents, some of whom have stayed for many years. I have known Joaquim since 2007, and he has shown me the ins and outs of this district and some of the tactical practices occasioned by inhabitation within it—something to which I will return shortly.

KasaVubu, named for a former head of state who was once the mayor of this commune, is a sprawling jumble of social composition, built environments, and capacities. It is not unlike many of the historical African popular neighborhoods that have accommodated large waves of incoming residents from different regions and backgrounds. Part of Kinshasa's massive Central Market now overflows into the district, morphing into the Marché Gambella, where traders from across West and Central Africa, Lebanon, Armenia, and Pakistan have for decades jostled with each other to win spaces and carve out niches. Like many such neighborhoods across West and Central Africa, KasaVubu has pulled many different kinds of people and activities into its orbit, generating coalitions, economic and social constellations, that various municipal powers have considered threatening and thus attempted to disentangle. Densities have made the district difficult to inhabit and navigate, and some residents have been propelled outward to elaborate new districts.

KasaVubu is a place full of residues, and without access to consistently functional municipal services, it is also a place full of litter and refuse, both material and symbolic. Its central location, however, guarantees the prospect of new built environments and economic games. The commercial area has been redeveloped several times, but each time these efforts seem to invite more overuse and overcrowding. The surrounding residential areas have some of the highest density levels in the city and are places of rough conditions and rough characters.

As in many rough districts of the world, the residents of KasaVubu have to simultaneously avoid everyday violence and take into account all of their friends, family members, and neighbors who have not "made it," who have not survived. Thus they must be cautious; they must scrutinize what they can say to whom and how they can "duck into" different worlds and alliances. At the same time, they have to do whatever it takes to not become poorer than the next person, not to become an object of charity or solely a beneficiary of the supports of others. They must take whatever is constant in their lives in unknown directions, experiment with it, but without "bringing down the house." What is important is the capacity to alternate continuously between acting in networks as if they are based on trust and cooperation and acting in them as if they are simply vectors of strategic manipulation where one opens spaces by immobilizing others.

As mentioned earlier, Joaquim has spent his entire life in the same place. He works in a skilled trade and, unlike almost all of his peers, earns a small but steady wage making high-end security gates for a growing nouveau riche. Each morning when he rises he buys a single cigarette from the small kiosk immediately down the road from his *parcele*—a practice he has engaged in every day for the past fifteen years.

As he steps outside the *parcele,* Joaquim always hesitates and looks up and down the surrounding streets, which remain pretty much the same from one day to the next. It is not clear that he is looking for anything in particular, as he also closes his eyes at some point so that his other senses may come to fore in his evidence gathering. This surveying is neither a semiconscious ritual implemented as a "good luck charm" nor a running down of a checklist of items or scenarios to be scrutinized. Joaquim is always serious and never rushes this investigation, no matter how alert or drowsy he may be or how intense his need for a nicotine fix. On occasions when I would rush out with him and simply offer to proceed to bring a few cigarettes back for both of us—no need for both of us to go for such a simple task—I would be instructed to hesitate, to get a sense of the day's "atmosphere."

As Joaquim explained, a person could never be too careful about how he or she started out the day. This was not a matter of individual preparation according to some kind of regimen, but rather a matter of getting a sense of how to associate with the street and all that had taken place on it during the previous hours. Even though Joaquim knew well the events and activities that almost always transpired in the same configurations each day, he never could know for sure whether what appeared to be consistent stability might not also hold an unusual combination of forces. Who knew for sure what swirling intersections of impact might ensue from the mixture of the all-night prayer services down the street with the gossip and profanations of the local bars? Who knew for sure all the possible implications of unprecedented meetings of spirits either welcomed or expelled from the daily scenarios of kin and strangers trying to find some way into each other's stories or to avoid each other's missteps and demands?

Even when the street looked almost exactly the same as it had done for days at a time, this sameness could never be a reliable sign of security. People could never know exactly what they were stepping into unless they "took their time," hesitated at the "gates" of a more public world where circulations of all kinds are more prolific and undomesticated. People had to take the "pulse" of things, not only to avoid unseen dangers but also to follow possibly advantageous streams where the fragments of good fortune might consolidate, bringing people and things into highly favorable associations.

Mostly, Joaquim, as he put it, "didn't want to get carried away," and in both senses of the term. He did not want to relinquish too much control about where his desires would take him. He did not want to be an unwitting participant in forces that could outmaneuver his discretion and the way he considered his chosen path in life. Neither did he want to be captivated by any new enthusiasms—that is, those shimmering events that draw a person in as relief from boredom or that promise quick fixes to seemingly intractable problems. Every day could be a fluidity to be used, a lubricant to the rough edges and grating irritations of people trying to get along and fit their frequently overwhelming lives together. But a person should not become too enamored of simply "going with the flow." Rather, it was a matter of how to open and close the "floodgates"—how the district could open itself to changes of all kinds without any one direction or outcome becoming inevitable and others irretrievable.

Virno (2009) reminds us that we should not make too much of the capacity of residents to be flexible and resilient, to become whatever they can be at any given moment. If to be human is to be nonspecialized, to exist without preset behaviors and without well-ordered environments within which to insert a series of innate capacities once and for all, then we all live with an incessant sense of untimeliness. But, as Virno indicates, this is precisely what characterizes the nature of work today—that is, a disorientation and instability that embodies the language faculty, "an inarticulate power, which is not reducible to a series of preset potential acts, acquires an extrinsic, or better pragmatic aspect in the commodity labour power" (101). In other words, the capacity to resiliently become many different things has become standard operating procedure, and so individuals repeatedly experience the very conditions that constitute the presuppositions for human experience in general. Of course, the relative absence of anchoring cultures, discourses, and norms does not open up complete freedom; instead, it ushers in a flood of guidelines, instructions, pointers, expectations, and indicators whose applicability is for the moment and then altered quickly.

I emphasize this point in order to reiterate the conundrum entailed in all discussions of urban life today, especially those that seek to valorize the efforts of urban residents in the near-South to put together cities that work for them. The potentials of those without access to substantial resources, authority, and autonomy are rooted in life's capacity to exceed any particular form of being—that is, the relations that are immanent outside any subject. Yet these same dynamics, the "stuff of life," are at work in the continuous reconfiguration of today's control society. Given this inseparability, Virno urges us to consider the ethical need to persist in putting together a "good life," and that endurance is attained through this persistence.

The Methods of Endurance

Endurance is different from survival. A lot of emphasis has been placed on how residents, particularly the urban poor, survive the city. Sometimes their survival efforts are realistically acknowledged—a great deal of resilience and street smarts are demonstrated under otherwise debilitating conditions. The celebratory sometimes gets out of hand, and the poor are hailed as urban heroes, proof of the resilience of human ingenuity and spirit against any hardships. There is nothing necessarily heroic about the demonstration of a willingness to rush to the bottom. On the other hand, a lot of disingenuousness is also conveyed in some people's apparent bafflement about how the poor manage to survive, as if only a truncated view of middle-class efficacy constitutes the terms of survival. An almost palpable sense of relief accompanies the reporting of high mortality and crime rates for the poor, as well as a host of psychological, medical, and social problems. Especially when cities are dangerous—as, for example, Karachi and Caracas are—stereotypical notions of survival seem predicated on residents' capacity to remain almost invisible, for if a person tries to be or have something of any significance, it is bound to attract all kinds of unwanted attention, and the chances are that the person is not going to be around for very long.

In contrast to survival, endurance is a means of continuing to continue that is not attributable to some inner force or underlying proposition. It is not the unfolding of a plan, or a well-put-together personality, full of fortitude, able to roll with the punches and flexibly duck and dive, avoiding all threats. Endurance depends on the continuous efforts of people to discover and reach each other. It is the willingness to suspend the familiar and even the counted-on in order to engage something unexpected. This engagement may sometimes be simply the reiteration of a commitment to what already is, a decision that it is better to stay put with what is familiar. At other times, it involves an effort to find a way to make what is discovered useful, to incorporate it into one's life or see it as another vehicle to be occupied; it entails the transfer of time and energy from one way of being in the world into another.

The concept of endurance is important for a consideration of how the desire for a radical urban politics might be reanimated. Notions of the "urban" and of "politics" need to be stretched, for the fundamental characteristic and dilemma of urban life has persisted for some time: In spaces and times where materials and matters intersect in ways that exceed the grasp of any particular set of analytical devices, vantage points, and controls, when and how do land, bodies, language, buildings, resources, and objects actually connect? What kinds of proximities and distances of connection are possible, and how are they affected? What do connections make possible, and how do they change? If politics is then a claim on the connections, on their implications and directions, then a broader sense of what brings these connections about is necessary.

Given this, the dogged persistence of intensely heterogeneous districts throughout central cities of the "majority world" constitutes a precondition for politics—not just a by-product. These districts exemplify the way in which density is not simply the proximity of bodies but also the intersection of various ways of doing things, of putting different materiality in contact, and of playing an often deceptive game of alternating the visible and the invisible—now you see it, now you don't. Differences in relations are thus configured that go beyond any specific formulation of a collective subject or of particular modes of identification or belonging. While such subjects must eventually be consolidated as the instruments of claim making and struggles with institutions, the "materials for rupture" are brought to life by this density of intersections. This is what I call an "implicit insurgency." Here the potentialities of radical political change run as a continuous undercurrent through urban life, regardless of whether they are actualized or not.

Such insurgencies are particularly evident in the "remains" of central districts of some major metropolitan areas of the near-South. In areas where distinctions among social classes have been significantly blurred for some time and where intensive mixtures of residence, commerce, and cultural practice have supported wide-ranging interchanges of ways of doing things, the issue of what actually connects in cities and how is not only brought into sharper view but also attains a marked political importance. For, as these areas substantially diminish under the weight of finance capital and speculative urban decision making, a certain productivity of urbanization also seems to fade—something that has important implications for how urban populations will be sustained. In significant ways these districts have endured, and this endurance has entailed the capacity to traverse various conceptualizations and divides that would seek to contain what urban dwellers think and do (Roy 2009; Jáuregui 2010; Raco, Imrie, and Lin 2011; Robinson 2011; Bayat 2012).

Under colonial rule and its various aftermaths, many cities of the near-South were subject to all kinds of impositions, forced down the throats of residents whose status in the cities was often unclear in one way or another. Usually these impositions failed to produce any positive results. They frequently broke down because they were ill conceived, ran out of money, or were not able to overcome the firestorms they provoked. This does not mean, however, that they had no effects (Bissell 2011). They consumed resources, made unnecessary divisions, and took up space and time. Often, their agendas and projects were just too excessive.

We must keep in mind that in the postcolonial world, the onus of constructing viable built environments and urban economies was placed largely on the "majority" itself—through well-known processes of autoconstruction. The very concretization of citizenship depended on the densification of techniques for materializing relations, such as I mentioned earlier—that is, the intermixing of measures, angles, calculations, impulses, hinges, screens, surfaces, soundscapes, exposures, folds, circuitries, layers, and tears as instruments for associating things, bringing things into association (Isin 2007, 2008).

Authorities often tried to limit the growth of urban populations or to defer the affordance of rights to exist in cities. Still, they had to manage city inhabitants according to specific conditions that made the actions, intentions, and aspirations of these inhabitants visible in terms of their responsibilities and claims being those of individuated persons or households. The technique of citizenship—in which every inhabitant is accorded rights and responsibilities as an individual, regardless of status or history—was often applied as a residual shadow of colonial rule and as a form of management without political substance. Individuals were to be enclosed, self-sufficient entities (King 1976; Cooper 1983; AlSayyad 1992; Chattopadhyay 2006; Legg 2008). In part, this approach derived from recognition of the intrinsic volatility of urban life, its tendencies to fracture and separate (Simmel 1972). Collective formations then were to be aggregations of individuals, who would functionally work out divisions of labor, roles, and hierarchies of authority. But this circumscribed concept of collective life made little provision for processes of imitation and contagion—the ways in which urban life engenders fascinations, curiosities, affective intensities, and proliferating intersections of "fugitive materials"—gestures, sounds, phrases, and ways of doing things unmoored from any particular sense or eligibility (Thrift 2004).

This presumption of self-sufficiency, unable to fully address concrete urban realities, brings to light the importance of the intricate intermeshing of bodies and materiality of all kinds, far from the subject positions that conventional notions of citizenship imply. Urban viability meant the willingness and capacity of residents to subsume—not subject—themselves within intercalibrations of materials and maneuvers. This meant displacing coherent cognitive orientations in favor of more dispersed ways of seeing and saying. In other words, people did not worry too much about being specific kinds of persons to specific kinds of others.

Descriptions of urban life also tend to focus on various agencies and structures and the play between them. Residents inhabit, navigate, and shape the city. They do something to it and with it within the constraints imposed by the decisions and forces exerted by different collective forces, whether they are forms of production, institutions, transactions, or ecological processes. Such action assumes the consolidation of ideas, energies, designs, and intentions that are instantiated as and in an environment. Residents, institutions, and economic activities impose agendas, objectives, schedules, stages, and anticipations. But the profusion of initiatives in urban life produces an incessant volatility such that it is often difficult for any actor to steer his or her objectives intact through the choppy waters of intersections, contestations, and collisions occasioned by agendas trying to make their way through and with each other (King 2008). Navigation here is a matter of drawing and feeling lines of connection between different horizons, vantage points, signals, and adjustments; it is not a matter of reading a map and pointing oneself along the shortest trajectory (Latour 2005; November, Camacho-Hübner, and Latour 2010). It is the reliance on a range of technical maneuvers that bring disparate and continuously shifting phenomena, domains, and operations into a momentary sense of coherence, a sense of being able to imagine an environment that makes sense. People's images of the city and the ways they deal with those images are pieced together from different sentiments, senses, affects, and bits and pieces of information and experience.

The impetus to consolidate space, enclose it, and limit its uses has been a long-term urban political project (Elden 2010). Contemporary megadevelopments are largely claims on space, driven by the exigency to tie up space before others do so. It might have been all right if developers had built a few shopping malls, but when a city is littered with several new ones every year, all the subsequent barely occupied space just is not worth the space these projects take up, as well as the social costs rung up for getting ahold of this space to begin with. But this excess has been taking place for a long time. For example, it was somewhat understandable that colonist households wanted to put some space between themselves and the natives, regardless of whether the colonists should have been in the cities they occupied in the first place. Similarly, it makes sense for regimes that want to hang on to power for whatever reason—whether to complete the revolution, to bring development to the people, or to get as rich off the state as possible—to put some distance between their zones of residence and administration and the more troublesome popular neighborhoods or populations. But political decisions have frequently been excessive: universities have often been located far from cities so as to prevent student demonstrations from having any effects; military bases have been located right in the centers of cities, severely interrupting their social and economic fabric.

These are some of the more obvious examples, but the tendency also filters down to more local everyday economic decisions. Social life is spurred by imitation, and imitation consolidates a sense of collective effort (Latour and Lépinay 2009). Imitation drives the formation of sectors, economies of scale, and social cohesion, yet it frequently gets out of hand. In one neighborhood in Jakarta where I work, Jembatan Lima, the reassembling of cloth patches and textile remainders is one of the main economic activities. It is something that has worked well for this area, but now almost everyone is trying to do it. They invest in some machines, make space in their residences or create new spaces, and garner the necessary contacts. But then they cannot find enough labor to keep up with demand or even get started. Each street is full of signs advertising jobs for different kinds of machine operators and semiskilled labor. Some workshops are humming twenty-four hours a day while others languish. Here imitation got carried away.

Because cities have often experienced the intensive separation of things, endurance is a matter of bridge building. These are not bridges that conjoin distinct entities into common purposes, resemblances, or mutualities, but rather bridges that point to breaks and particular procedural frictions in the putting to work of different operating systems (Tsing 2005). Without such frictions there is little motivation to work out ways of associating things that have no overarching reason to be associated (Simondon 2009b). There are also no occasions to come up with practical interventions in a wide range of problematic situations (Riles 2010). These are bridges that reiterate the separateness of things. Yet this is a separateness "within view," where different domains and practices are concrete possibilities of parallel lives that need not warrant continuous accommodation but are still accessible to both parties as disruptions of routinized assumptions. They can be experienced without the compulsion to try to understand all that is taking place within them.

As such, these bridges articulate a wide range of possible futures that people could assume, whether this ever actually happens or not. These positions do not connote underlying points of commonality prior to relations. The relations are not dependent on the isomorphism of what is brought together; nor do they integrate. What is maintained is an intensive proximity, an offering of different perspectives to the other (Strathern 2011). These intersections, then, are lived through as a means of continuance. This notion of endurance points to the ways

Signs seeking skilled labor for the different machines that fabricate textiles. In Jembatan Lima so many households are involved in this business that there are frequent shortages of workers.

in which residents of many mixed-income, mixed-use central-city districts have been able to "recognize" themselves, to maintain a sense of coherence across many different activities and conditions and in the midst of others with whom they do not easily identify or associate.

Citizens, denizens, ethnic groups, administrative districts, and institutions are defined by their transactions with each other and enter into specific transactions based on the various legal and cultural statuses of their personhood. But each also retains separate "insides" that are continuously reshaped through the application of various techniques, stylization, and efforts to reconcile the frictions generated by the different operating systems to which they are exposed and that they incorporate. No matter how accountable and compliant residents may be to larger authorities, no matter how much external institutions intrude and appropriate, it has been possible for residents to develop "insides" of their neighborhoods and districts that enable them to experiment, to explore opportunities of livelihood and sociality other than the hegemonic (Gray 2004; Telles and Hirata 2007; Whitson 2007; Bayat 2009; Holston 2009; Kudva 2009; Nielsen 2010; Perlman 2011).

The Deceptions of Endurance

My interest in the notion of endurance comes from thinking about how the heterogeneous districts of the near-South have managed to persist as mixed-use, mixed-income, and "mixed-up" ways of being in the city. As I have emphasized, things have been changing fast, and these districts are vulnerable to the radical remaking of urban space that has been under way in cities across the world. Is it possible for them to endure, and what would endurance look like? In addition, the question is, endurance for whom? Who endures, and under what circumstances?

Jakarta largely remains a city full of different ways of doing things and residents of different incomes and backgrounds, even as a middle class rapidly expands. To become middle-class might appear to be synonymous now with the capacity to endure. According to the Central Statistics Agency, Indonesia's average annual per capita income was $2,271 in 2008. In 2007 Goldman Sachs predicted that the nation's GDP would reach $700 billion in 2020, with average incomes at $3,000—a level that was attained ten years earlier, in 2010 (*Jakarta Globe,* December 11, 2011). Nielsen Indonesia defines middle-class households as those that spend between 1 million rupiah and 2 million rupiah ($110 and $220) a month for basic needs, such as food, transportation, and electricity. This accounts for 48 percent of the country's population of nearly 240 million. The World Bank (2011) has reported that Indonesia's middle-class population increased by 7 million people per year in the period 2003–10, according to its definition of a minimal monthly income of 2.5 million rupiah. But despite this expanding demographic, the middle class is still dominated by lower-middle-class people who spend $2 to $4 a day. This subgroup represents 38.5 percent of the entire middle class. In contrast, the upper-middle class—consisting of those who spend $10 to $20 a day on average—makes up only 1.3 percent of the middle-class demographic.

Still, the appearances of cities can be deceiving, and Jakarta is certainly no exception. It seems to waver between being a city of full-speed-ahead ascendancy into supermodernity, with its now conventional looks of spectacular buildings, global sheen, and high-end productivity, and a city falling apart, overbuilt, with too many demands, as well as aspirations and capacities to consume more. In the districts in which I work, a more cavalier attitude does emerge, a willingness to exchange almost anything for situations of greater comfort and less exertion and responsibility.

What has been striking in our interviews, conversations, and exchanges with residents across the mixed districts of central Jakarta is that even as the residents want simpler lives with greater material comfort, they recognize that they have come as far as they have because they have forgone the guarantees of unilateral trajectories. In other words, they have been willing to take risks of things not working, and that has often included taking risks on dealing with people and situations different from themselves. This does not mean that they have necessarily worked out long-term affiliations or forged a sense of ongoing community. Often quite the opposite has occurred. But time and time again, residents would talk about how the ability to "keep going" depends on "interrupting the routine, everything that was expected," as Heni, a forty-year-old civil servant, put it.

Again, looks are deceiving, as popular representations of Indonesian behavior usually emphasize the need to "go along with the proper appearance of things," as Fauzi, a fifty-five-year-old restaurant owner, expressed it:

> We seriously believe in the myth of things; the fact that everyone is religiously devout, serious about taking care of their families, and maintaining the basic order of things. But look around you, look at this city, look at how almost everything in the *kampungs* [neighborhoods] barely looks the same when put next to each other, and how that basic pattern of things looking different is then repeated across the city. We came this far because we were willing to go further than anyone thought possible, and we did this by making sure that when you left your house you were not going to go anywhere that was going to be the same place every day you went past it.

In much of Jakarta, then, the capacity to endure seems predicated not on practices of integration or harmonization but on ways of maintaining a certain conceptual distance. Everything that transpires in a particular locality need not necessarily fit, and in the deployment of household and individual initiatives residents need not be excessively preoccupied with the reactions of others. Such localities demonstrate an overall capacity to absorb a plurality of economic and social activities. As Wita, a thirty-seven-year-old administrative clerk in a local government office, pointed out, "We have seen a lot of things come and go, and people are always coming up with this scheme or that, and you know, a lot of it just never works, but it doesn't just change the fact that we like this area, it keeps going no matter what happens." Or as Narima, a young visual arts student staying with her parents, put it:

> No matter what happens between us, the bridges hold. But never, never take it for granted. This is a city that seems to have gone out of its way to look as ugly as possible. . . . The city can be pretty strange, given just how much we trust in what people seem to be doing, the way that things look so easily normal, but that's just the point, you never know for sure what is going on. The challenge for us has always been how to make this uncertainty a good thing, a way in which to thrive, instead of falling apart.

So endurance does have something to do with the look of things, and the ways in which looks can always deceive. For example, no matter which direction I take from the door of my house in Tebet, and no matter how far I might venture, I always encounter people standing, sitting, or lying still, their faces showing something between contentment and dejection, between a longing to be a part of something always just out of reach and a relief of detachment from the myopic conceit that human endeavor will overcome all obstacles. It is as if a space has been cut open to include them, still as they are, in no hurry to do much of anything and oblivious to any resentment that their inclusion should entail some exertion of initiative, some kind of striving. Should their stillness warrant some kind of overview? Is there really any need for them to stare into an abyss or to reassure themselves that rationale choices and entrepreneurial effort are possible in the face of a city wreaking havoc on their lives?

After all, for many residents, the accomplishment of the city was the possibility to attend to small matters—the profusion of small bucklings, leaks, cracks, additions, and encounters. These are the runoffs that skirt the operations of grand plans, no matter how greedy or generous. Among these runoffs, these tiny fissures in the fabric of the sense of things, lurk zones of indeterminate sovereignty and capture.

As Rahman, the guardian of a lot vacant for decades, remarked, "I have never crossed this place the same way twice, for it is important that a person never get too far ahead of themselves." For indeed, the problem of the entrepreneurial self has always been to anticipate the outcomes, to attempt to surpass the outlook that is there right now.

One of the most common remarks heard these days in Jakarta is "People are lazy; they want the easy way out." As Rika, a thirty-five-year-old visual artist, indicated: "Traffic gridlock, flooding, bureaucratic ineptness are some of the greatest gifts to Jakarta people, for it gives them a ready-made excuse for their preference for inertia. For a country so determined not to let the rest of Asia or the other 'BRICs' [Brazil, Russia, India, and China] pass them by, this is a place where people want to slow down everything." But again, looks can be deceiving. Lassitude, ennui, malaise, and anxiety do not slow things down as much as they mark the velocity of things passing by. The impossibility of keeping up with the information that one needs, as well as the impossibility of resisting the seduction of pursuing the different angles and trajectories of sentience coming from all directions, may tactically encourage a kind of fast-framing of experience, the whizzing by of events so as to make them almost imperceptible.

So participation in the same menus, shopping bags, Twitter chatter, lackadaisical couplings, and pharmaceutically enhanced convictions elongates a vast "middle" requiring little effort. There are few barriers to entry. At the same time, for the thousands of citizens milling about, standing around, seemingly taking the easy way out, and waiting out the periods when nothing much happens, there is always a need to do something now. As Miya, a sixty-five-year-old owner of a small textile factory, put it: "We always had a sense of urgency, always felt the need to do something, even when we did not have much of an idea about exactly what to do; but it was important not to stand still. It was our way of being together, our always trying out things. But where is the opportunity for this now?" So in the apparent stillness of fatigue, lack of initiative, or the desertion of imagination, it may not be clear whether residents are being left behind, biding their time, refusing easy solutions, completely at a loss as to what to do, or simply holding out for something else.

In part, there is a willingness simply to settle for what one has. Deni has been driving a motorcycle taxi for nearly twenty years. He said that he has never really considered doing much else: "As long as I make enough to feed myself, my wife, and three kids each day, that's enough. I know by now that waiting by on this corner will give me at least five customers a day, guaranteed. I know if I don't protect my spot there are hundreds that are going to take my place, so better to secure what I have." On the other hand, his wife, Jaie, spends her days not only scrutinizing the prices and styles of small trinkets popular with young female junior high school students, buying them in bulk, and selling them outside schools, but also picking out different students to walk with, accompanying them to local hangout spots where she tries to introduce them to new styles and small products. She tries to start new trends, often losing out and making mistakes, often being made fun of or considered a nuisance by some students, but she keeps on trying and pushing. Over the course of a year, she cultivated a niche of schools where it is now well-known that new styles will start and spread.

If this context of a single couple might be generalized, then, there are intersections between the static and the dynamic, the sedentary and the mobile. They need not be integrated, their distance can be maintained, but somehow they are kept in view. Of course, the seeming inactivity of many residents indicates the problem of providing sufficient work as well as the difficulties caused by overcrowding in informal sectors; it also reflects the fact that certain kinds of selling are seasonal or happen intensely only at certain times of day.

Sometimes milling about leads to something specific. Johnny used to sleep on an overpass that crosses a busy thoroughfare, and he started to sweep the bridge from 5:30 a.m. to 7:30 a.m. every day. Nobody officially paid him for his work. There were passing donations, and people appreciated his presence on a bridge that had a reputation for being dangerous at night. His willingness to do this job gave him a vantage point from which to witness the comings and goings of different residents. For example, he found out that a nearby building housed many sex workers who returned early in the morning before he started his "shift," and that they would often cross the bridge to take breakfast before going to sleep for the morning. Over time, he organized a small fleet of motorbikes to pick them up from the clubs where they worked and bring them home, having developed a relationship of trust. Eventually, he even managed to buy the building where they lived.

The sedentary and the frenetic seem to dance with and around each other. There are residents who have their places, careers, and life trajectories. They are on their way somewhere; they have definitive points of departure and arrival. But this busyness, this elaboration of selling, buying, residing, and transacting, also opens up other spaces. Nothing much may happen in these spaces, or they may exist as spaces between things, but they become their own particular vantage points and modes of occupancy, even when those who do the occupying do not appear to be doing much of anything.

Deception as Method

Here it is useful to consider Deleuze's (1989) notion of the "power of the false" in his reflections on cinema. The cinematic event generates interstices that are basically uncertain in that any given frame or scenario need not follow from the preceding; angles, vantage points, temporalities, and arrays of images can be recombined. Instead of an indirect image of time being derived from how actual things move, a direct time-image generates its own sense of movement, through sound and optical intensities that exist outside any story line or objective. Multiple experiences of the present, logically impossible in any simultaneity, can come to the fore. Story lines can be modified by disconnected places and moments out of any clear temporal sequence. Each interstice in cinema then comes to question its own truth, its own limit of what is possible, and thus unleashes a wide range of possibilities, what Deleuze calls the power of the false. Such an interstice "replaces and supersedes the form of the true, because it poses the simultaneity of incompossible presents, or the coexistence of not-necessarily true pasts" (131).

Additionally, Deleuze characterizes contemporary cinema as that in which "the people are missing"—for the political characterization of "the people" of the past is not adequate to either the potentials opened up by cinematic events or the unfolding politics of urban life. As such, the people will have to be invented. This, as Vincente Rafael (2010) puts it, is a different kind of state of exception, perhaps akin to a miracle. Writing about Filipino vernacular experiences of freedom, he argues that the self-constitution of that missing people occurs in the very inviting and welcoming of their arrival in a process that is never completed and is always under way. In the struggles for liberation, when people were on the move all the time and had to circulate through places and regions where they did not belong, they had to count on some kind of welcoming. The welcoming itself is always surprising, for how and when it takes place always go beyond whatever sense of political calculation we are able to make. In analyzing the landscape of reception across the struggle for liberation in the Philippines, Rafael asserts that the people struggled for were being made in these welcomed arrivals, whose eventfulness went beyond any available logic of political calculation, whether it be self-interest, demographic composition, or regional specificity. The seeming salience of social factors, while at work in some form or another, as *the* form of explication had to be set aside.

The exigency of dealing with the uncertainties of urban life today means that one simply cannot rely on inherited notions about people of the past—such as the conventional stories about modernity, development, and progress. Nor can one count on long-standing notions of identity. There must be a way of seeing between the lines. This is a space that is not so much interstices but substantial in its own right. It is no longer a metaphor for an opaque space between the figures of dominant visibility, but the turbulent leftovers produced by different trajectories of intensely discordant urban growth.

Sometimes it seems obvious that city life everywhere is heading in an increasingly convergent, unified direction, and there is evidence for this. But with such evidence, it is all the more striking that minor differences can still be so powerful and inequities so pronounced. Poverty is being both successfully addressed and ignored; well-being is increasing, as is the intensity of dissatisfaction and alarm. Life is enacted through images of people as objects of class position and cultural, national, and religious identity; as expressions of probabilistic behavior, risk, and development "careers"; and as indicators of complex configurations of demographic, biochemical, and biopolitical variables. Yet these are all inadequate modes of enunciation for how urban life is experienced and acted upon. What Deleuze suggests, then, in his observations on cinema, is a way of trying to creatively posit a sensory, cognitive, and discursive relationship with the city that generates lines of commonality, conveyance, and intensity among different facets of urban life that on the surface and in convention are either not amenable to or not eligible for such lines.

Deception, then, provokes thought. What is visible is not necessarily intelligible, and what is intelligible is not necessarily visible. The apparent certainties of the past dissipate rapidly in the very forms that are most able to document and preserve them (technological proficiencies) as these modalities of preservation entangle them in thickets of vast cross-referencing that make it almost impossible for them to retain any discrete autonomy. All kinds of questions are thus raised about exactly what did happen; how did we get here? Likewise, the elaboration of the future is already crowded with concretizations of anticipation and speculation that assume the form of megadevelopments and long-term indebtedness, much of which will inevitably have to be converted to something else. So how do urban inhabitants navigate the excessive piling up of significations of the past and the leveraged buyouts of deceptively homogeneous futures?

Endurance: Where to Put Things

Part of the issue of deception concerns absorption. It is a matter of how well people and things absorb what is taking place around them. Often it seems that the fabric of the city is being torn because different uses, occupations, and materials do not fit well together or act at cross-purposes. Discrepant uses cannot absorb one another's presence. Things are not in their proper places, and the task of policy is to ensure or restore the proper places of activities. When conditions fracture, seem to fall apart, seem overburdened by different uses, this is a sign that things are outside their proper places, that they cannot assume the same places at the same times. But again, looks may be deceiving.

In Jakarta the questions and struggles about where to put things remain open. This is something more than the imposition of the tools of particular interests and agendas. People have to make a living, and they do so with materials—materials that designs and policies have tried to assign to their proper places, just as people themselves are expected to know their places, which they mark with the materials to which they have access. But the questions and struggles of where to put things are more than a matter of the constant jockeying for space to make a living, although these supplementary dimensions may remain associated with the primacy of this task. The piling of belongings on a street, the ranking of a small line of taxis in the middle of a crowded thoroughfare, the unfolding of a tarpaulin between trees to shelter an outdoor eating place, the circling of rats around scattered debris, the hollowing out of a wall intended to shield a construction site—each of these brings to visibility a sense of space that otherwise would not exist. However discordant, decayed, or exhausted things might be, however little sense they might make in their proximity, they seem to lean toward each other, support each other's most outrageous and inexplicable claims, claims that their persistence makes on both attention and indifference. It is not just that there are aspects of things that remain withdrawn from any attempt to make them take their places in the relationships of the imaginary; there are also things that do not want to be noticed, that seem to want to be left alone in inscrutable contiguity with things to which no conceivable or useful relationship could be drawn.

In Jakarta, the extractions from materials and their concomitant leftovers and waste are massive. On terrain inscribed with competing layers of rules, expectations, claims, functions, and propriety, the interstices created by the limits of available management can be wide. As such, there are many instances in which provisional authorizations neither permit nor forbid particular uses for spaces and things. They bring spaces and things together in ways that could never be consensual. Relations among occupants, both human and nonhuman, never shed their vulnerability. If those operating in any kind of official capacity muster sufficient force, whatever occurs in these temporary intersections is quickly eliminated. As urban politics increasingly prioritizes the rush to making things noticeable—whether deteriorating infrastructure, neglected populations, escalating violence, or styles and fashions—it is important always to question the endurance of things positioned in particular incongruities, wild attractions, and repulsions.

How to keep these improbable juxtapositions going? The most likely and rational response would be to simply invoke neglect: the city is far too expansive and complicated to put everything into its proper

Jalan Tebet Raya, a busy commercial street in central Jakarta. A sign on the phone indicates that money was left with a street seller to encourage use of the public phone so that the local authorities will not remove it.

place, even if there were general agreement as to the terms of propriety. With few exceptions, most mega-urban regions are characterized by highly limited selections of zones that stand in for nearly the entirety of the cities' efficacy and promoted self-images. Resources are overstretched or misappropriated; dilapidation and misuse can act as hedges or as insulation for deeply entrenched interests and claims.

Yet there are supple arrangements that might exceed these calculations of efficiency. Materials, spaces, and people may come together, wrap themselves around each other, and get themselves tangled up in impenetrable knots that can be undone only by expenditures of violence and coordination that for one reason or another prove too costly. So Jakarta is full of different things that seem to "lean into each other" as improbable existences side by side. Particular looks, styles of construction, leftovers of past projects, and temporary initiatives to make or sell things all get tangled up with each other. The remnants of old construction—residences, workshops, sheds, dead-end streets, switchbacks built both to avoid and to accommo-date different claims and interests—meet head-on with the vestiges of public parks never used but that bear the names of national heroes whose memories could never be affronted. These meet head-on with the intricate constructions of dwellings whose unfinished upper stories are intertwined across pylons and wires and planks that act as alternative thoroughfares to those at street level. These meet head-on with the massive vacancies of parastatal landholdings long intended for every conceivable development project but in the end simply used to make up for interminable budget deficits. And these meet head-on with tightly drawn and dense quarters that now abut major commercial zones and hurriedly add on whatever rooms they can to available living quarters in order to accommodate low-wage service workers.

Any particular space or instance may not have sufficient reason or force on which to stake any kind of long-term security. But it is the "meeting head-on," with all of the discrepant, bewildering, and frequently unappealing convergences of things and their arrangements, that produces confounding visibilities and not easily decipherable story lines. These story lines induce hesitation, even paralysis, in those who might otherwise be convinced of their ambition to clean up the whole mess, to impose all the trappings of the profitable city. Certainly tears are made in this fabric of intersections all the time. Feelings of the uncanny do not necessarily stop the big shots from firing randomly into the crowd. But as one *kelurahan* (district chief) told us:

> We could be making some really big money straightening out our territories and selling them off to investors. But sometimes it is much too risky to just go in and start new projects because you don't always know whose prerogatives you might be interrupting. Besides, the developers always like to make sure things happen without a lot of risk, and they want clear access to land and roads, but in much of this district, things are much too mixed in; it is hard to simply identify clear spaces to develop without interfering with the properties and activities of people you don't want to make angry or don't have a very good idea about how they will respond.

Thus critical to the notion of endurance is the fact that there is something about the strange intersections of things and the ways in which proximities that are not clearly prohibitive, functional, useless, explicable, or monstrous slow down rationalizing impulses. They can confuse the apportionment of clear jurisdictions, the assignment of designated responsibilities, and the calculation of the implications resulting from disentangling the mess. Jakarta certainly has not hesitated to get rid of the unwanted and continues to push more of its population to the periphery, yet the obdurate holding on of the intertwining of places with far too many uses with those seemingly abandoned of any constitutes a field of vision that may not be seen in the same way by any critical mass of authorities necessary to get rid of them.

Even in the approval of licenses for new businesses that takes place at the district level, I have repeatedly witnessed arguments among staff about the implications of granting certain licenses. What seemingly should be a perfunctory administrative task sometimes turns into heated deliberations over the possible impacts of a new store, workshop, or restaurant on the surrounding area. These deliberations have little to do with concerns about proper planning or community consultation. Rather, they reflect a desire to maintain a delicate equilibrium among things, and the fact that the powerful and not so powerful, the resourced and underresourced, and the new and the old are still significantly intermeshed. This is in part why, in the very same approval process, some administrative staff will approve almost anything regardless of the consequences, especially for a small "informal" fee. As one local official pointed out: "If we were to try and think about what effect anything we do has on this place, we probably couldn't do anything, for consequences are still going to come at you from where you least expect them. So our job is pretty much just to let anything happen as long as it looks legal and seems to abide by all of the rules, otherwise any other course of action is nearly impossible."

Certainly the way that any street or district looks is the condensation of many stories and struggles, many starts and stops, and many protracted deliberations, as well as decisions and promises continuously deferred to a more optimal time. The intricacies of local politics, the convolution of chains of command, and the gridlock of bureaucracies all play their part in the temporalities of endurance and change applicable to any place within the city. Still, it is important to recognize the actions at the surface of things, for the way their improbable juxtapositions look and the ways they might deceive us—through the appearance of things not working, or of being "on their way out," or even of being impervious to anyone doing anything about them— are facets of their endurance.

Free without a World

A large part of Jakarta then involves the inability to identify what things really are. Sometimes popular mythologies prevail such that things are construed as looking bad on the surface, but if one scratches a little bit, other dimensions come to life. As an example, consider the figure of the *preman* that is pervasive throughout Jakarta. In its most simplistic rendering, the word means "freeman," someone without substantial social ties who was available for protracted renegade warfare against colonial authority, someone who need not garner respect or social capital in predetermined ways and thus can engage in various underhanded activities. In the postcolonial period competing political authorities could mobilize this figure for different purposes. But *preman* (the word is both singular and plural) have generally been vilified as thugs, and they often seem to exaggerate and relish this connotation. In popular vernacular, the *preman* is often simply a criminal, one who tends to originate from the more marginal parts of the Indonesian archipelago, such as Ambon, Flores, or Papua. Thus the word takes on a racial dimension as well.

Yet, in the contemporary history of Jakarta urban politics, the *preman* has been an important figure largely in part because he remains "free" of being tied down to a specific, overarching definition. He is considered to be without a world. Any definitive rendering inevitably acts as a "deception." The *preman* is criminal, entrepreneur, philanthropist, enforcer, local political leader, gambler, sage, mercenary, guerrilla, mediator, broker, entertainer, conciliator, historian, insider, and outsider. Any specific *preman* commonly embodies contradictory roles, and the *preman* works these divergent roles as foils for each other. While any totalizing signification ends up producing a deceptive result, the *preman* himself does not deceive so much as he produces a sense of uncertainty as to what is taking place. He embodies the condition that things may not be what they appear to be. They may not be graspable simply through the elimination of considerations and networks of association that might appear tangential to or immune from such associations with the condition or event being considered. In this way, the uncertainty approximates the *reality* of the situation, and the *preman* becomes the figure that enables this reality to be thought about and engaged.

This is by definition a volatile preoccupation. During the three decades of the New Order, the *preman* symbolized both the degree to which an unpopular government could reach deep inside urban neighborhoods and the degree to which urban neighborhoods could exist out of the government's reach. Specific "regimes" of "*preman*-ship" will assume particular directions: some *preman* will terrorize a district with violent, highly exploitative rackets; some will mobilize collaborative relationships among enterprises of different sizes and ways of working but that all produce for the same market; some will encourage landowners to hold on to their property and mobilize the resources that enable them to do so; some will expedite the evacuation of an area, applying pressure on local residents to sell property; some will facilitate ongoing cooperative activities and balances among distinct ethnic and regional groupings in a neighborhood, and some will foster conflict among them. Additionally, *preman* may circulate through different districts, articulating varying projects and "styles of management" with both intricate competitions and complicities.

Because *preman* are both purveyors of insecurity and guarantors of security, security becomes much less a defensive proposition, instead taking the form of risk-laden maneuvers of experimental triangulations and conjunctions among actors and activities that are not usually viewed as compatible or relevant. This is important, since it means that in order for many residents to attain a sense of stability and consolidate perhaps hard-won gains, they will have to extend their interest and consideration into areas of activity and decision making that on the surface may not seem to have any obvious relationship to them, just as they themselves become potentially implicated in maneuvers that they could reasonably assume they have nothing to do with. What on a macro-urban level are the twists and turns of wildly different futures, developments, imaginations, and memories mingling with each other in seemingly arbitrary companionship are translated into the exigencies of seeing urban life in more provisional, speculative, and sometimes impulsive ways at the level of households and neighborhoods.

To be "free" of social anchorage or a world may inevitably mean being considered a criminal and thug. This is the price to be paid for such autonomy. But what an individual does from that position, while never completely shaking off the designation as criminal, is also open. It need not assume a fixed relationship to the prevailing standards of normality and legality. This, in turn, disrupts the fixed positions these designations have as well. But more important, the popular understanding of what constitutes the authority of *preman* to operate across so many ambiguities and sectors is their willingness to act as the repositories of stories. *Preman* have interests and turfs to defend, both theirs and those of the various parties they may come to work for, but they also know that their maneuverability largely derives from the persuasiveness of the narratives they generate about how people within particular markets, neighborhoods, or economic sectors are connected to each other, how they are implicated in each other's lives. Hercules, one of Jakarta's most notorious *preman,* long considered the "sovereign" of the city's largest market, said, "The only thing sellers in this market don't know about themselves is themselves." Loosely translated, there is just no way they can keep track of everything they are becoming in the ins and outs of the relationships that are necessary to keep the market going.

Preman rarely sit behind closed doors; they are found most often in places that make them highly visible and also give them opportunities to witness what is going on. They are "exposed to the elements," as a popular saying goes. They watch what comes and goes, and one of their major "businesses" is to regulate various flows into and out of markets, traffic intersections, and entertainment districts. But again, their most important activity is the gathering of stories. They sit in *warung* and *kaki lima,* markets, mosques, and warehouses, offering snacks, cigarettes, and small loans while they garner pieces of gossip, news, and reports. People in turn ask them for their impressions as to what is going on and who might be behind certain events. *Preman* are sources of information about what property might be for sale, what official might be persuaded to cooperate in a particular venture, how best to expedite an application, where a particular volume of goods might be accessed at a good price, where a spouse may be spending his or her time, and what specific figures in the neighborhood are doing elsewhere.

Sometimes people ask *preman* to intervene in troubling situations, to "straighten out" recalcitrant bosses or employees, neighborhoods, or relatives. *Preman* use the links they have cultivated across the city to supplement the information they have and to intervene in situations beyond their own immediate competence.

As the "attractors" of stories, and without owing any overarching obligation to anyone in the ways these stories are assembled and intersected, *preman* can shape the narrative threads in many different ways, and they often do so in order to bring many different actors within a common orbit. The intent of the narration is not to represent events and daily life according to strictures of official intelligibility or in tropes that favor the ranking hierarchies of sense and authority within a given district. Nor is the intent to stick close to a linear unfolding of temporality, where the sequence of events is rendered in a strict order of "before and after," for this is a process that tends to favor "causes" that protect the alignments of power and meaning that residents are accustomed to. Rather, the accounts related by *preman* are often uncanny, speculative readings of what might be transpiring behind the visible chain of associations.

Preman may be relied upon for authoritative accounts of what is taking place based on their exposure to multiple events and angles, the long hours they spend watching what is unfolding around them, the steps they take to intervene in trouble and conflict, and their opportunistic seizing of unanticipated openings. Yet the accounts they usually render fall outside the conventional assumptions about what makes accounts authoritative. In a city where the exigencies of survival tend to now dissociate individuals and households, *preman* are likely to give accounts that pull them back together. At times, they invent accounts of how the actions of different individuals are related to each other. At other times, they actively stage scenarios where those implications are performed. If, for example, residents are worried that a new business on their lane is going to fill the area with unwanted traffic, *preman* may actually stage a scenario where trucks break down in the area, clog the street, and force those launching the new business venture to reconsider.

But usually the actions are more nuanced. *Preman* will incessantly hint, rumor, and suggest in ways that implant a sense of caution or determination, a sense of being emboldened or restrained. Everything the *preman* uses comes from the surrounds, and it is calculated to have some degree of resonance with the recipients of the narrative no matter how it is arranged. All the *preman* does is to reflect back to an audience that which the audience members themselves have provided, but in ways that destabilize the audience's sense of what is going on and what it is possible to do in relationship to it.

Of Eligibility and Risk

Of course, the members of that audience may become increasingly convinced that they know what is good for them, without reservation. In our discussions with residents, I noticed that younger people, especially, referred to the need not to "deceive themselves." As Ade, a twenty-four-year-old graduate student, explained: "We have seen generations before us trying to get by in any way they can for so long that they seemed to have lost the purpose for what they were doing this for. Now if one is to be successful, you have to be eligible for it, you have to prove to the world that you have what it takes." A renewed sense of eligibility seems to again put the onus of dealing with the complexities of urban life squarely on the individual—that is, it is the individual's moral responsibility to achieve, to attain some kind of success. So it is important that one not deceive oneself, and often the best way to do this is to put oneself in a situation where one can follow the good examples of others.

Indra and Faras are a couple in their late twenties with a small child. Indra is a nursery assistant and Faras repairs air conditioners in a large office building. They rent a small house in in a crowded lower-middle-class section of Johar Baru. The rent takes up about 20 percent of their income, which they supplement by preparing sweets for special events sponsored by the many schools in the surrounding area. They are generally satisfied with the conditions of their neighborhood and have no difficulties with the fact that there are many new residents coming from all over the country to work in nearby factories and shopping malls. But they feel that the people they aspire to emulate would undoubtedly look down on their living context.

Faras said, "My seniors at work wouldn't like it here because there are a lot of unmarried couples, and many neighbors drink and the pious ones complain to no avail; still everyone gets along, and I am able to earn more because my neighbors have different connections to places which always need their air-cons fixed." Indra stated that she relies on her neighbors to pick her son up after school if she is late getting home, and this is never a problem. "But it is not the right kind of place to really think about making sure our son lives the right kind of life; in this life you have to be worthy in order to succeed, and we worry whether or not living here will make us worthy."

Rather than assessing the prospects of future viability in terms of what a person is capable of doing and the networks of support and information that person has available, Indra was saying that a person has to be "eligible" for success, and that eligibility can literally be a matter of where one is located in the city. She and Faras are saving hard to accumulate enough for a down payment on a small flat in Pondok Bambu in East Jakarta, which they believe to be a more Islamically correct place to live. Although they do not consider themselves any more religiously devout than most, they think that living in Pondok Bambu will maximize their eligibility for eventual success, even though they both know that they will go into long-term debt paying for the apartment and that their opportunities for supplemental income and child care will also be reduced.

Other residents worry that they will increasingly have no choice but "to play it safe," as Rani, the twenty-eight-year-old proprietor of a small computer shop, put it. Rani went on:

> For my parents, they tried a lot of different kinds of economic activities, and when they didn't work, well, there was always the opportunity to try other things because we lived around a lot of other people who were also trying to do things; they took different ideas and ways of doing things from each other, and even more important, the neighborhood seemingly could take it all in; a person wasn't going to ruin anything, because things were being changed all of the time. But when I move to an apartment, who am I going to see and what am I going to do there except just eat and sleep?

Denny, a sixty-year-old owner of several *warung* (local shops selling basic food and supplies), indicated that "it wouldn't be bad to have everything you need managed well, but realistically, we took so many risks to get this far, had to try and get along with so many people we were not prepared to deal with, but it got us somewhere, made us better people. I look at all of those people in those towers and have no idea who they are."

Dita, a fifty-year-old manager of a small textile workshop, explained: "We might have had our specific hopes or specific ideas about what we thought we could do, but we also knew that other people with more money and more connections probably had the same ideas as well, and that we could never go from point A to point B without making adjustments along the way. But when we did this, we found out not only that we could make compromises, but that we were quite excited to discover different plans that we hadn't thought of before." Andi, a fifty-eight-year-old owner of a fleet of *bajaj* (three-wheeled covered motorbikes), noted, "It was always a risk finding the activity that worked for you."

A sense of risk pervades a lot of the residents' comments. I am mindful of the slippery connotations associated with risk. I am mindful of the way that risk becomes knowledge critical to practices of governance in that it renders visible the actions of populations in a field of chance. Here differences among people and situations are instrumentalized and abstracted from the ways in which they are produced by economy and politics. Such instrumentalization then permits accumulation to proceed without having to take into consideration the vast range of negative impacts it induces. More significantly, it illustrates the overall condition as that which only capitalist production is capable of rectifying (Stanley 2013).

But again, risk is something that can be deceptive. So instead of risk being the language of contingency that obscures the processes through which a household reality has been constructed—a language that abstracts that experience in terms of particular appearances in statistical calculations—contingency for many of the residents I work with seemed to become a means of "freeing" up livelihoods from a limiting commitment to specific modalities of self-recognition. Residents could get on with negotiating complicated interactions with different facets of the city without necessarily being hindered by the defense of "ultimate bottom lines" or "territories of belonging." They could get by without taking on cascading social obligations that would limit the kinds of perspectives and information they had available.

Endurance is a tricky matter. It is common in Jakarta to remark that given the way the city looks now, it will be unrecognizable in ten years. Things are simply changing too much. But the dominant narratives of this change are deceptive. Yes, things are changing, but to a large extent the change is ordinary—ordinary in the sense that things have always been changing, and in the sense that residents have made change something ordinary. For example, new buildings are going up all the time, but the majority of these constructions are not high-rise towers, but more modest dwellings that rarely go beyond ten stories. At the same time, these are multipurpose constructions, sometimes clearly demarcated into residential and commercial sections, but just as often left vague and undetermined as if final uses have not yet been figured out. Some of these constructions are completed in a matter of weeks, almost seeming to appear from nowhere. Others appear to be built without clear plan or schedule. Those who finance the construction are both long-term residents and outsiders, often working together. In some instances it may seem that residents are vacating their homes to live farther from the central city, but they then convert their former residences into commercial spaces that they continue to control.

Much of Jakarta has endured because the way it looks at any given point in time is full of deception. The global entrepreneurial engine chugs along, seeming to wipe out everything in its path, and to a certain extent this has happened in Jakarta. Many residents I work with are obsessed with the price they should hold out for in terms of giving up their property to this juggernaut. They seem to think of nothing else. They do not think of their histories together or the relationships they have built over time. They just seem greedy, willing to take the big money and run. But the obsession with price also reflects a long-term willingness not to hold on to the trappings of sentiment or conviviality simply because these are comfortable or familiar. In addition, the focus on price makes it difficult for developers to trigger a snowballing effect by either buying off community leaders or creating a collective sense of inevitability that everyone will have to relocate.

Many residents in central Jakarta have long taken risks; others seem to have avoided them at all costs. Some residents are constantly on the move; others appear never to go anywhere. There is the exigency to do something, just as there is sometimes an urgency to do nothing, to wait. All of these tendencies lean into one another. They are materialized in the shaping of the built environment and give rise to juxtapositions of all kinds. The pieces do not necessarily fit and may provoke many problems, but these improbabilities and the deceptive ways that things never seem able to work may be the very means through which much of Jakarta has endured.

Living without a World

Endurance entails living without holding a particular ground, since, as Joaquim has taught us, the ground that is familiar to you is always shifting under your feet. Endurance means building bridges across chasms that will never be integrated, where you keep the other side in view if not fully incorporated into your everyday life. It means, as we learn from Deleuze, conjoining yourself with others in the possibility of "saying something" that need not be summed up, that need not have specific parameters of efficacy or objectivity, something that "keeps people going" in and through transformations that are without precedent in the sense that they need not represent the culmination of a goal or necessity. It means the capacity to risk what is familiar, in part because what is familiar may not be what it seems to be; every ground and appearance is deceptive. If all of this is the case, then endurance means to live without a world.

It is to live within the give-and-take of small efforts, recombinant materials, continuous rehearsals and adjustments. It is to live in the midst of things that do need to be connected, or that do have to have something to do with each other but where the end result is not a rational and ready-made map or an arena that constrains and potentiates because it acts as a container. Worlds are constituted in order to encompass and leave out what is necessary for the continuous engagement of surrounds that both grow and shrink depending on how one operates in relationship to them. There is no need to include or exclude specific things. Rather, people and cities can deal with certain complexities and processes only given what they have done and are doing at the moment. As such, there are some people, events, objects, and processes that cannot be taken into consideration right now. Perhaps in the future a more opportune time for such engagement will come. But the point here is that sometimes it is as important to leave things alone as it is to take them on, and what is more important is to create the conditions whereby people and things can come back to each other, so that there can be a return of possibilities and what is now separate is not ordered or segmented in ways that permanently put those possibilities into oppositions or irrelevance.

So to live without a world is to live in the midst of the uncertainty of urbanization, where certain articulations are clear and opaque, where all kinds of visibilities exist as they by implication render invisible much of what the city is and could be. But invisibility always remains a device, and a device with many different political implications. This is why it is important to acknowledge the extent to which inhabitants of the near-South live simultaneously in different versions of themselves and the city. This simultaneity, with its contradictory features—for example, the importance and irrelevance of specific identities and attributions; the city's tendency to individuate and aggregate—cannot be summed up as a world. It is not a world that puts everything in its place. This is in part because, as Achille Mbembe (2011) indicates, a world with the capacity to do this is a world that is dead or, rather, a world that valorizes death above anything.

Particularly as the places of urban populations in many parts of the world are faced with the prospect of extinction, it is important to live without the conceit that there is always some kind of organic whole of life, some larger framework of moral imperatives or human capacity that can come to the rescue. As Claire Colebrook (2012) has noted, the very notions of the world, with all of the scientific tools, imaginations of social coherence, and psychologies of completeness that have enabled the capacity of human beings to aspire to ongoing development, are the very same orientations and practices that enable people to distance themselves from the prospect of extinction all humans face in light of the anthropocene.

I want to make one final brief comment on the notion of endurance. In Jia Zhangke's famous 2004 film set in one of Beijing's original theme parks, *The World*, death is never far away. The world, as conveyed through the construction of replicas, indeed can come into the lives of everyone and intensify individuals' desire to be part of "it." But as Jia shows, this kind of inclusion, this infrastructural connection, always comes at a price—in the film, the price includes the accidents that inevitably occur in round-the-clock labor, gas leaks, and the deployment of young illiterate men who repeat the same mechanical operations on fake architectural wonders. Yet in the park's simulation of many of the world's key sites—the Eiffel Tower, the Taj Mahal, Big Ben, and so forth—and its constant spectaculars (giant floor shows) that bring "representatives" of the world's peoples onto a single stage in displays of global harmony, all of the apparent ontological separations between present and past, primitive and modern, first and third worlds are undone (Hayot 2012). For many of the people working the show do not speak a common language; they cannot understand each other. Yet, in their daily transactions, they try to make the best of their encounters; they accord each other some recognition and try to act generously toward each other, despite how unintelligible all aspects of the setting, the world, might be. As Jean-Luc Nancy (2007) has said, only ordinary existence is without a price.

] 5 [

INVENTIVE POLICY
Integrating Residents into Running the City

The Uncertain Stories of Urban Policy

The relational economies discussed in chapter 4 raise significant questions about the future direction of urban development and economic policy. The presumptions of clarity in economic transactions attained through the devices of price, securitization, leverage, and guarantees intended to distribute risk efficiently no longer hold (Clark 2011; Bryan et al. 2012; Gillespie 2013). We know the general criteria for agglomeration and its relationship to economic innovation, and that agglomeration is contingent on the supply of housing and amenities, as well as the productivity effects of the worker skills available. But there are no adequate explanations of how agglomeration really gets going in specific places (Storper 2010). We know that sustainability in cities will largely depend on the reduction of demand and a more even distribution of demand across both collective consumption and production.

But the politics of how these shifts are to be actualized remains uncertain. While the management of urban populations has been oriented toward the enumeration of capabilities, how are things in complex and fluid situations, like cities and their relational economies, made available to be counted?

The emphasis regarding issues of land tenure, property relations, and cadastral matters was that these were potentially unambiguous. A specific person was legally attributed the rights to use a specific territory for a sanctioned purpose. Thus the complicated externalities that characterized other forms of market relations, such as the impact of transactions of third parties and social and political conditions, could be attenuated through the monopolistic relationship that property establishes between actor and good. Neoliberal logic has attempted to deal with the cascading ramifications potentiated by transactions, where the conjunction of things and actors generates unanticipated effects that are not specifiable by the instrumental uses that are made of them. This logic has tried to bring back the predominance of instrumentalism by putting assets, problems, ideas, future possibilities, natural events, and policy challenges under private management.

But as Davies and McGoey (2012) point out, this has been a self-defeating process. The conversion of everything into forms of property, where things are emplaced within specified rights of use and become instrumentalized as the property of individuals or groups, was supposed to displace the salience of externalities in economic transactions. But the ability of banks to trade and own risks they could neither afford nor legally had to pay for, as well as the existence of central banking and limited liability, ensured the failure of property as a device of absolute clarity. Faith in private ownership has gotten turned around so as to highlight a wider range of different and unquantifiable social costs despite the presence of legal property rights.

In Jakarta, prevailing policy fashions may repeatedly advocate the need for the rationalization of property. But it is not clear whether such policy makes sense in a city like Jakarta, where land has many different possible statuses and uses. Additionally, the experience of China, where land is subject to a wide variety of both formal and informal, specified and unspecified rights and responsibilities, points out the fact that the privatization of property reflects and take place only with considerable coercion (Haila 2007; Hsing 2012). Are there other ways, then, to work out the need to maximize not only the use value of urban space in relationship to the past obsession with ground rent but also the relational value of space—that is, the ability of the city to maximize the value of the energies, sensations, efforts, and intensities of human interactions? In contrast to the way property relations enumerate individuated rights and responsibilities as the preconditions of interchange, relational value cannot anticipate what is to be produced by an ongoing series of multivalent encounters.

Whereas the play of property rights has often acted to undermine any concretization of property ownership, increasingly the law is being invoked as a tool to protect the "integrity" of specific definitions of space, to secure space against incursions and operations of lower-income residents. This is ironic given how large-scale land acquisition and transactions could play havoc with the law. The judiciary is now an active collaborator in "conjuring a state of emergency to justify punitive actions against the underclass" (Gidwani and Reddy 2011, 1649).

In addition, the privatization of a development device, such as land, water, or energy, is not self-explanatory. In their work on water supply systems in Jakarta, Kooy and Bakker (2008) point out that privatization is a complicated "tapestry of overlapping strategies." These include the industrialization of water supply production, the territorialization of corporate power, where a high degree of noncorporate power already exists, and the internationalization of the control of bulk water supply. Neither are water markets self-evident, as both national and multilateral institutions have to ensure investor confidence, provide seed loans, and foster appropriate regulatory frameworks. Given existing historical disparities in water supply, the poor often start out with a disadvantage in terms of the sunk costs necessary to connect to the larger system. Privatization has also been a means for the state to capture larger amounts of groundwater extraction as artisanal activities are displaced, in what Kooy and Bakker call "the formalization of the enclosure of the hydro-commons." This is an intensely social activity as it entails evaporation, runoff, leakages, demand patterns and expectations, pipes, water law, and quality standards.

Any urban management process needs to attribute costs to the operations of essential services, and this means having a pretty good idea about who will use them and how they will get paid for, with the latter necessitating the attribution of particular responsibilities of cost sharing to individuals and households. At the same time, does such accounting of responsibilities necessarily need to be fixed as the exclusive responsibility of either individuals or households? Various formulas of landholding, collective tenure, limited partnerships, and customary title certainly exist and might, with creative elaboration, facilitate the intensive and simultaneous usage of urban space by multiple sectors and actors. Instead of legal guarantees for specific properties, perhaps a more efficient deployment of such instruments would be in the guarantees of development rights—that is, the capacity of specific territories to develop along consensually worked-out trajectories. These trajectories would specify the basic frameworks of land use and development, as well as various cost formulas and trade-offs, given commitments to contribute to the management of particular supply and service systems related to sewage, water, and power. Challenges would center on whether a local district has the will and capacity to undertake particular projects of locally distributed supply and manage economic incubators and public facilities, what kinds of mixtures of commercial activities and residences are considered viable, and to what extent commercial areas are to be developed by local and external actors.

Public subsidies would then be set to provide minimal levels of financial support. Supplements to this minimum would be contingent on the financial viability of proposed development trajectories, the trade-offs that can be secured through the realistic self-management of various aspects of the local distribution system, and the establishment of a hierarchy of preferences. For example, district residents may have a preference to maintain substantial areas of green space. With the urgency to make urban areas denser, what kinds of trade-offs can be made to distribute a particular volume of such green space along with systematic in-fills of new housing? The concretization of development rights would require belabored and tedious negotiations, but specific time frames for step-by-step accomplishments could be enforced. To a large extent, an activist national and municipal state is needed to propel and steer the process, even if the elaboration of specific development plans falls largely under the ambit of public–private local development corporations established to administer these plans.

As for the development of infrastructure, competencies and conditionality require more extensive regional planning mechanisms and data-driven simulations. These constitute the platform that is necessary if any more localized elaboration is to take place; there is no way around this. Still, it is difficult to specify an overarching framework whereby all the pieces will fit; this is largely a matter of working out the interfaces and conjunctions of local needs and projects once specific deliberations at the district level are ready to be materialized. In other words, cities and regions will have to draft spatial development plans as instruments so that they will know how to make specific investments and manage material flows. At the same time, however, individual districts will have to find ways of doing what they have done all along, which is to continuously adjust their economies, political arrangements, and social practices to the changing dynamics of the larger city. Overall spatial plans then reflect a kind of image or summation of such dynamics, and districts must then make self-assessments about what they are prepared to do to find ways of connecting to these overall orientations. Rather than such comprehensive plans being specific maps to guide thousands of local adjustments, they are prompts, incentives, and compulsions to induce districts into examining what they do and how they do it and identifying specific ways of fitting into the larger surrounds.

Both environment performance adaptation (the ability of the energy, water, and sanitation systems to endure under changing environmental conditions) and socioeconomic adaptation (the ability of the locale to support the economic productivity of inhabitants, provide livelihoods, and foster social cohesion) should underpin urban investment strategies. Too often calculations are made in terms of discrete spatial products rather than based on assessments of how different elements within a place might potentially work together.

Such place-based, district-wide recalibration requires a multiplicity of financial tools applicable to particular facets of the district. These tools may include land swaps, revolving loan funds, land leases, tax-increment financing (in which future gains in taxes are used to subsidize current improvements, which create the conditions for such gains), value capture (in which the completion of a development project often results in an increase in the value of surrounding property, and this value can be converted into public revenue), and bonus incentives (in which municipal government grants bonuses, usually in the form of density or the size of the development, in exchange for amenities such as increased open space or pedestrian paths or a higher quality of required provisions such as enhanced storm-water management facilities or landscaping). The multiplicity and complexity of such instruments usually require special purpose vehicles—local institutions invested with special powers and the capacities to mobilize and administer them (Brugmann 2012).

Land valuation should be based on real costs to constitute property and to develop and service whatever use is made of the land, as well as its location and the implications of the land's conversion into a particular type of property or use for the general welfare of the city—infrastructural and social considerations. This differentiated approach to the assessment of value can then inform the calculation of appropriate development fees. Incorporating the social costs generated by particular dispositions of land use into the formulation of taxation and development fees generates income that can be deployed to secure land for housing low-income residents.

Deliberative bodies at the district level have to be carefully thought-out. In some instances the bulk of the work may take place in specially constituted bodies, perhaps mirroring some of the institutional forms developed by participatory budgeting models. Pioneered in Brazil, participatory budgeting is a process in which citizens are consulted at the local level regarding decisions about how to use municipal capital expenditures (Santos 1998). In other instances, the process may have to work its way through a mélange of existing institutions, where this agenda becomes a necessary supplement to the work they already take on. This is especially important in areas where there is a danger that the process will become dominated by a limited number of powerful interests. This is a tendency that has plagued many participating planning processes across the world. Long-standing competition among key religious and civil associations may infuse these deliberations. Time may be required to institutionalize more informal, long-standing associations among entrepreneurs, residential groupings, and youth that can act as counterweights to organizations that have the power and money to assert an overarching representational authority. But this requires effective local government councils, which in many cities are only in the initial stages of development. In Jakarta such councils are still, for the most part, nonexistent.

In Jakarta, the absence of any municipal democratic politics until the first gubernatorial and municipal parliament election in 2008 has been both a handicap and a blessing. While Jakartans have been kept out of the loop of local decision making, the various decision-making processes that do exist at a daily level have not yet been completely captured by the formal political parties. In Indonesia, political competition usually means simply a distribution of rent-seeking activities among a growing number of political parties. It is difficult to imagine that any effective long-range development planning for the city will take place without a complete and democratic overhaul of local government.

A highly decentralized management system remains a holdover from the days of Japanese colonial rule. The most basic administrative unit is the *rukun tetangga* (RT), which represents ten to twenty households. At the next level is the *rukun warga* (RW), which comprises five to ten RTs. Twenty to thirty RWs are then administered under a district government office, or *kelurahan*. The RW is largely responsible for the collection of fees for basic services such as sanitation and security. The head of each district office is an appointed civil servant, in charge of the official supervision of the district, including the management of demographic information, the issuance of housing permits and commercial licenses, and the enforcement of municipal regulations. As mentioned previously, small attempts have been made to democratize local governance through the election of district-wide advisory committees, but these *dekel* have minimal responsibilities.

The main function of this local governance process is to enumerate the population, with the RT responsible for processing major identity functions, such as birth, death, and marriage, and for ensuring that residents have the proper certification to live in the city. This latter function has gone by the wayside as the changing demographic profiles of districts and the infusion of a new generation of young and migrant workers have overwhelmed the possibility of functional surveillance. While these structures of decentralization may be simply geared to bureaucratic management, it is possible to appropriate them as a component in any development planning process, particularly as they operate as platforms of local associability. Everyone tends to know the RT and RW leaders, who are increasingly being drawn from a more educated and activist pool of residents. Whereas such leadership in the past had the tendency to curtail local political and social initiative, a major reversal is under way as residents reach toward formal mechanisms to address concerns about the long-term security and viability of their residential areas.

Whereas residents in a city like Mumbai continuously force locally elected councillors to provide basic services through the pressure that these councillors can exert on engineers and other bureaucrats, Jakarta's residents have historically had to pose uncertainties as to their own governability in order to levy such pressure. Again, the absence of a widely disseminated political game cuts both ways. Jakarta is a city where residents have a long history of doing things for themselves, but at the same time, particularly as consumption capabilities have expanded, they have been vulnerable to being complacent. This is a habit cultivated over the long years of national authoritarian rule. In both Mumbai and Jakarta, however, service provisioning has depended greatly on dissimulation and circumvention of rules. While rules governing the uses of water, power, land, and other resources and services may be clear and publicized, many different kinds of actors pretend not to know them. This active not knowing about what is really taking place becomes a critical facet for sustaining the very authoritativeness of rules and regulations. For in order for things to function, to balance out competing, often vociferous demands for services that, given a lack of adequate infrastructure and administration, can never be provided equally to everyone at the same time, the rules simply cannot apply.

As Nikhil Anand (2011, 552) points out, ignorance is deployed as a technology of government: "Knowing not to know particular violations of the city's water rules allows the city's rules to remain unchallenged, even as it permits engineers to remain open to allowing profitable, political, and sympathetic systems of access for the urban poor." An obsession with abiding by the rules, and even in some cases knowing them well, is made possible by the many instances in which they are not applied. This point should caution against having too great a faith in the salience of the "rule of law" and the transparency of regulations if viewed as a generalized framework of commonality, as something capable of promoting equal opportunities across the board. Inventive ways of devising relations among the highly differentiated facets and residents of urban life still need to be conjured.

Inventive Policy

Using the analysis of *preman* in chapter 4, I want to make a few brief comments on how this might apply to the nature of urban policy. In a related sense, the efficacy of policy is the ability to tell a story that attempts to capture the possible articulations among people and places in ways that exceed the usual formats of intelligibility and narrative familiarity. At the same time, it is a story that is graspable, whether through affect, through a sense of curiosity or engaged puzzlement, or, perhaps more important, through the sense that one needs to know more. Far from boiling down complex issues to their simplest formulations and then telling citizens what to do in relationship to them, policy work takes all of the different stories being told about why water, power, land, politics, buildings, transport, money, and people act the way they do and draws creative lines of conjunction among them—plausible, attainable, but not necessarily self-evident. It takes the assumptions and language of existing policy and stretches it into implications it is not prepared to deal with but that nevertheless must be reckoned with in order to retain the integrity and sense of that language.

So policy work does not simply entail what is written down in policy papers, guidelines, and frameworks. The language of these documents and resolutions may be simple, establishing the commonly understood parameters in which different actors and institutions have to work. Policy is attached to entities and processes so as to convey the conclusion that these entities and processes are "spoken for." Housing, transportation, poverty, health care, employment, and so forth are "spoken for" in that they are taken up to be addressed with a particular set of attitudes, approaches, measurements, visibilities, and solutions. Specific collectives that produce policy "speak for" these entities on the presumption that the collectives' deliberations entail a process of "listening" to what these entities "say"–how communities or organizations present themselves, how they become visible and intelligible at this particular point in time, and how they can exist in a complicated and crowded field of action. While the use of policy may be assumed to consolidate diverse efforts and interests into a common cause, or to be the means of steering the attention of institutions and groups toward the realization of particular outcomes, the actual work of policy implicitly authorizes the influx of different voices and temporalities.

Policies must be instantiated through pilot and demonstration projects, provisional buy-ins by targeted groups, monitoring processes, and "riders" that specify adjustments. They must reframe various occurrences in the present as preliminary indicators of specific directions to be pursued, as initial stages, or simply as temporary, time-limited measures. In other words, if policy is to do its work, no matter how precise the wording of documents may be, it has to open up a space of partial measures and partial objects. There must be instances and entities that are not part of either the old or the new dispensation, as well as a wide range of deals, negotiations, experiments, and improvised practices that do not follow from the "policy prescriptions" themselves.

In Indonesia, for example, many important policy shifts in housing, social welfare, and urban development have occurred in the past several years. But every policy shift requires a sequence of accompanying articles that provide a range of sanctioned options for how these policy changes will be actualized. This is the hard part—not because there is a lack of imagination or technical competence, but because it is difficult for those involved to work out what all the implications will be, a process that is facilitated by partial demonstrations, different ways of testing the waters. As the policy shifts exist on the books, however, they acquire the status of "new gospel" even though their miracles have yet to appear. But as new gospel, they can mobilize new "flocks" not only to witness the awaiting new kingdom but also to usher in its appearance through bits and pieces of activities informed by the spirit of the new policy. Thus a key emphasis of urban development work is the publicizing of findings, policies, and new rules and regulations through various instruments of popularization.

While this in-between space may be colonized by technocrats, politicians, big business, and academics, it is a space that is theoretically open to multiple formulations, advocacy, trial and error, proposals, and demonstrations. Not only are the entities and processes that policy "speaks for" continuously presenting themselves in ways that are not completely intelligible, but also the very work of policy, trying to concretize itself in the new conditions it seeks to bring about, inevitably relies on a process of tinkering, adjusting, and demonstrating that alters the grounds of intelligibility.

Policy still insists on the authority to "speak for," but by default it opens up the space of many different kinds of speaking and acting in order to retain this authority. This is why, instead of being shunned, policy work could be viewed as an important locus of engaging many different kinds of places and actors. A wide range of initiatives could be elaborated as efforts to pursue and realize specific policy guidelines, undertaken in the interest of demonstrating the applicability of policy to particular contexts and situations. Regardless of whether a given set of policy prescriptions is within the interests of particular areas of the city or groups of actors, what is important is to identify ways in which the multifaceted process of trying to implement the policy provides an occasion for actors to demonstrate their existence in ways that were not previously available.

Policy work should not be confused with mapping or probabilities. A vast wealth of software is now available that allows researchers, analysts, and the general public to access a wide range of data sets and to map interrelationships among them, almost at will. It is now possible to visualize interrelationships of all kinds. Through data mining and innovative mapping design, it is possible to gain fresh perspectives on and substantially reimagine the worlds that we live in. Relations once out of view or too complex to represent can now be rendered in various interactive formats. It is possible to map in real time the flows of events, resources, traffic, and various transactions as they occur in cities. It is also possible to anticipate the probable trajectories of urban development for particular cities by summing up the relative impacts of multiple variables in simulated prospective scenarios.

The sophistication of tracking systems institutionalizes what Jordan Crandall (2010) labels the predominance of "mathematical seeing"— the ability to insert multiple attributes into a regression formula that produces a historical trajectory from which subsequent behaviors and events can be extrapolated. By amassing large amounts of scanned observations and establishing algorithmic patterns among the environment's components, these systems can establish "norms" from which they can predict deviational outcomes based on real-time tracking of any event in progress.

While such technical proficiencies of mapping and anticipation are certainly important resources for planning, and planning is certainly an important affiliate of policy work, policy work is not the precise representation of current realities or an attempt to generate the probabilities of future outcomes. It may try to map conditions as a means of pointing out problems, challenges, and potentialities, but it is not interested in the precision of representations. Policy work is not a practice of planning, although planning may be necessary as a means of preparing and steering the efforts of institutions and groups in certain directions, mobilizing time and resources to try to get their part of the job done.

Policy work is more a practice of active translation. It is enrolling attention, effort, bodies, money, and various tools, objects, and devices into a process whereby the present is "converted" into a new present, where entities now appear and "speak" in different ways, are repositioned in their relationships with each other. New uses are derived from familiar components, and strange behaviors are "familiarized." Conversion may entail step-by-step practices, but it also means that the "moment" of conversion can never be precisely predicted even when particular rituals, standards, or formulas of recognition exist. It is never quite clear what it will take to get a "people" to the "other side," so this space is infused with much uncertainty. The uncertainty is addressed through various techniques that attempt to demonstrate that the goal remains in sight, that it is getting closer, even though no clear benchmarks may exist.

This space is then cacophonous, and in the actual realm of day-to-day urban policy work there probably exists insufficient cacophony; it could be more crowded with different demonstrations, experiments, and initiatives. Most trial runs will in any objective assessment be mere approximations of what the intended policy should look like according to its own terms of reference. There will be plenty of hucksters and tricksters and manipulators who are more than willing to try to sell anything that look like the intended outcome. Marked inequities will exist among potential stakeholders. Big developers will not be sidelined, but they may have to concede space to other actors or take a lesser share of profits from involvement in different kinds of projects. In a crowded field, participants will have to move in relationship to each other; they will push and pull, and use elbows, and try to act when others are not looking, but this is always the risk of city life.

Policy is something that people should be seen as doing even when it appears they are not doing it, even when they do not recognize themselves doing it, and this is where campaigns of popularization might focus: on inculcating the sensibility that whatever people are doing, they are doing the work of the city; that they are emitting contributions that will be recognized somewhere; and that the job of local government, sectoral agencies, and analyst institutions is to connect themselves to these contributions, either through on-site engagements in schools, associations, and other civic and religious venues where people spend time or through online crowdsourcing platforms. Rather than trying to mobilize participation in a limited number of set formats, an endeavor that often seems like pulling teeth, policy work should assume that people are already participating and then look for ways to register this participation, just as different actors could use this moment to bring themselves to the stage as participants in the pursuit of "policy objectives."

While this may seem like a game of deception, it is more a matter of generating stories with exciting twists and turns that involve juicy complicities among different characters from around the town. It is a process of keeping things moving in ways that it is difficult for people to stay away from. Unlike games in which the players are condemned to chase each other around, to pin each other down, the policy game, at its best, is the discovery of new plotlines, where the unexpected is to be expected, but where this expectation does not temper the surprise at what actually shows up. It is a game with limited self-reflexivity. Participants do not moan and groan about how dissatisfied and stuck they are. After all, the policy game entails the turbulent "middle," where it is not clear just how the collective is going to get to that new horizon it has laid out for itself, and where the inevitable sense of urgency outstrips patience by running around and designating all kinds of things as important pieces of the puzzle or as impediments to future. This is an unsettling process, and there is little time to generate continuous updates on personal status.

Ultimately, the trade-offs necessary to make things happen themselves become important pieces of the picture, as institutions have to give up something to others they never thought they would have to deal with in order to continue to be important players in any new dispensation. There is plenty of intrigue around these deals, but they manage to generate their own flows of impressions and determinations that make up an interesting cross fire for anyone who wants to remake the "crime scene." For all of the venues of formal deliberation that exist to pronounce, resolve, plan, and decide, the city proliferates spaces of indecision, hesitation, impulse, changes of opinion, seduction, enchantment, and serious "heart-to-hearts." As one of Jakarta's most illustrious *preman* once told me, "All I have to do many times is just show up" and things seem to change course. Of course, a man in such a position perhaps can be a little flippant with a hard-won arrogance. But his comment does illustrate the point that policy work is a locus where various actors in different assemblages, disguises, and pretenses do important things just by showing up.

Enrolling Residents in the Work of the City

While the current administration of Jakarta's municipal government, the team of Governor Joko Widodo and Vice Governor Basuki Tjahaja Purnama, is clearly dedicated to a wide range of progressive policies geared toward enhancing the quality of life for all residents, various urgent needs tend to result in overly sweeping decisions and programs. For example, the commitment to rehabilitate substandard housing, which is defined in unnecessarily stringent ways, has led to attempts to take on too much at once. Given the capacity of the municipal housing department, such sweeping endeavors inevitably produce gridlock, debilitating shortcuts, or cosmetic interventions aimed at addressing political considerations rather than at effecting changes that will be sustainable in the long run. Similar problems are evident in the commitment to provide health care for all low-income citizens of Jakarta, which has been bogged down by the logistical problems of printing health cards.

Similarly, the municipality has attempted to reclaim operational control of facilities within its jurisdiction. For example, a high-stakes standoff ended with a victory for the municipality when hundreds of traders who had been operating outside the official facility at Tanah Abang—Indonesia's largest market—were forced to move into a new wing of the market. In part, the city undertook this move to break the backs of the *preman* who controlled the apportioning of space and the extraction of fees in the extension outside the official market and often ruled over it as their private domain. While the municipality certainly has the right and responsibility to manage the market, there was little room for negotiation in this process, and it remains to be seen how well the official management structure can incorporate a different type and capacity of retail trade and also maintain the strategic advantage, in terms of including traders operating at lower profit margins and costs, within the official ambit of the market. Too often, municipal governments do not learn from the incremental practices of residents who have pieced together workable residential and economic districts over time. They have a tendency to try to do everything at once, imposing all-in kinds of solutions that are homologous to the conceits of the all-in-one residential commercial complexes that proliferate across Asia.

The current Jakarta governor, Widodo, has the political savvy to know that markets are political spaces and largely won election in 2012 by virtue of his ability to "work" the markets, to speak to traders and customers. Implicitly, he knows that markets are not simply economic spaces—they can also be used as instruments of discussion, information transmission, and debate. The heavy-handedness subsequently displayed at Tanah Abang, however, seemed to contradict such political wisdom, mitigating the potentialities of using the market as a means of instrumentally reaching across wider spaces and networks of the city and of maintaining the market as an intensely heterogeneous domain of transaction.

It is true that too much is left to chance in the running of the city. Too many deals require the deployment of resources simply to make the deals work; too many off-the-books accords are made. As a result, the city loses both money and authority. The new administration of Jakarta's government rightly seeks to win these back, but it has been clumsy in doing so. The government needs to put effort into thinking of approaches that are more attuned to the various histories of real implementation and management that have been prevalent across the city, where different figures have taken it upon themselves or have been unofficially delegated to smooth rough edges, to disentangle tie-ups in dense interactions in crowded spaces, and to ensure compliance with agreements that have been consensually worked out but are not written down anywhere. While many of these figures once did the "dirty work" for past municipal administrations and many are used to throwing their weight around regardless of the costs or sentiments of others, they largely remain emplaced not simply because they may instill fear and are willing to take up the slack where no one else ventures. As pointed out before, they also in most cases institute their authority through their knowledge of the ground, of everyday practices and the ways in which they are articulated to other spheres of activity and influence. It is not inconceivable that these figures could be made partners in municipal efforts to attain comprehensive and sweeping changes in service delivery and upgrades in the built environment through their potential comparative advantage of knowing how to instantiate such changes within specific contexts.

In significant ways, residents in many districts of Jakarta have already "solved" the problem of composing sustainable densities. While housing shortages exist and worsen, the basic outlines of doubling housing capacity are already implanted within central and near-suburban areas. Infrastructure will have to be retrofitted to increase carrying capacity, and greater diligence will be required in the management of solid wastes (which have compromised most of the existing evacuation systems), but much of Jakarta already demonstrates the combination of compactness, sustainable carbon footprints, and decent living environments.

In general, a wide range of residents, not just *preman,* are well accustomed to making incremental changes in their living environments, implementing continuous repairs and adjustments, and spurring various initiatives to beautify the physical surrounds, supplement income, and care for children, youth, the aged, and the infirm. Maximizing the possibilities of employment in urban contexts where many sectors are already crowded and overtraded, where trade liberalization reduces the outputs of local production, and where value is increasingly derived from high-end, high-skilled sectors will necessarily entail the incorporation of more urban residents in the provision of everyday care, training, and maintenance services. Such employment may constitute a way for municipalities to circumvent many of their responsibilities as providers of basic services, cheapen the delivery of those services, and raise issues about quality and accountability. But if such employment were, for example, to be supplemented by universally distributed basic income grants (Standing 2011), a platform would then exist for ongoing renovation and upscaling of the practices in which many residents are already engaged.

While Indonesia has implemented numerous schemes of unconditional cash transfers to the poor in the past, widespread tax avoidance, weak collection mechanisms, and low corporate rates make the necessary revenue generation for such basic income grants difficult to envision. The country still lacks even an effective pension system. On the other hand, widespread corruption in the public sector consumes a large share of public funds, and the now-withdrawn government subsidy of fuel consumption cost more than the budgets devoted to health, education, and social welfare combined. So there is a general capability of moving toward such a basic income.

With some form of basic income residents would essentially be accorded the security to venture even further in the initiatives they already undertake, as the government would provide the platform from which they could be enrolled as partners in the implementation of policy aims. Here the government would not be paying residents directly to fix up houses, repair roads, provide child care, organize youth groups, or provide transportation for the sick to relevant health care facilities. Rather, with their minimal needs of shelter, water, power, and food met through the allocation of a basic income, residents would win the opportunity of space and time to pursue concrete transformations of the efforts they have already been making, here and there, perhaps in a piecemeal fashion, with perhaps now too-limited gains. New opportunities for accumulation opened up by these efforts would thus supplement their income, and those supplements would then be taxable.

Finding practical means of enrolling the efforts of residents that are already under way into the realization of specific policy aims—something that will usually require equipping residents with more skill, time, validation, technical support, and legitimacy—does not obviate the responsibilities of the municipal, metropolitan, regional, and national governments to do what only they can do. Theirs is the job of mobilizing planning and provision at the scale necessary to ensure a concrete sense of coherence within the city, to tend to its infrastructure and manage material inflows and outflows, the sources, evacuations, and footprints of which far exceed the city's boundaries and the competencies of any one institution or sector. Jakarta currently faces several large-scale needs: the construction of a massive seawall to protect the northern and mostly densely populated part of the city from rising sea levels, the construction of the first (and probably only) leg of a public metro system to deter the city from grinding to a traffic-induced halt, the substantial expansion of the port and its connecting road systems, and the establishment of a functional regional planning administration to coordinate the basic management of transportation, infrastructure, and material resources with the municipalities of Tangarang, Bekasi, Bogor, Cianjur, and Depok.

There is broad recognition that the organizations responsible for sanitation, health care, housing, education, social welfare, taxation, and infrastructure services will have to intensify and broaden their interactions with one another. Of course this is easier said than done, as such organizations have settled into particular understandings and approaches to their domains of responsibility and have developed internal cultures that influence how they manage their ambits, draw boundaries between themselves and others, ward off scrutiny, and, often, pretend to efficiencies that do not really exist. Interactions among these organizations are increasingly shaped by market considerations and political trade-offs, but at the same time they can have significant impacts (Marwell and McQuarrie 2013). They frame and affect whatever residents can do and the processes of integration that exist among them.

The tasks ahead for Jakarta are massive and costly undertakings that exceed anything the municipality has attempted in the past; they require the wholesale acquisition of land, extensive rearrangement of existing settlement patterns, and unparalleled mobilization of political efficacy. In this sense, the city's future rests in levels of action far beyond the comprehension, let alone actions, of most residents. Still, the city is lived on a day-to-day basis in hundreds of "trenches," where myriad interpretations of macro-level morphological considerations are inscribed in people's relationships with each other and the built environment. Here residents' aspirations, understandings, and potentials are materialized, exert an impact on the city, and—in the midst of seemingly adverse, even toxic, conditions—elaborate maneuvers and ways of existing that continuously reframe the massive challenges of climate change, transportation, and sustainable livelihood into the "next step," the next increment. How viable and efficacious these "next steps" are over the long run will inevitably be the stuff of stochastic modeling, future scenarios, cost-benefit analyses, and so forth. But they embody the ability of residents to think ahead, to shift gears, to realign themselves with the implications—hard to predict or to contain—of the intersection of working, resting, extracting, believing, cajoling, resisting, declaring, submitting, expelling, consuming, and demanding, which is just the city.

Conclusion
Reimagining a Commons

Urban thought today places great emphasis on the notion of the urban commons. As spaces of all kinds are valued primarily as financial assets, this emphasis on the commons attempts to make spaces accessible to a wide range of uses and actors. The commons is not just a collection of things. It is not just the buildings and infrastructure, with their various uses, shared among residents, not just the specific public spaces identified through a checklist of green areas, squares, and facilities. The commons is not just an assortment of public goods that have in recent decades been privatized or put under intensive surveillance and limiting codes of access. Rather, the sense of the commons lies more in the use of space, civic culture, and infrastructure as a process that modulates the diverse and frequently contradictory trajectories of everyday urban life. In other words, the commons is a form of orchestration that interweaves the tendencies of residents to differentiate themselves from each other, to articulate specialized and particular aspirations and ways of doing things, and to compete with each other for access to resources, but also to find ways of coexisting, of melding differences into complementary objectives and practices.

The work of making a commons has in recent years been envisioned as a matter of reoccupying particular urban spaces and then using that occupation as a means of experimenting with different ways of engendering a public, of building mechanisms for a concrete sense of inclusiveness for inhabitants of the city long socialized into hierarchies and privileged consideration of their own needs. At times, it is presumed that the sheer act of occupying space makes that space a commons. Although such occupation is an important step in the cultivation of an urban commons, sometimes it is too easy to assume that solidarity necessarily follows.

As Indonesian critics have repeatedly pointed out, Jakarta is a city woefully lacking in public space. For a city that is purportedly unaccustomed to public congregation, however, Jakarta provides outpourings of its display when opportunities arise. I have tried to emphasize in this work the capacity of the city's inhabitants to forge workable modalities of commonality in conditions that have long militated against an urban commons. Through tough struggles of give-and-take, of incremental adjustments and adaptations, and through intricate uses of the material environment, many residents of the city have built working relationships with each other. These are often far from perfect solidarities, but they still manage to keep diverse walks of life in view, to make them pieces of larger if mostly provisional collaborations. I have considered these residents heuristically as an "urban majority"—a substantial force of city making that continues to exist between the lines, between the conventional demarcations of space and power. No matter how tentative and imperfect, these efforts nevertheless say something important about the urban commons as a process of continuous rehearsal, as something that must be constantly attended to and worked on.

These Jakarta attainments are important especially in light of the ways in which the operating procedures of contemporary financial capitalism attempt to render so many aspects of everyday life beyond the necessities of social interaction and negotiation. As theorist and activist Franco Berardi (2009) repeatedly emphasizes, finance capital is not simply about exotic forms of exchange value; it is also the elaboration of mathematical languages as the primary means of reading the world, assessing what is important, and making decisions. Determinations of efficacy are taken out of the realm of messy human quotidian deliberation and instead rendered as probabilistic calculations, algorithmic screenings of increasingly massive data sets that situate human actors as interoperable profiles and coding systems. As such, precarity is not simply the increasing informalization of labor but also the stripping away of people's capacities to desire and imagine ways of being with each other, of feeling empathy for each other. For Berardi, the important feature of the urban commons is its ability to revitalize the ways in which inhabitants can imagine acting in concert, for collaborative action is impossible unless the potential participants can envision such collaboration, imagine it, sense its incipient outlines. A large part of this effort, then, is to live amid things, people, situations, and materials that do not seem to go together, to use inhabitation itself as a device that keeps things in some kind of proximity. Discordant elements need not be integrated in some kind of overarching perspective, but they must be sufficiently related so as to pay attention to each other, to be available to different uses.

The practices in Jakarta that I have emphasized are continuous efforts to activate such a social imagination. While in many instances such imagination may be compelled by the sheer fact that incomes and security are not sufficient for households to make it on their own, to live in their own compartmentalized worlds, even when the shape of collaboration is largely motivated by self-interest it is effective only when people imagine some form of working in concert. Vital if not sufficient is the conclusion I want to draw. Residents could do more with supportive municipal and national governments behind them. While it may be surprising that they have been able to do much at all, given the many instances in which Indonesian public authorities have acted against the welfare of Jakarta's inhabitants, long periods of neglect have become the norm, creating vacuums that residents use and occupy in ways that authorities cannot easily figure out. What residents have done follows a logic that necessarily differs from what municipal institutions, by virtue of their remit to provide a kind of blanket coverage to a self-constructed territory, have been able to conceive and implement.

Whereas processes of resident self-construction and governance tend to be viewed as compensations for the abnegated responsibilities of the state, residents largely have done what the state has been unable to do, which does not mean that the state should be excused from doing the things for which it is constituted. As I have repeatedly emphasized, the efforts of residents to construct shelter, infrastructure, services, employment, and general well-being often do not go anywhere, but these "failures" do not prevent residents from continuing to try. The process of trying, sometimes with limited results, is indicative of the faith residents have in each other and, above all, in the city. Here the city is an always mutating and unpredictable world, something that will not always be either for you or against you; it is something that cannot be domesticated by routine or specific understandings or formulas. Thus, even when things work out and residents manage somehow to calibrate their different histories, perspectives, and assets, they cannot take this for granted. The inverse is also the case—next time, maybe, things will work out differently. The city is something that is hard to know, hard to get a handle on, but it also gives residents something to work with, even those with limited means.

A great deal of analysis of the relationship between neoliberalism and urban life over the past decade has incisively pointed out how the transformation of the city into a patchwork of premium, privatized, and enclave domains has been facilitated through the valorization of resilience and flexibility. Urban life, from work to school to worship to leisure time to civic engagement, is engineered to roll with the punches and to change gears constantly, but instead of affirming individuals' self-confidence, these capacities and give rise to an incessant sense of dread and insufficiency. That self-responsibility for managing the contours of a life that must be prepared for virtually anything has become entrenched in the minds of most urban residents, and the collective initiatives that many residents have long relied on to make cities work for them have become doubly tainted. Municipal institutions, for the most part, do not understand what residents are up to or are even threatened by their actions, and these endeavors are now too easily seen as signs of complicity with the dismantling of public goods and social value.

To emphasize that resident initiatives are vital but not sufficient is to reiterate the need for the simultaneity of different elaborations of space in which practices that adhere to different logics might be able to operate. While there are many examples of programs in which municipal states draw on the broad-based participation of residents in planning and decision making, what I am talking about here are not grand partnerships, not the folding of resident endeavors into a framework specified and managed by public institutions. These affiliation and conjoint efforts are important, but equally important are the ways in which residents have been able to experiment with different scenarios, different ways of intersecting their lives, resources, time, efforts, and knowledge that may or may not have clear-cut objectives, may or may not know where they are headed.

What transpires among residents across different localities may have impacts that are difficult to anticipate but often become important mechanisms for interrelating discrepant spaces and actors. Sometimes local endeavors remain highly local, and at other times they spread like wildfire; in each instance, they reveal something important about circuitries of information flow and the forces of attraction and constraint. While municipal institutions must perform their demographic surveys, cost-benefit analyses, and political calculations about what kinds of policies will "fly" or be rejected, there are other strata of articulations that point out areas of fruitful conjunction or persistent disconnection. The capacity to govern justly and efficiently remains imperative, but governing well entails more than simply prescribing and prohibiting; it also involves helping to create opportunities for the larger city—its inhabitant, needs, problems, potentials, and resources—to have real traction in people's lives and the spaces they elaborate and work within. Municipality means making a larger sphere of consideration and opportunity available to those who, through their own efforts, try to be a part of this larger sphere. The "halfway mark" may always shift, even when formal structures are designated for the confluence of these reciprocal efforts, and municipal institutions must continuously work out a sense of fairness that is not amenable to definitive standards yet is communicable across the different domains of the city.

The stories of Jakarta presented here illustrate the willingness of residents to live amid differences as long as differences in kind do not connote differences of worth. There is a widely shared sense that the city is complicated and that, as in Islam, fairness lies mostly in the intention involved, the process of setting out to be fair. People are sometimes able to live with substantial divergences in terms of status and income as long as the presence of wealthier households does not exclude the presence of others. In our discussions with residents of many different backgrounds, it became evident that Jakarta is worth paying attention to. In other words, there is something about daily life in the city, with all of its awkward travails and clamor, that is important to watch and engage. Residents can afford some missteps, some wasted time, because they can learn much from engaging the to-and-fro of daily events. The city is a rich world in itself, even with its layers of dissimulation and opacity, all the games of hiding and engaging various authorities, and all the manipulations put into play. Gradually this sense of interest has waned for many residents who now find the daily transactions necessary to tend to everyday life in intensely mixed-up districts to be too much work. With the growing professionalization of the workforce, increases in purchasing power, and the adoption of more standardized imaginaries of middle-class status, some residents who can afford to do so move on to more homogeneous living environments. They frequently profess that they made the move so that they can better pay attention to a larger world, a world that seems to count more than the messy manners, incessant gossip, highly stylized performances, and intricate intermeshing of routines and attention that characterize Jakarta's inner-city life.

Indeed, urban inhabitants are increasingly compelled to turn their attention to a larger world of information flows, commodity chains, media transmissions, cultural contagions, and transurban powers. As city economies are themselves opened up to a larger world of transactions and events, so will be the attention spans of those who live within them. They will seek niches and specializations in this larger arena; they will increasingly focus on continuous processes of self-fashioning and adaptation. Eventually many will be able to navigate effectively across different parts of the world. But also something is lost in this turning away from Jakarta as something important in and of itself. While everyday life in a district can certainly become claustrophobic, there is a sense of incompleteness, of something else that could also be made, and residents to a large extent are oriented to this possibility. To keep going, to keep residing in such a place, people have to rehearse new skills, new versions of themselves, and do so without a clear map of where they might be headed.

They have to keep a wide range of memories and ways of doing things near to them, and this nearness is inscribed into the city itself, which is why I have attempted to elaborate the notion of a near-South. Here everything is kept "near": modernity, colonialism, post-colonialism, neocolonialism, informality, translocality, development, and underdevelopment—all of the labels that are not quite sufficient for engaging interurban differences and similarities. They are kept in view, not discarded nor discredited, but also not completely relevant or operable.

The meaning of such capacities for urban studies is not so much a reiteration of the context or locally specific. It is not so much an understanding of how global processes of urbanization are inscribed in particular environments or how different parts of cities might compare across particular dynamics of change. Rather, it is the ability to see a larger world of possibilities within the circumscribed confines of these districts. It is not a confirmation of particular theoretical frameworks or how global capitalism seeps its way into the pores and metabolisms of quotidian operations. While these are significant concerns and points of analysis, these stories of Jakarta have something else to offer: a sense of what cities still might be aiming for—that is, a sense of vitality based on the elaboration of spaces and practices able to make the most of the differences and resources with which they have contact.

The stories of Jakarta presented here do not ask people to return to enriched local textures or to focus simply on the here and now of where they are located. Rather, these stories point to all that is yet to be made from what already exists, and how what already exists is open to and prepared for these futures. They show how the residents of these districts do not try to stabilize themselves within specific codes and procedures, but rather apply themselves to steering the inevitable fluctuations and uncertainty of a plurality of individual and household efforts in ways that allow room for maneuver while keeping everyone in close view, if not always constant contact.

Urban residents from different walks of life may be increasingly burdened by, uncertain of, dismissive of, or preoccupied with highly individual concerns. But the urgency of Jakarta is not just all of the things that do indeed need fixing, and that may be beyond repair. The urgency is also that a multiplicity of propositions, skills, inclinations, hunches, and convictions remain untapped even though they are deployed every day. This is not a matter of celebrating the informal; it is not a matter of the subaltern getting their due. This is discovering in the intricate relational meshes of how things get done the incipient formation of a new city, a city that is more inclusive and that maximizes the resourcefulness of its inhabitants, that suggests new ways for institutions to connect concretely with their constituents and for the practices of residents to inform the operations of those very institutions. After all, these are just the city's procedures, the procedures of a city that attempts to realize itself through the very lives of those who live it, day in and day out.

Bibliography

Aalbers, Manuel. 2009. "The Sociology and Geography of Mortgage Markets: Reflections on the Financial Crisis." *International Journal of Urban and Regional Research* 33: 281–90.

Abbas, Ackbar. 2000. "Cosmopolitan De-scriptions: Hong Kong and Shanghai." *Public Culture* 12: 769–86.

Abeyasekere, Susan. 1987. *Jakarta: A History*. Singapore: Oxford University Press.

Abidin, Hasanuddin Z., Heri Andreas, Irwan Gumilar, Yoichi Fukuda, Yusuf E. Pohan, and T. Deguchi. 2011. "Land Subsidence of Jakarta (Indonesia) and Its Relation with Urban Development." *Natural Hazards* 59: 1753–71.

Abramson, Daniel Benjamin. 2011. "Places for the Gods: Urban Planning as Orthopraxy and Heteropraxy in China." *Environment and Planning D: Society and Space* 29: 67–88.

Ajidarma, Seno Gumira. 2008. *Kentut kosmopolitan*. Depok: Koekoesan.

Aksit, Elif Ekin. 2010. "Politics of Decay and Spatial Resistance." *Social and Cultural Geography* 11: 343–57.

Allard, Scott W., and Mario L. Small. 2013. "Reconsidering the Disadvantaged: The Role of Systems, Organizations, and Institutions." *Annals of the American Academy of Political and Social Science* 647: 6–20.

Allen, John. 2011. "Topological Twists: Power's Shifting Geographies." *Dialogues in Human Geography* 1: 283–98.

Allewaert, Monique. 2013. *Ariel's Ecology: Plantations, Personhood, and Colonialism in the American Tropics*. Minneapolis: University of Minnesota Press.

Alonso-Villar, Olga. 2001. "Large Metropolises in the Third World: An Explanation." *Urban Studies* 38: 1359–72.

AlSayyad, Nezar, ed. 1992. *Forms of Dominance: On the Architecture and Urbanism of the Colonial Enterprise*. Aldershot, England: Avebury.

———. 2004. "Informality as a 'New' Way of Life." In *Urban Informality: Transnational Perspectives from the Middle East, Latin America, and South*

Asia, edited by Ananya Roy and Nezar AlSayyad, 7–30. Lanham, Md.: Lexington Books.

Amin, Ash. 2013. "Telescopic Urbanism and the Urban Poor." *City: Analysis of Urban Trends, Culture, Theory, Policy, Action* 17: 476–92.

Anand, Nikhil. 2011. "Pressure: The PoliTechnics of Water Supply in Mumbai." *Cultural Anthropology* 26: 542–63.

Ancien, Delphine. 2011. "Global City Theory and the New Urban Politics Twenty Years On." *Urban Studies* 48: 2473–93.

Anderson, Ben. 2009. "Affective Atmospheres." *Emotion, Space and Society* 2: 77–81.

Anderson, Benedict R. O'G. 1972. *Java in a Time of Revolution: Occupation and Resistance, 1944–1946.* Ithaca, N.Y.: Cornell University Press.

Anderson, Benedict R. O'G., and Ruth T. McVey. 1971. *A Preliminary Analysis of the October 1, 1965, Coup in Indonesia.* Ithaca, N.Y.: Cornell University, Modern Indonesia Project.

Asian Development Bank. 2010. *Key Indicators for Asia and the Pacific 2010.* Manila: Asian Development Bank.

Askew, Marc. 1994. "Bangkok: Transformation of the Thai City." In *Cultural Identity and Urban Change in Southeast Asia: Interpretative Essays,* edited by Marc Askew and William S. Logan, 85–115. Geelong, Victoria, Australia: Deakin University Press.

———. 2002. *Bangkok: Place, Practice and Representation.* London: Routledge.

Aspinall, Edward. 2005. *Opposing Suharto: Compromise, Resistance, and Regime Change in Indonesia: Contemporary Issues in Asia and the Pacific.* Stanford, Calif.: Stanford University Press.

Banerjee-Guha, Swapna, ed. 2010. *Accumulation by Dispossession: Transformative Cities in the New Global Order.* New Delhi: Sage.

Barker, Joshua. 2001. "State of Fear: Controlling the Criminal Contagion in Suharto's New Order." In *Violence and the State in Suharto's Indonesia,* edited by Benedict R. O'G. Anderson, 20–53. Ithaca, N.Y.: Cornell University Press.

———. 2009a. "Introduction: Street Life." *City and Society* 21: 155–62.

———. 2009b. "*Negara Beling*: Street-Level Authority in an Indonesian Slum." In *State of Authority: The State in Society in Indonesia,* edited by Gerry van Klinken and Joshua Barker, 47–72. Ithaca, N.Y.: Cornell University, Southeast Asia Program.

Barry, Andrew, and Nigel Thrift. 2007. "Gabriel Tarde: Imitation, Invention and Economy." *Economy and Society* 36: 509–25.

Baviskar, Amita. 2003. "Between Violence and Desire: Space, Power, and Identity in the Making of Metropolitan Delhi." *International Social Science Journal* 55: 89–98.

Bayat, Asef. 2007. "Radical Religion and the Habitus of the Dispossessed: Does

Islamic Militancy Have an Urban Ecology?" *International Journal of Urban and Regional Research* 31: 579–90.

———. 2009. *Life as Politics: How Ordinary People Change the Middle East.* Stanford, Calif.: Stanford University Press.

———. 2010. "Tehran: The Paradox City." *New Left Review* 66 (November/ December).

———. 2012. "Politics in the City Inside-Out." *City and Society* 24: 110–28.

Beall, Jo, and Sean Fox. 2009. *Cities and Development.* London: Routledge.

Beasley-Murray, Jon. 2010. *Posthegemony: Political Theory in Latin America.* Minneapolis: University of Minnesota Press.

Benjamin, Solomon. 2000. "Governance, Economic Settings and Poverty in Bangalore." *Environment and Urbanization* 12: 35–56.

———. 2008. "Occupancy Urbanism: Radicalizing Politics and Economy beyond Policy and Programs." *International Journal of Urban and Regional Research* 32: 719–29.

Berardi, Franco. 2009. *The Soul at Work: From Alienation to Autonomy.* Los Angeles: Semiotext(e).

Berner, Erhard, and Rüdiger Korff. 1995. "Globalization and Local Resistance: The Creation of Localities in Manila and Bangkok." *International Journal of Urban and Regional Research* 19: 208–22.

Berney, Rachel. 2011. "Pedagogical Urbanism: Creating Citizen Space in Bogota, Colombia." *Planning Theory* 10: 16–34.

Bhan, Gautam. 2009. "'This Is No Longer the City I Once Knew': Evictions, the Urban Poor and the Right to the City in Millennial Delhi." *Environment and Urbanization* 21: 127–42.

Birch, Eugene, and Susan Wachter. 2011. *Global Urbanization.* Philadelphia: University of Pennsylvania Press.

Bishop, Ryan, John Phillips, and Wei-Wei Yeo. 2003. *Postcolonial Urbanism: Southeast Asian Cities and Global Processes.* London: Routledge.

Bissell, William Cunningham. 2011. "Between Fixity and Fantasy: Assessing the Spatial Impact of Colonial Urban Dualism." *Journal of Urban History* 37: 208–29.

Blundo, Giorgio. 2006. "Dealing with the Local State: The Informal Privatization of Street-Level Bureaucracies in Senegal." *Development and Change* 37: 799–819.

Boellstorff, Tom. 2004. "The Emergence of Political Homophobia in Indonesia: Masculinity and National Belonging." *Ethnos* 69: 465–86.

Boucher, Nathalie, Marianna Cavalcanti, Stefan Kipfer, Edgar Pieterse, Vyjayanthi Rao, and Nasra Smith. 2008. "Writing the Lines of Connection: Unveiling the Strange Language of Urbanization." *International Journal of Urban and Regional Research* 32: 989–1027.

Boudreau, Julie-Anne. 2007. "Making New Political Spaces: Mobilizing Spatial

Imaginaries, Instrumentalizing Spatial Practices, and Strategically Using Spatial Tools." *Environment and Planning A* 39: 2593–611.

Bourdeau-Lepage, Lise, and Jean-Marie Huriot. 2008. "Megapolises and Globalization: Size Doesn't Matter." *Les Annales de la Recherche Urbaine* 105: 81–93.

Brenner, Neil. 2004. *New State Spaces: Urban Governance and the Rescaling of Statehood*. Oxford: Oxford University Press.

Brenner, Neil, and Christian Schmid. 2013. "The 'Urban Age' in Question." *International Journal of Urban and Regional Research*. Online December 4. doi:10.1111/1468-2427.12115.

Bridge, Gary. 2008. "City Senses: On the Radical Possibilities of Pragmatism in Geography." *Geoforum* 39: 1570–84.

Brighenti, Andrea Mubi. 2010. "On Territorology: Towards a General Science of Territory." *Theory, Culture & Society* 27 (1): 52–72.

Brown, Allison, Michal Lyons, and Ibrahima Dankoco. 2010. "Street Traders and the Emerging Spaces for Urban Voice and Citizenship in African Cities." *Urban Studies* 47: 666–83.

Brown, David, and Ian Douglas Wilson. 2007. "Ethnicized Violence in Indonesia: Where Criminals and Fanatics Meet." *Nationalism and Ethnic Politics* 13: 367–403.

Brugmann, Jeb. 2012. "Financing the Resilient City." *Environment and Urbanization* 24: 215–32.

Bryan Dick, Martin Randy, Johanna Montgomerie, and Karel Williams. 2012. "An Important Failure: Knowledge Limits and the Financial Crisis." *Economy and Society* 41: 299–315.

Bunnell, Tim. 2002. "*Kampung* Rules: Landscape and the Contested Government of Urban(e) Malayness." *Urban Studies* 39: 1686–1701.

Bunnell, Tim, and Anant Maringanti. 2010. "Practicing Urban and Regional Research beyond Metrocentricity." *International Journal of Urban and Regional Research* 34: 415–20.

Burdett, Ricky, and Deyan Sudjic, eds. 2007. *The Endless City*. London: Phaidon.

Caldeira, Teresa, and James Holston. 2005. "State and Urban Space in Brazil: From Modernist Planning to Democratic Interventions." In *Global Assemblages: Technology, Politics, and Ethics as Anthropological Problems*, edited by Aihwa Ong and Stephen J. Collier, 393–416. Malden, Mass.: Blackwell.

Callon, Michel, Yuval Millo, and Fabian Muniesa. 2007. *Market Devices*. Oxford: Wiley-Blackwell.

Çelik, Zeynep. 1997. *Urban Forms and Colonial Confrontations: Algiers under French Rule*. Berkeley: University of California Press.

Centner, Ryan. 2010a. "Cities and Strategic Elsewheres: Developments in the

Transnational Politics of Remaking Urban Space." *New Global Studies* 4: 1–7.

———. 2010b. "Spatializing Distinction in Cities of the Global South: Volatile Terrains of Morality and Citizenship." *Political Power and Social Theory* 21: 281–98.

Chant, Sylvia, and Cathy McIlwaine. 2009. *Geographies of Development in the 21st Century: The Global South.* Cheltenham, England: Edward Elgar.

Chatterjee, Partha. 2004. *The Politics of the Governed: Popular Politics in Most of the World.* New York: Columbia University Press.

Chattopadhyay, Swati. 2006. *Representing Calcutta: Modernity, Nationalism, and the Colonial Uncanny.* London: Taylor and Francis.

Chu, Yin-wah. 2009. "Deconstructing the Global City: Unraveling the Linkages That Underlie Hong Kong's World City Status." *Urban Studies* 45: 1625–46.

Clark, Gordon. 2011. "Myopia and the Global Financial Crisis: Context-Specific Reasoning, Market Structure, and Institutional Governance." *Dialogues in Human Geography* 1: 4–25.

Cochrane, Allan. 2012. "Making Up a Region: The Rise and Fall of the South-East of England as a Political Territory." *Environment and Planning C: Government and Policy* 30 (1): 95–108.

Coe, Neil M., Martin Hess, Henry Wai-chung Yeung, Peter Dicken, and Jeffrey Henderson. 2004. "'Globalizing' Regional Development: A Global Production Networks Perspective." *Transactions of the Institute of British Geographers* 29: 468–84.

Colebrook, Claire. 2010. "Creative Evolution and the Creation of Man." *Southern Journal of Philosophy* 48: 109–32.

———. 2012. "Extinction: Framing the End of the Species." In *Extinction*, edited by Claire Colebrook. Open Humanities Press. http://www.livingbooksaboutlife.org/books/Extinction.

Colliers International. 2011. "Indonesia: Jakarta Property Market Report." http://www.colliers.com.

———. 2012. "Research and Forecast Report: Jakarta Real Estate." http://www.colliers.com.

Colombijn, Freek. 2010. *Under Construction: The Politics of Urban Space and Housing during the Decolonization of Indonesia, 1930–1960.* Leiden: KITLV Press.

———. 2011. "Public Housing in Post-colonial Indonesia: The Revolution of Rising Expectations." *Bijdragen tot de Taal-, Land- en Volkenkunde (BKI)* 167: 437–58.

Connolly, William. 2002. *Neuropolitics: Thinking, Culture, Speed.* Minneapolis: University of Minnesota Press.

Cooper, Fred. 1983. "Urban Space, Industrial Time, and Wage Labor in Africa."

In *Struggle for the City: Migrant Labor, Capital, and the State in Urban Africa*, edited by Fred Cooper. Beverly Hills, Calif.: Sage.

Cooper, Melinda. 2010. "Turbulent Worlds: Financial Markets and Environmental Crisis." *Theory, Culture & Society* 27 (2/3): 167–90.

Coordinating Ministry of Economic Affairs, Republic of Indonesia, and Japan International Cooperation Agency. 2012. *JABODETABEK Urban Transportation Policy Integration Project in the Republic of Indonesia* (Final Report). Jakarta: Republic of Indonesia, March 2012.

Coward, Martin. 2012. "Between Us in the City: Materiality, Subjectivity, and Community in the Era of Global Urbanization." *Environment and Planning D: Society and Space* 30: 468–81.

Cowherd, Robert. 2002. "Planning or Cultural Construction? The Transformation of Jakarta in the Late Soeharto Period." In *The Indonesian Town Revisited*, edited by Peter J. M. Nas, 17–40. Münster: Lit Verlag.

Crandall, Jordan. 2010. "The Geospatialization of Calculative Operations: Tracking, Sensing and Megacities." *Theory, Culture & Society* 27 (6): 68–90.

Cross, John, and Alfonso Morales. 2007. "Introduction: Locating Street Markets in the Modern/Postmodern World." In *Street Entrepreneurs: People, Place and Politics in Local and Global Perspective*, edited by John Cross and Alfonso Morales. London: Routledge.

Curran, Winifred. 2007. "From the Frying Pan to the Oven: Gentrification and the Experience of Industrial Displacement in Williamsburg, Brooklyn." *Urban Studies* 44: 1427–40.

Daniels, Timothy. 2010. "Urban Space, Belonging, and Inequality in Multiethnic Housing Estates of Melaka, Malaysia." *Identities* 17: 176–203.

Davies, William, and Linsey McGoey. 2012. "Rationalities of Ignorance: On Financial Crisis and the Ambivalence of Neo-liberal Epistemology." *Economy and Society* 41: 64–83.

Davis, Diane. 1994. *Urban Leviathan: Mexico City in the Twentieth Century*. Philadelphia: Temple University Press.

———. 2005. "Cities in Global Context: A Brief Intellectual History." *International Journal of Urban and Regional Research* 29: 92–109.

Dawson, Ashley. 2009. "Surplus City." *Interventions* 11: 16–34.

De Boeck, Filip, and Marie-Françoise Plissart. 2006. *Kinshasa: Tales of the Invisible City*. Antwerp: Ludon.

de Certeau, Michel. 1998. *The Capture of Speech, and Other Political Writings*. Minneapolis: University of Minnesota Press.

Deleuze, Gilles. 1989. *Cinema 2: The Time-Image*. Minneapolis: University of Minnesota Press.

———. 1995. *Difference and Repetition*. New York: Columbia University Press.

Deleuze, Gilles, and Felix Guattari. 1980. *A Thousand Plateaus: Capitalism and Schizophrenia*. London: Continuum International.

Derrida, Jacques. 2000. *Demeure: Fiction and Testimony.* Stanford, Calif.: Stanford University Press.

Desai, Vandana, and Alex Loftus. 2013. "Speculating on Slums: Infrastructural Fixes in Informal Housing in the Global South." *Antipode 45: 789–808.*

Dick, Howard, Vincent Houben, J. Thomas Lindblad, and Thee Kian Wie. 2002. *The Emergence of a National Economy: An Economic History of Indonesia, 1800–2000.* Honolulu: University of Hawaii Press.

Dick, Howard, and Peter Rimmer. 1998. "Beyond the Third World City: The New Urban Geography of South-east Asia." *Urban Studies* 35: 2003–23.

Dieleman, Marlene. 2011. "New Town Development in Indonesia: Renegotiating, Shaping and Replacing Institutions." *Bijdragen tot de Taal-, Land- en Volkenkunde* 167: 60–85.

Dikeç, Mustafa. 2005. "Space, Politics, and the Political." *Environment and Planning D: Society and Space* 23: 171–88.

———. 2007. *Badlands of the Republic: Space, Politics and Urban Policy.* London: Blackwell.

Dill, Brian. 2009. "The Paradoxes of Community-Based Participation in Dar es Salaam." *Development and Change* 40: 717–43.

DiMuzio, Timothy. 2008. "Governing Global Slums: The Biopolitics of Target 11." *Global Governance* 14: 305–26.

Dixon, Adam. 2011. "Variegated Capitalism and the Geography of Finance: Towards a Common Agenda." *Progress in Human Geography* 35: 193–210.

Dosh, Paul. 2010. *Demanding the Land: Urban Popular Movements in Peru and Ecuador 1990–2005.* University Park: Pennsylvania State University Press.

Douglass, Michael. 2010. "Globalization, Mega-projects and the Environment: Urban Form and Water in Jakarta." *Environment and Urbanization Asia* 1: 45–65.

Duke, Joanna. 2009. "Mixed Income Housing Policy and Public Housing Residents' 'Right to the City.'" *Critical Social Policy* 29: 100–120.

Durand-Lasserve, Alain, and Lauren Royston. 2002. "International Trends and Country Contexts: From Tenure Regularization to Tenure Security." In *Holding Their Ground: Secure Land Tenure for the Urban Poor in Developing Countries,* edited by Alain Durand-Lasserve and Lauren Royston. London: Earthscan.

Eckstein, Susan. 2001. "Poor People versus the State and Capital: Anatomy of a Successful Community Mobilization for Housing in Mexico City." In *Power and Popular Protest: Latin American Social Movements,* expanded ed., edited by Susan Eckstein, 329–51. Berkeley: University of California Press.

Edensor, Tim, and Mark Jayne, eds. 2011. *Urban Theory beyond the West: A World of Cities.* London: Routledge.

Elden, Stuart. 2010. "Land, Terrain, Territory." *Progress in Human Geography* 34: 799–817.

Elsheshtawy, Yasser. 2008. "Transitory Sites: Mapping Dubai's 'Forgotten' Urban Spaces." *International Journal of Urban and Regional Research* 32: 968–88.

Elyachar, Julia. 2005. *Markets of Dispossession: NGOs, Economic Development, and the State in Cairo.* Durham, N.C.: Duke University Press.

———. 2011. "The Political Economy of Movement and Gesture in Cairo." *Journal of the Royal Anthropological Institute* 17: 82–99.

Emrence, Cem. 2008. "After Neo-liberal Globalization: The Great Transformation of Turkey." *Comparative Sociology* 7: 51–67.

Escobar, Arturo. 1995. *Encountering Development: The Making and Unmaking of the Third World.* Princeton, N.J.: Princeton University Press.

Evans, Robert, and Simon Marvin. 2006. "Researching the Sustainable City: Three Modes of Interdisciplinarity." *Environment and Planning A* 38: 1009–28.

Fawaz, Mona. 2008. "An Unusual Clique of City-Makers: Social Networks in the Production of a Neighborhood in Beirut." *International Journal of Urban and Regional Research* 32: 565–85.

Fernandes, Edesio. 2007. "Urban Land Regularization Programs: State of Knowledge." In *Global Urban Poverty: Setting the Agenda,* edited by Allison M. Garland, Mejgan Massoumi, and Blair A. Ruble, 181–88. Washington, D.C.: Woodrow Wilson International Center for Scholars.

Fernandes, Sujatha. 2010. *Who Can Stop the Drums? Urban Social Movements in Chávez's Venezuela.* Durham, N.C.: Duke University Press.

Firman, Tommy. 1999. "From 'Global City' to 'City of Crisis': Jakarta Metropolitan Region under Economic Turmoil." *Habitat International* 23: 447–66.

———. 2002. "Urban Development in Indonesia, 1990–2001: From the Boom to the Early Reform Era through the Crisis." *Habitat International* 26: 229–49.

———. 2004. "New Town Development in Jakarta Metropolitan Region: A Perspective of Spatial Segregation." *Habitat International* 28: 349–68.

Foucault, Michel. 2008. *The Birth of Biopolitics: Lectures at the College de France, 1978–1979.* Basingstoke: Palgrave Macmillan.

Friedmann, John. 2007. "The Wealth of Cities: Towards an Assets-Based Development of Newly Urbanizing Regions." *Development and Change* 38: 987–98.

Garmany, Jeff. 2010. "Religion and Governmentality: Understanding Governance in Urban Brazil." *Geoforum* 41: 908–18.

Ghannam, Farha. 2002. *Remaking the Modern: Space, Relocation, and the Politics of Identity in a Global Cairo.* Berkeley: University of California Press.

Gibson-Graham, J. K. 2008. "Diverse Economies: Performative Practices for 'Other Worlds.'" *Progress in Human Geography* 32: 613–32.

Gidwani, Vinay, and Rajyashree N. Reddy. 2011. "The Afterlives of 'Waste': Notes from India for a Minor History of Capitalist Surplus." *Antipode* 43: 1625–58.

Gillespie, Ryan. 2013. "From Circulation to Asymmetrical Flow: On Metaphors and Global Capitalism." *Journal of Cultural Economy* 6: 200–216.

Glissant, Édouard. 1999. *Caribbean Discourse: Selected Essays*. Charlottesville: University of Virginia Press.

Goldfrank, Benjamin, and Andrew Schrank. 2009. "Municipal Neoliberalism and Municipal Socialism: Urban Political Economy in Latin America." *International Journal of Urban and Regional Research* 33: 443–62.

Goldman, Michael. 2011. "Speculative Urbanism and the Making of the Next World City." *International Journal of Urban and Regional Research* 35: 555–81.

Goldstein, Daniel M. 2004. *The Spectacular City: Violence and Performance in Urban Bolivia*. Durham, N.C.: Duke University Press.

González de la Rocha, Mercedes. 2006. "Vanishing Assets: Cumulative Disadvantage among the Urban Poor." *Annals of the American Academy of Political and Social Science* 606: 68–94.

Gooptu, Nandini. 2001. *The Politics of the Urban Poor in Early Twentieth-Century India*. Cambridge: Cambridge University Press.

Grant, Ursula. 2004. "Economic Growth, Urban Poverty and City Governance." In *Urban Governance, Voice and Poverty in the Developing World*, edited by Nick Devas, 37–52. London: Earthscan.

Gray, Obika. 2004. *Demeaned but Empowered: The Social Power of the Urban Poor in Jamaica*. Kingston: University of the West Indies Press.

Grillo, Ralph. 2000. "Plural Cities in Comparative Perspective." *Ethnic and Racial Studies* 23: 957–81.

Grosz, Elizabeth. 2012. "Deleuze, Ruyer and Becoming-Brain: The Music of Life's Temporality." *Parrhesia* 15: 1–13.

Guarneros-Meza, Valeria. 2009. "Mexican Urban Governance: How Old and New Institutions Coexist and Interact." *International Journal of Urban and Regional Research* 33: 463–82.

Haber, Paul Lawrence. 2006. *Power from Experience: Urban Popular Movements in Late Twentieth-Century Mexico*. University Park: Pennsylvania State University Press.

Hadiz, Vedi. 2000. "Retrieving the Past for the Future? Indonesia and the New Order Legacy." *Southeast Asian Journal of Social Science* 28: 10–23.

Hadiz, Vedi, and Richard Robison. 2005. "Neo-liberal Reforms and Illiberal Consolidations: The Indonesian Paradox." *Journal of Development Studies* 41: 220–41.

Haila, Anna. 2007. "The Market as the New Emperor." *International Journal of Urban and Regional Research* 31: 3–20.

Hakim, Ikhwan, and Bruno Parolin. 2009. "Spatial Structure and Spatial Impacts of the Jakarta Metropolitan Area: A Southeast Asian EMR Perspective." *International Journal of Human and Social Sciences* 4: 397–405.

Halkort, Monika. 2012. "Taming the Insurgent City: On the Political Ontology of Ownership in the Reconstruction of a Palestinian Refugee Camp." Ph.D. thesis, Department of Sociology, University of Belfast.

Hanlon, Joseph, Armando Barrientos, and David Hulme. 2010. *Just Give Money to the Poor: The Development Revolution from the Global South.* Sterling, Va.: Kumarian Press.

Hansen, Thomas Blom. 2001. *Wages of Violence: Naming and Identity in Postcolonial Bombay.* Princeton, N.J.: Princeton University Press.

Hansen, Thomas Blom, and Oskar Verkaaik. 2009. "Urban Charisma: On Everyday Mythologies in the City." *Critique of Anthropology* 29: 5–26.

Harms, Erik. 2011. *Saigon's Edge: On the Margins of Ho Chi Minh City.* Minneapolis: University of Minnesota Press.

Harriss, John. 2006. "Activism and the Politics of the Informal Working Class: A Perspective on Class Relations and Civil Society in India." *Critical Asian Studies* 38: 445–65.

Harvey, David. 2006. *Space of Global Capitalism: Towards a Theory of Uneven Geographical Development.* London: Verso.

Hayot, Erick. 2012. "Cosmologies, Globalization and Their Humans." *Social Text* 29: 81–105.

Healey, Patsy. 2007. *Urban Complexity and Spatial Strategies: Towards a Relational Planning for Our Times.* London: Routledge.

Hefner, Robert. 1993. "Islam, State, and Civil Society: I.C.M.I. and the Struggle for the Indonesian Middle Class." *Indonesia* 56: 1–35.

———. 1999. "Islam and Nation in the Post-Suharto Era." In *The Politics of Post-Suharto Indonesia,* edited by Adam Schwarz and Jonathan Paris, 40–72. New York: Council of Foreign Relations.

———. 2006. "State, Society, and Secularity in Contemporary Indonesia." In *Religion and Religiosity in the Philippines and Indonesia: Essays on State, Society, and Public Creeds,* edited by Theodore Friend, 39–51. Washington, D.C.: School of Advanced International Studies and Brookings Institution Press.

———. 2011. "Human Rights and Democracy in Islam: The Indonesian Case in Global Perspective." In *Religion and the Global Politics of Human Rights,* edited by Thomas Banchoff and Robert Wuthnow, 39–69. Oxford: Oxford University Press.

Heller, Patrick, and Peter Evans. 2010. "Taking Tilly South: Durable Inequalities, Democratic Contestation, and Citizenship in the Southern Metropolis." *Theory and Society* 39: 433–50.

Heller, Patrick, and K. N. Harilal. 2007. "Building Local Democracy: Evaluating the Impact of Decentralization in Kerala, India." *World Development* 35: 626–48.

Henderson, J. Vernon, and Ari Kuncoro. 2004. *Corruption in Indonesia* (NBER Working Paper 10674). Cambridge, Mass.: National Bureau of Economic Research. http://www.nber.org/papers/w10674.pdf.

Hesse, Markus. 2010. "Cities, Material Flows and the Geography of Spatial Interaction: Urban Places in the System of Chains." *Global Networks* 10: 75–91.

Hillier, Jean. 2002. *Shadows of Power: An Allegory of Prudence*. London: Routledge.

Hirsch, Joachim, and John Kannankulam. 2011. "The Spaces of Capital: The Political Form of Capitalism and the Internationalization of the State." *Antipode* 43: 12–37.

Hodson, Mike, and Simon Marvin. 2009. "'Urban Ecological Security': A New Urban Paradigm?" *International Journal of Urban and Regional Research* 33: 193–215.

Hogan, Trevor, Tim Bunnell, Choon-Piew Pow, Eka Permanasari, and Sirat Morshidi. 2012. "Asian Urbanisms and the Privatization of Cities." *Cities* 29: 59–63.

Holston, James. 1991. "Autoconstruction in Working-Class Brazil." *Cultural Anthropology* 6: 447–66.

———. 2008. *Insurgent Citizenship: Disjunctions of Democracy and Modernity in Brazil*. Princeton, N.J.: Princeton University Press.

———. 2009. "Insurgent Citizenship in an Era of Global Urban Peripheries." *City and Society* 21: 245–67.

Houweling, Tanja A. J. 2002. "At the Low End of the Ladder: Resilience, Treatment-Seeking Behaviour and the Impact of the Economic Crisis in a Poor Neighbourhood in Jakarta." In *The Indonesian Town Revisited,* edited by Peter J. M. Nas, 296–318. Münster: Lit Verlag.

Hsing, You-tien. 2012. *The Great Urban Transformation: Politics of Land and Property in China*. Oxford: Oxford University Press.

Huchzermeyer, Marie. 2007. "Tenement City: The Emergence of Multi-storey Districts through Large-Scale Private Landlordism in Nairobi." *International Journal of Urban and Regional Research* 31: 714–32.

Hudalah, Delik, and Tommy Firman. 2012. "Beyond Property: Industrial Estates and Post-suburban Transformation in Jakarta Metropolitan Region." *Cities* 29: 40–48.

Human Rights Watch. 2006. "Condemned Communities: Forced Evictions in Jakarta" (C1810). http://www.refworld.org/docid/4517cc404.html.

Hunt, Stacey. 2009. "Citizenship's Place: The State's Creation of Public Space and Street Vendors' Culture of Informality in Bogotá, Colombia." *Environment and Planning D: Society and Space* 27: 331–51.

Hutabarat Lo, Ria. 2010. "The City as a Mirror: Transport, Land Use and Social Change in Jakarta." *Urban Studies* 47: 529–55.

Huyssen, Andreas, ed. 2008. *Other Cities, Other Worlds: Urban Imaginaries in a Globalizing Age.* Durham, N.C.: Duke University Press.

International Housing Coalition. 2010. *The Challenge of an Urban World.* Washington, D.C.: International Housing Coalition.

Isin, Engin F. 2007. "City, State: Critique of Scalar Thought." *Citizenship Studies* 11: 211–28.

———. 2008. "The City as the Site of the Social." In *Recasting the Social in Citizenship,* edited by Engin F. Isin, 261–80. Toronto: University of Toronto Press.

Jacobs, Jane M. 1996. *Edge of Empire: Postcolonialism and the City.* New York: Routledge.

James, William. 1976. *Essays in Radical Empiricism.* Cambridge, Mass.: Harvard University Press.

Jáuregui, Jorge Mario. 2010. "Urban and Social Articulation: Megacities, Exclusion and Urbanity." In *Rethinking the Informal City: Critical Perspectives from Latin America,* edited by Felipe Hernández, Peter Kellett, and Lea K. Allen. New York: Berghahn Books.

Jellinek, Lea. 1991. *The Wheel of Fortune: The History of a Poor Community in Jakarta.* Honolulu: University of Hawaii Press.

———. 2000. "Jakarta, Indonesia: Kampung Culture or Consumer Culture?" In *Consuming Cities: The Urban Environment in the Global Economy after the Rio Declaration,* edited by Nicholas Low, Brendan Gleeson, Ingemar Elander, and Rolf Lidskog, 271–86. London: Routledge.

———. 2002. *My Neighbour, Your Neighbour: Governance, Poverty and Civic Engagement in Five Jakarta Communities.* Jakarta: British Embassy, Department for International Development.

Jensen, Ole B., and Tim Richardson. 2004. *Making European Space: Mobility, Power and Territorial Identity.* London: Routledge.

Jones, Gavin W. 2002. "Southeast Asian Urbanization and the Growth of Mega-urban Regions." *Journal of Population Research* 19: 119–36.

Jones, Martin. 2009. "Phase Space: Geography, Relational Thinking, and Beyond." *Progress in Human Geography* 33: 487–506.

Juliastuti, Nuraini. 2008. "Understanding Movie Piracy in Indonesia: Knowledge and Practices of Piracy." Thesis, University of Amsterdam.

Kamete, Amin. 2009. "In the Service of Tyranny: Debating the Role of Planning in Zimbabwe's Urban 'Clean-up' Operation." *Urban Studies* 46: 897–922.

Keil, Roger. 2011. "The Global City Comes Home." *Urban Studies* 48: 2495–517.

Khondker, Habibul Haque. 2009. "Dhaka and the Contestation over the Public Space." *City: Analysis of Urban Trends, Culture, Theory, Policy, Action* 13: 129–36.

King, Anthony D. 1976. *Colonial Urban Development: Culture, Social Power, and the Environment*. London: Routledge & Kegan Paul.

———. 1991. *Urbanism, Colonialism and the World Economy: Cultural and Spatial Foundations of the World Urban System*. London: Routledge.

King, Ross. 2008. "Bangkok, Space, and Conditions of Possibility." *Environment and Planning D: Society and Space* 26: 315–37.

Kipfer, Stefan. 2007. "Fanon and Space: Colonization, Urbanization, and Liberation from the Colonial to the Global City." *Environment and Planning D: Society and Space* 25: 701–26.

Kirkpatrick, L. Owen, and Michael Peter Smith. 2011. "The Infrastructural Limits to Growth: Rethinking the Urban Growth Machine in Times of Fiscal Crisis." *International Journal of Urban and Regional Research* 35: 477–503.

Konings, Piet, Rijk van Dijk, and Dick Foeken. 2006. "The African Neighbourhood: An Introduction." In *Crisis and Creativity: Exploring the Wealth of the African Neighbourhood*, edited by Piet Konings and Dick Foeken. Leiden: Brill.

Kooy, Michelle, and Karen Bakker. 2008. "Technologies of Government: Constituting Subjectivities, Spaces, and Infrastructures in Colonial and Contemporary Jakarta." *International Journal of Urban and Regional Research* 32: 375–91.

Kothari, Uma. 2008. "Global Peddlers and Local Networks: Migrant Cosmopolitanisms." *Environment and Planning D: Society and Space* 26: 500–516.

Krank, Sabrina, Wicaksono Sarosa, and Holger Wallbaum. 2009. "Coping with Growth and Sustainable Development? Urban Management Indicators in Jakarta." Paper presented at the Eighth International Symposium of the International Urban Planning and Environment Association, Kaiserslautern, Germany, March 23–26.

Kudva, Neema. 2009. "The Everyday and the Episodic: The Spatial and Political Impacts of Urban Informality." *Environment and Planning A* 41: 1614–28.

Kusno, Abidin. 2000. *Behind the Postcolonial: Architecture, Urban Space and Political Cultures in Indonesia*. London: Routledge.

———. 2003. "Remembering/Forgetting the May Riots: Architecture, Violence, and the Making of 'Chinese Cultures' in Post-1998 Jakarta." *Public Culture* 15: 149–177.

———. 2010. *Appearances of Memory: Mnemonic Practices of Architecture and Urban Form in Indonesia*. Durham, N.C.: Duke University Press.

———. 2011. "Runaway City: Jakarta Bay, the Pioneer and the Last Frontier." *Inter-Asia Cultural Studies* 12: 515–30.

———. 2012. "Housing the Margin: *Perumahan Rakyat* and the Future Urban Form of Jakarta." *Indonesia* 94: 23–56.

Kusumawijaya, Marco. 2004. *Jakarta: Metropolis tunggang-langgang*. Jakarta: Gagas Media.

———. 2006. *Kota rumah kita*. Jakarta: Borneo.

Latour, Bruno. 2005. *Reassembling the Social: An Introduction to Actor-Network-Theory*. Oxford: Oxford University Press.

Latour, Bruno, and Valery Lépinay. 2009. *The Science of Passionate Interests: An Introduction to Gabriel Tarde's Economic Anthropology*. Chicago: Prickly Paradigm Press.

Law, John. 2002. "Objects and Spaces." *Theory, Culture & Society* 19 (5/6): 91–105.

Leaf, Michael. 1993. "Land Rights for Residential Development in Jakarta, Indonesia: The Colonial Roots of Contemporary Urban Dualism." *International Journal of Urban and Regional Research* 17: 477–91.

Lee, Doreen. 2007. *Turun ke jalan/Taking the Streets: Activism and Memory Work in Jakarta* (Indonesian Studies Working Paper 3). Sydney: University of Sydney.

Leeuwen, Lizzy van. 2011. *Lost in Mall: An Ethnography of Middle-Class Jakarta in the 1990s*. Leiden: KITLV Press.

Lefebvre, Henri. 2004. *Rhythmanalysis: Space, Time and Everyday Life*. London: Continuum.

Le Galès, Patrick. 2002. *European Cities: Social Conflicts and Governance*. Oxford: Oxford University Press.

Legg, Stephen. 2007. *Spaces of Colonialism: Delhi's Urban Governmentalities*. Malden, Mass.: Blackwell.

———. 2008. "Ambivalent Improvements: Biography, Biopolitics, and Colonial Delhi." *Environment and Planning A* 40: 37–56.

Lewis, Martin W. 2010. "Locating Asia Pacific: The Politics and Practice of Global Division." In *Remaking Area Studies: Teaching and Learning across Asia and the Pacific*, edited by Terence Wesley-Smith and Jon Goss, 41–65. Honolulu: University of Hawaii Press.

Lim, Merlyna. 2008. "Transient Civic Spaces in Jakarta Demopolis." In *Globalization, the City and Civil Society in Pacific Asia*, edited by Mike Douglass, K. C. Ho, and Giok Ling Ooi, 211–30. London: Routledge.

Lindell, Ilda. 2008. "The Multiple Sites of Urban Governance: Insights from an African City." *Urban Studies* 45: 1879–1901.

———. 2010. "Informality and Collective Organising: Identities, Alliances and Transnational Activism in Africa." *Third World Quarterly* 31: 207–22.

Logan, John R., Yiping Fang, and Zhanxin Zhang. 2009. "Access to Housing in Urban China." *International Journal of Urban and Regional Research* 33: 914–35.

Lomnitz, Larissa. 1977. *Networks and Marginality: Life in a Mexican Shantytown*. New York: Academic Press.

Lora, Eduardo. 2010. "Latin American Cities: Their Origins, Achievements, and Problems." In *The Quality of Life in Latin American Cities: Markets and Perception,* edited by Eduardo Lora, Andrew Powell, Bernard M. S. van Praag, and Pablo Sanguinetti, 1–30. Washington, D.C.: World Bank.

Lovell, Peggy. 2006. "Race, Gender, and Work in São Paulo, Brazil, 1960–2000." *Latin American Research Review* 41: 63–87.

Low, Murray. 2007. "Political Parties and the City: Some Thoughts on the Low Profile of Partisan Organisations and Mobilisation in Urban Political Theory." *Environment and Planning A* 39: 2652–67.

Lund, Christian. 2006. "Twilight Institutions: Public Authority and Local Politics in Africa." *Development and Change* 37: 685–705.

Lyons, Michal, and Colman Titus Msoka. 2010. "The World Bank and the Street: (How) Do 'Doing Business' Reforms Affect Tanzania's Micro-traders?" *Urban Studies* 47: 1079–97.

MacLeod, Gordon. 2011. "Urban Politics Reconsidered: Growth Machine to Post-democratic City?" *Urban Studies* 48: 2629–60.

Mahon, Rianne, and Laura Macdonald. 2010. "Anti-poverty Politics in Toronto and Mexico City." *Geoforum* 41: 209–17.

Marcuse, Peter. 2011. "The Forms of Power and the Forms of Cities: Building on Charles Tilly." In *Contention and Trust in Cities and States,* edited by Michael Hanagan and Chris Tilly, 339–53. Dordrecht, Netherlands: Springer.

Maricato, Erminia. 2010. "The Statute of the Peripheral City." In *The City Statute of Brazil: A Commentary,* edited by Celso Santos Carvalho and Anaclaudia Rossbach, 5–22. São Paulo: Cities Alliance and Ministry of Cities.

Marques, Eduardo. 2011. "Do Social Networks Matter in Gaining Access to Goods and Services Obtained from Outside Markets?" *International Sociology* 41: 10–27.

Marwell, Nicole, and Michael McQuarrie. 2013. "People, Place, and System: Organizations and the Renewal of Urban Social Theory." *Annals of the American Academy of Political and Social Science* 647: 126–43.

Mbembe, Achille. 2011. "Provincializing France?" *Public Culture* 23: 85–119.

McCann, Eugene, and Kevin Ward, eds. 2011. *Mobile Urbanism: Cities and Policymaking in the Global Age.* Minneapolis: University of Minnesota Press.

McFarlane, Colin. 2007. "Urban Shadows: Materiality, the 'Southern City' and Urban Theory." *Geography Compass* 2: 340–58.

———. 2008a. "Postcolonial Bombay: Decline of a Cosmopolitanism City?" *Environment and Planning D: Society and Space* 26: 480–99.

———. 2008b. "Sanitation in Mumbai's Informal Settlements: State, 'Slum,' and Infrastructure." *Environment and Planning A* 40: 88–107.

————. 2009. "Translocal Assemblages: Space, Power, and Social Movements." *Geoforum* 40: 561–67.

————. 2011. *Learning the City: Knowledge and Translocal Assemblage.* Oxford: Wiley-Blackwell.

McGranahan, Gordon, Diane Mitlin, and David Satterthwaite. 2008. "Land and Services for the Urban Poor in Rapidly Urbanizing Countries." In *The New Global Frontier: Urbanization, Poverty and Environment in the 21st Century,* edited by George Martine, Gordon McGranahan, Mark Montgomery, and Rogelio Fernández-Castilla, 77–98. London: Earthscan.

McVey, Ruth. 2006. *The Rise of Indonesian Communism.* Jakarta: Equinox.

Meagher, Kate. 2010a. *Identity Economics: Social Networks and the Informal Economy in Nigeria.* London: James Currey.

————. 2010b. "The Tangled Web of Associational Life: Urban Governance and the Politics of Popular Livelihoods in Nigeria." *Urban Forum* 21: 299–313.

Mehrotra, Rahul. 2002. "Bazaar City: A Metaphor for South Asian Urbanism." In *Kapital and Karma: Recent Positions in Indian Art,* 95–110. Vienna: Kunsthalle Wien.

Meillassoux, Quentin. 2008. *After Infinitude: An Essay on the Necessity of Contingency.* London: Continuum.

Melly, Caroline. 2010. "Inside-Out Houses: Urban Belonging and Imagined Futures in Dakar, Senegal." *Comparative Studies in Society and History* 52: 37–65.

Mitchell, Timothy. 2002. *Rule of Experts: Egypt, Techno-politics, Modernity.* Berkeley: University of California Press.

Mohamad, Goenawan. 1994. "City." In *Sidelines: Thought Pieces from Tempo Magazine,* translated by Jennifer Lindsay, 28–29. Jakarta: Lontar Press.

Mohan, Giles. 2006. "Embedded Cosmopolitanism and the Politics of Obligation: The Ghanaian Diaspora and Development." *Environment and Planning A* 38: 867–83.

Moncada, Eduardo. 2013. "The Politics of Urban Violence: Challenges for Development in the Global South." *Studies in Comparative International Development* 48: 217–39.

Mongin, Olivier. 2004. "Globalization and Urban Metamorphosis: 'Megacities,' 'Global Cities' and Metropoles." *Esprit* 303: 175–200.

Moss, Timothy. 2009. "Intermediaries and the Governance of Sociotechnical Networks in Transition." *Environment and Planning A* 41: 1480–95.

Mrázek, Rudolf. 2002. *Engineers of Happy Land: Technology and Nationalism in a Colony.* Princeton, N.J.: Princeton University Press.

————. 2004. "Bypasses and Flyovers: Approaching the Metropolitan History of Indonesia." *Social History* 29: 425–43.

————. 2010. *A Certain Age: Colonial Jakarta through the Memories of Its Intellectuals.* Durham, N.C.: Duke University Press.

Nancy, Jean-Luc. 2007. *The Creation of the World; or, Globalization.* Albany: State University of New York Press.

Nas, Peter J. M. 1992. "Jakarta, City Full of Symbols: An Essay in Symbolic Ecology." *Sojourn: Journal of Social Issues in Southeast Asia* 7: 175–207.

Nas, Peter J. M., and Pratiwo. 2003. "The Streets of Jakarta: Fear, Trust and Amnesia in Urban Development." In *Framing Indonesian Realities,* edited by Peter J. M. Nas, Gerard A. Persoon, and Rivke Jaffe, 275–94. Leiden: KITLV Press.

Ndjio, Basile. 2008. "Millennial Democracy and Spectral Reality in Postcolonial Africa." *African Journal of International Affairs* 11: 115–56.

Nicholls, Walter J. 2006. "Associationalism from Above: Explaining Failure through France's Politique de la Ville." *Urban Studies* 43: 1779–1802.

Nielsen, Morten. 2010. "Contrapuntal Cosmopolitanism: Distantiation as Social Relatedness among House-Builders in Maputo, Mozambique." *Social Anthropology* 18: 396–402.

November, Valérie, Eduardo Camacho-Hübner, and Bruno Latour. 2010. "Entering a Risky Territory: Space in the Age of Digital Navigation." *Environment and Planning D: Society and Space* 28: 581–99.

Oyama, Susan. 2000. *The Ontogeny of Information: Developmental Systems and Evolution.* Durham, N.C.: Duke University Press.

Padawangi, Rita. 2013. "The Cosmopolitan Grassroots City as Megaphone: Reconfiguring Public Spaces through Urban Activism in Jakarta." *International Journal of Urban and Regional Research* 37: 849–63.

Parisi, Luciana. 2012. "Digital Design and Topological Control." *Theory, Culture & Society* 29 (4/5): 165–92.

Parr, John. 2008. "Cities and Regions: Problems and Potentials." *Environment and Planning A* 40: 3009–26.

Peck, Jamie, and Nik Theodore. 2007. "Variegated Capitalism." *Progress in Human Geography* 31: 731-72.

———. 2010a. "Mobilizing Policy: Models, Methods, and Mutations." *Geoforum* 41: 169–74.

———. 2010b. "Recombinant Workfare, across the Americas: Transnationalizing 'Fast' Social Policy." *Geoforum* 41: 195–208.

Peck, Jamie, Nik Theodore, and Neil Brenner. 2010. "Postneoliberalism and Its Malcontents." *Antipode* 41: 1236–58.

Perera, Nihal. 2009. "People's Spaces: Familiarization, Subject Formation and Emergent Spaces in Colombo." *Planning Theory* 8: 51–75.

Perlman, Janice E. 2004. "Marginality: From Myth to Reality in the Favelas of Rio De Janeiro, 1969–2002." In *Urban Informality: Transnational Perspectives from the Middle East, Latin America, and South Asia,* edited by Ananya Roy and Nezar AlSayyad, 105–46. Lanham, Md.: Lexington Books.

————. 2011. *Favela: Four Decades of Living on the Edge in Rio de Janeiro.* New York: Oxford University Press.

Peters, Robbie. 2009. "The Assault on Occupancy in Surabaya: Legible and Illegible Landscapes in a City of Passage." *Development and Change* 40: 903–25.

Phelps, Nicholas A., and Andrew M. Wood. 2011. "The New Post-suburban Politics?" *Urban Studies* 48: 2591–610.

Pieterse, Edgar. 2008. *City Futures: Confronting the Crisis of Urban Development.* London: Zed Books.

Pine, Adam. 2010. "The Performativity of Urban Citizenship." *Environment and Planning A* 42: 1103–20.

Pløger, John. 2010. "Presence-Experiences: The Eventalisation of Urban Space." *Environment and Planning D: Society and Space* 28: 848–66.

Portes, Alejandro, and Bryan Roberts. 2005. "The Free-Market City: Latin American Urbanization in the Years of the Neoliberal Experiment." *Studies in Comparative International Development* 40: 43–82.

Pries, Ludger. 2005. "Configurations of Geographic and Societal Spaces: A Sociological Proposal between 'Methodological Nationalism' and the 'Spaces of Flows.'" *Global Networks* 5: 167–90.

Protevi, John. 2009. *Political Affect: Connecting the Social and the Somatic.* Minneapolis: University of Minnesota Press.

Pryke, Michael. 2011. "Geographies of Economic Growth: Money and Finance." In *The SAGE Handbook of Economic Geography,* edited by Andrew Leyshon, Roger Lee, Linda McDowell, and Peter Sunley. Thousand Oaks, Calif.: Sage.

Purcell, Mark. 2006. "Urban Democracy and the Local Trap." *Urban Studies* 43: 1921–41.

Raco, Mike, Steven Henderson, and Sophie Bowlby. 2008. "Changing Times, Changing Places: Urban Development and the Politics of Space-Time." *Environment and Planning A* 40: 2652–73.

Raco, Mike, Rob Imrie, and Wen-I Lin. 2011. "Community Governance, Critical Cosmopolitanism and Urban Change: Observations from Taipei, Taiwan." *International Journal of Urban and Regional Research* 35: 274–94.

Rafael, Vincente. 2010. "Welcoming What Comes: Sovereignty and Revolution in Colonial Philippines." *Comparative Studies in Society and History* 52: 157–79.

Rakodi, Carole, and Tommy Firman. 2009. "Planning for an Extended Metropolitan Region in Asia: Jakarta, Indonesia." Case study prepared for United Nations Human Settlements Programme, *Planning Sustainable Cities: Global Report on Human Settlements 2009.* London: Earthscan.

Rancière, Jacques. 2010. *Dissensus: On Politics and Aesthetics.* New York: Continuum.

Riles, Annelise. 2010. "Collateral Expertise: Knowledge in the Global Financial Markets." *Current Anthropology* 51: 795–818.

Roberts, Bryan. 2010. "Moving on and Moving Back: Rethinking Inequality and Migration in the Latin American City." *Journal of Latin American Studies* 42: 587–614.

Roberts, Bryan, and Robert Wilson. 2009. *Urban Governance and Segregation in the Americas*. New York: Palgrave.

Robinson, Jennifer. 2004. "In the Tracks of Comparative Urbanism: Difference, Urban Modernity and the Primitive." *Urban Geography* 25: 709–23.

———. 2008. "Developing Ordinary Cities: City Visioning Processes in Durban and Johannesburg." *Environment and Planning A* 40: 74–87.

———. 2011. "Cities in a World of Cities: The Comparative Gesture." *International Journal of Urban and Regional Research* 35: 1–23.

Robison, Richard, and Andrew Rosser. 2000. "Surviving the Meltdown: Liberal Reform and Political Oligarchy in Indonesia." In *Politics and Markets in the Wake of the Asian Crisis,* edited by Richard Robison, Mark Beeson, Kanishka Jayasuriya, and Hyuk-Rae Kim, 171–91. London: Routledge.

Rodgers, Dennis. 2009. "Slum Wars of the 21st Century: Gangs and the New Urban Geography of Conflict in Central America." *Development and Change* 40: 949–76.

Roitman, Janet. 2005. *Fiscal Disobedience: An Anthropology of Economic Regulation in Central Africa*. Princeton, N.J.: Princeton University Press.

Rolnik, Raquel. 1999. *Territorial Exclusion and Violence: The Case of São Paulo, Brazil* (Comparative Urban Studies Occasional Paper 26). Washington, D.C.: Woodrow Wilson Center for Scholars.

Roosa, John. 2006. *Pretext for Mass Murder*. Madison: University of Wisconsin Press.

Rose, Nikolas. 2000. "Governing Cities, Governing Citizens." In *Democracy, Citizenship and the Global City,* edited by Engin F. Isin, 95–109. London: Routledge.

Roy, Ananya. 2009. "The 21st Century Metropolis: New Geographies of Theory." *Regional Studies* 43: 819–30.

———. 2011a. "Postcolonial Urbanism: Speed, Hysteria, Mass Dreams." In *Worlding Cities: Asian Experiments and the Art of Being Global,* edited by Ananya Roy and Aihwa Ong, 307–35. Oxford: Blackwell.

———. 2011b. "Slumdog Cities: Rethinking Subaltern Urbanism." *International Journal of Urban and Regional Research* 35: 223–38.

Roy, Ananya, and Aihwa Ong, eds. 2011. *Worlding Cities: Asian Experiments and the Art of Being Global*. Oxford: Blackwell.

Sanchez, Andrew. 2012. "Questioning Success: Dispossession and the Criminal Entrepreneur in Urban India." *Critique of Anthropology* 32: 435–57.

Sandercock, Leonie. 2003. *Cosmopolis 2: Mongrel Cities in the 21st Century.* London: Continuum.

Santos, Boaventura de Sousa. 1998. "Participatory Budgeting in Porto Alegre: Toward a Redistributive Democracy." *Politics and Society* 26: 461–510.

Santoso, Jo. 2011. *Jakarta's Fifth Layer.* Jakarta: University of Tarumanagara.

Sassen, Saskia. 2006. *Territory, Authority, Rights: From Medieval to Global Assemblages.* Princeton, N.J.: Princeton University Press.

———. 2010. "Global Inter-city Networks and Commodity Chains: Any Intersections?" *Global Networks* 10: 150–63.

Savitch, H. V., and Paul Kantor. 2002. *Cities in the International Marketplace: The Political Economy of Urban Development in North America and Western Europe.* Princeton, N.J.: Princeton University Press.

Scott, Allen J. 2009. *Social Economy of the Metropolis: Cognitive-Cultural Capitalism and the Global Resurgence of Cities.* New York: Oxford University Press.

Secor, Anna. 2004. "There Is an Istanbul That Belongs to Me: Citizenship, Space, and Identity in the City." *Annals of the Association of American Geographers* 92: 352–68.

Segre, Roberto. 2010. "Formal Informal Connections in the Favelas of Rio de Janeiro." In *Rethinking the Informal City: Critical Perspectives from Latin America,* edited by Felipe Hernández, Peter Kellett, and Lea K. Allen. New York: Berghahn Books.

Shatkin, Gavin. 2008. "The City and the Bottom Line: Urban Megaprojects and the Privatization of Planning in Southeast Asia." *Environment and Planning A* 40: 383–401.

———. 2009. "The Geography of Insecurity: Spatial Change and the Flexibilization of Labor in Metro Manila." *Journal of Urban Affairs* 31: 381–408.

Shih, Mi. 2010. "The Evolving Law of Disputed Relocation: Constructing Inner-City Renewal Practices in Shanghai, 1990–2005." *International Journal of Urban and Regional Research* 34: 350–64.

Shin, Kyoung-Ho, and Michael Timberlake. 2000. "World Cities in Asia: Cliques, Centrality and Connectedness." *Urban Studies* 37: 2257–85.

Sidaway, J. D. 2012. "Geographies of Development: New Maps, New Visions?" *Professional Geographer* 64: 49–62.

Sidel, John T. 1998a. "Indonesia: Economic, Social, and Political Dimensions of the Current Crisis." WriteNet papers, United Nations High Commissioner for Refugees, Geneva, Switzerland.

———. 1998b. "*Macet Total*: Logics of Circulation and Accumulation in the Demise of Indonesia's New Order." *Indonesia* 66: 158–95.

———. 2006. *Riots, Pogroms, Jihad: Religious Violence in Indonesia.* Ithaca, N.Y.: Cornell University Press.

Siegel, James T. 1998. *A New Criminal Type in Jakarta: Counter-revolution Today*. Durham, N.C.: Duke University Press.

Silver, Christopher. 2008. *Planning the Megacity: Jakarta in the Twentieth Century*. London: Routledge.

Silver, Hilary, Alan Scott, and Yuri Kazepov. 2010. "Participation in Urban Contention and Deliberation." *International Journal of Urban and Regional Research* 34: 453–77.

Simmel, Georg. 1972. *On Individuality and Social Forms*. Edited by Donald Levine. Chicago: University of Chicago Press.

Simondon, Gilbert. 2009a. "The Position of the Problem of Ontogenesis." *Parrhesia* 7: 4–16.

———. 2009b. "Technical Mentality." *Parrhesia* 7: 17–27.

Singerman, Diane, ed. 2009. *Cairo Contested: Governance, Urban Space, and Global Modernity*. Cairo: American University Press.

Smart, Alan, and George C. S. Lin. 2007. "Local Capitalisms, Local Citizenship and Translocality: Rescaling from Below in the Pearl River Delta Region, China." *International Journal of Urban and Regional Research* 31: 280–302.

Smith, David A. 2004. "Global Cities in East Asia: Empirical and Conceptual Analysis." *International Social Science Journal* 56: 399–412.

Smith, Michael Peter. 2000. *Transnational Urbanism: Locating Globalization*. Oxford: Wiley-Blackwell.

Soegijoko, Budhy T. S., and B. S. Kusbiantoro. 2001. "Globalization and the Sustainability of Jabotabek, Indonesia." In *Globalization and the Sustainability of Cities in the Asia Pacific Region*, edited by Fu-chen Lo and Peter J. Marcotullio. Tokyo: United Nations University Press.

Soja, Edward. 2010. *Seeking Spatial Justice*. Minneapolis: University of Minnesota Press.

Sparke, Matthew. 2008. Political Geography—Political Geographies of Globalization III: Resistance." *Progress in Human Geography* 28: 423–40.

Srinivas, Smita. 2010. "Industrial Welfare and the State: Nation and City Reconsidered." *Theory and Society* 39: 451–70.

Standing, Guy. 2011. *Work after Globalization*. Cheltenham, England: Edward Elgar.

Stanley, Anna. 2013. "Natures of Risk: Capital, Rule, and Production of Difference." *Geoforum* 45: 5–16.

Stengers, Isabelle. 2010. "Including Nonhumans in Political Theory: Opening Pandora's Box?" In *Political Matter: Technoscience, Democracy, and Public Life,* edited by Bruce Braun and Sarah J. Whatmore, 3–33. Minneapolis: University of Minnesota Press.

Stiegler, Bernard. 1998. *Technics and Time: The Fault of Epimetheus*. Stanford, Calif.: Stanford University Press.

Stoler, Ann. 2009. *Along the Archival Grain: Epistemic Anxieties and Colonial Common Sense.* Princeton, N.J.: Princeton University Press.

Storper, Michael. 2010. "Why Does a City Grow? Specialisation, Human Capital or Institutions?" *Urban Studies* 47: 2027–50.

Strassler, Karen. 2010. *Refracted Visions: Popular Photography and National Modernity in Java.* Durham, N.C.: Duke University Press.

Strathern, Marilyn. 2011. "Binary License." *Common Knowledge* 17: 87–103.

Sundaram, Ravi. 2010. *Pirate Modernity: Delhi's Media Urbanism.* London: Routledge.

Swyngedouw, Erik. 2009. "The Antinomies of the Post-political City: In Search of a Democratic Politics of Environmental Production." *International Journal of Urban and Regional Research* 33: 601–20.

Swyngedouw, Erik, Frank Moulaert, and Arantxa Rodriguez. 2010. "Neoliberal Urbanization in Europe: Large-Scale Urban Development Projects and the New Urban Policy." In *Masstab,* edited by A. Moravánsky, J. Hopfengärtner, A. Kirchengast, and L. Stanek. Zurich: Department of Architectural Theory, ETH.

Tadie, Jerome. 2006. *Les Territoires de la violence á Jakarta.* Paris: Belin.

Taussig, Michael. 1999. *Defacement: Public Secrecy and the Labor of the Negative.* Stanford, Calif.: Stanford University Press.

Taylor, Peter. 2001. "Distributed Agency within Intersecting Ecological, Social, and Scientific Processes." In *Cycles of Contingency: Developmental Systems and Evolution,* edited by Susan Oyama, Paul E. Griffiths, and Russell D. Gray, 313–32. Cambridge: MIT Press.

Telles, Vera da Silva, and D. V. Hirata. 2007. "The City and Urban Practices: In the Uncertain Frontiers between the Illegal, the Informal, and the Illicit." *Estudos Avançados* 21: 173–91.

Thery, Clement. 2012. "Making Money off People, Making Money with People: Economic Action and Moral Order among Landlords in Low-Income Minority Neighborhoods in Brooklyn, NY." Paper presented at the annual meeting of the American Association of Geographers, New York, February 26.

Thompson, E. P. 1968. *The Making of the English Working Class.* Harmondsworth: Penguin.

Thorburn, Craig. 2004. "The Plot Thickens: Land Administration and Policy in Post-New Order Indonesia." *Asia Pacific Viewpoint* 45: 33–49.

Thrift, Nigel. 2004. "Movement-Space: The Changing Domain of Thinking Resulting from the Development of New Kinds of Spatial Awareness." *Economy and Society* 33: 582–604.

———. 2009. "Different Atmospheres: Of Sloterdijk, China, and Site." *Environment and Planning D: Society and Space* 27: 119–38.

————. 2012. "Insubstantial Pageants: Producing an Untoward Land." *Cultural Geographies* 19: 141–68.

Torrance, Morag I. 2008. "Forging Glocal Governance? Urban Infrastructures as Networked Financial Products." *International Journal of Urban and Regional Research* 32: 1–21.

Tsing, Anna. 2005. *Frictions: An Ethnography of Global Connections*. Princeton, N.J.: Princeton University Press.

Tunas, Devisari. 2009. *The Spatial Economy in the Informal Settlement*. The Hague: Papiroz.

Turner, Sarah. 2009. "Hanoi's Ancient Quarter Traders: Resilient Livelihoods in a Rapidly Transforming City." *Urban Studies* 46: 1203–21.

Turok, Ivan. 2009. "The Distinctive City: Pitfalls in the Pursuit of Differential Advantage." *Environment and Planning A* 41: 13–30.

Uhlin, Anders. 1997. *Indonesia and the "Third Wave" of Democratization. The Indonesian Pro-democracy Movement in a Changing World*. New York: St. Martin's Press.

United Nations Human Settlements Programme. 2010. *State of the World's Cities 2010/2011: Bridging the Urban Divide*. London: Earthscan.

Vargas, Joao Costa, and Jaime Amparo Alves. 2010. "Geographies of Death: An Intersectional Analysis of Police Lethality and the Racialized Regimes of Citizenship in São Paulo." *Ethnic and Racial Studies* 33: 611–36.

Vickers, Adrian. 2005. *A History of Modern Indonesia*. Cambridge: Cambridge University Press.

Vind, Ingeborg, and Niels Fold. 2010. "City Networks and Commodity Chains: Identifying Global Flows and Local Connections in Ho Chi Minh City." *Global Networks* 10: 54–74.

Virno, Paolo. 2009. "Natural-Historical Diagrams: The 'New Global' Movement and the Biological Invariant." *Cosmos and History* 5: 92–104.

Wang, Ya Ping, Yanglin Wang, and Jiansheng Wu. 2009. "Urbanization and Informal Development in China: Urban Villages in Shenzhen." *International Journal of Urban and Regional Research* 33: 957–73.

Ward, Kevin, David Imbroscio, Deborah Martin, Clarence Stone, Robert Whelan, Faranak Miraftab, and Allan Cochrane. 2011. "Urban Politics: An Interdisciplinary Dialogue." *International Journal of Urban and Regional Research* 35: 853–71.

Weber, Samuel. 2009. "Between Part and Whole: Benjamin and the Single Trait." *Paragraph* 32: 364–81.

Whitson, Risa. 2007. "Hidden Struggles: Spaces of Power and Resistance in Informal Work in Urban Argentina." *Environment and Planning A* 39: 2916–34.

Wieringa, Saskia. 2003. "The Birth of the New Order State in Indonesia: Sexual Politics and Nationalism." *Journal of Women's History* 15: 70–91.

Wigle, Jill. 2010. "Social Relations, Property and 'Peripheral' Informal Settlement: The Case of Ampliación San Marcos, Mexico City." *Urban Studies* 47: 411–36.

Williams, Gavin. 2002. *The Other Side of the Popular: Neoliberalism and Subalternity in Latin America.* Durham, N.C.: Duke University Press.

Wilson, Ara. 2008. "The Sacred Geography of Bangkok's Markets." *International Journal of Urban and Regional Research* 32: 631–42.

Wilson, Ian Douglas. 2006. "Continuity and Change: The Changing Contours of Organized Violence in Post-New Order Indonesia." *Critical Asian Studies* 38: 265–97.

———. 2011. "Reconfiguring Rackets: Racket Regimes, Protection and the State in Post–New Order Jakarta." In *The State and Illegality in Indonesia,* edited by Edward Aspinall and Gerry van Klinken, 239–60. Leiden: KITLV Press.

———. 2012. "The Biggest Cock: Territoriality, Invulnerability and Honour amongst Jakarta's Gangsters." In *Men and Masculinities in Southeast Asia,* edited by Michele Ford and Lenore Lyons, 121–38. London: Routledge.

Winarso, Haryo. 2005. "City for the Rich." Paper presented at the Eighth International Conference of the Asian Planning Schools Association, Penang, Malaysia, September 11–14.

———. 2011. "Urban Dualism in the Jakarta Metropolitan Area." In *Megacities: Urban Form, Governance, and Sustainability,* edited by A. Sorensen and J. Okata, 163–91. New York: Springer.

Winarso, Haryo, and Tommy Firman. 2002. "Residential Land Development in Jabotabek, Indonesia: Triggering Economic Crisis." *Habitat International* 26: 487–506.

Woodward, Keith, John Paul Jones, and Sallie Marston. 2012. "The Politics of Autonomous Space." *Progress in Human Geography* 36: 204–24.

World Bank. 2009. *World Bank Development Report 2009.* Washington, D.C.: World Bank.

———. 2011. *Indonesia Economic Quarterly: Turbulent Times: Perkembangan triwulanan perkonomian* (Working Paper 6). Jakarta: World Bank.

Wright, Gwendolyn. 1992. *The Politics of Design in French Colonial Urbanism.* Chicago: University of Chicago Press.

Yeoh, Brenda. 2001. "Postcolonial Cities." *Progress in Human Geography* 25: 456–68.

———. 2005. "The Global Cultural City: Spatial Imagineering and Politics in the (Multi)cultural Marketplace of Southeast Asia." *Urban Studies* 42: 945–58.

Young, Douglas, and Roger Keil. 2010. "Reconnecting the Disconnected: The Politics of Infrastructure in the In-Between City." *Cities* 27: 87–95.

Zaki, Saeed, and A. T. M. Nurul Amin. 2009. "Does Basic Services Privatisation Benefit the Urban Poor? Some Evidence from Water Supply Privatisation in Thailand." *Urban Studies* 46: 2301–27.

Zhang, Li. 2001. *Strangers in the City: Reconfigurations of Space, Power, and Social Networks within China's Floating Population.* Stanford, Calif.: Stanford University Press.

Index

capital: devices associated with global, 172; maximizing accumulation of, 164

capitalism, 238; operating procedures of contemporary financial, 262; planetary urbanization structured by global, 32–33, 267. *See also* neoliberalism

captivation, space of, 166, 167; undercurrents of change and, 167–68

car theft, 141

cash transfers to poor: conditional, 63; unconditional, 258

Cavalcanti, Marianna, 163

Çelik, Zeynep, 27

Centner, Ryan, 28

central-city development, x; trajectories of, 164–65

Central Statistics Agency, 220

Chan, Fruit, 195

change: undercurrents of, 167–68

Chant, Sylvia, 28

Chatterjee, Partha, 102

Chattopadhyay, Swati, 168, 216

China: privatization of property in, 244

Chinese Indonesians: economic power of, 14; entrepreneurs, 95–96; May riots of 1998 and, 14; in Pademangan district, 184; in printing industry, 203–5

Christian–Muslim violence: avoidance of, 15, 16

Chu, Yin-wah, 32

cinema: Deleuze on, 225–27

Ciputra (developer), 41

circulation in Jakarta: declining physical, 143–44

citizenship, 137–40; concretization of, 215–16; as matter of accords and deals, 147; salience of ethnic

identity over, 137; technique of, presumption of self-sufficiency in, 216

city(ies): absence of North–South divide in terms of world's major, 26–27; as hinges, 162–63; indiscipline in, 147–49; as locus of aspiration, 147; mutual recognition among, across disparate national contexts, 117–18; of near-South, as "crossroads" of conflicting trajectories of urbanization, 163; of the North, "Souths" embedded within, 33–34; periphery of, development of, 165; persisting differences among, 27–30, 31, 34, 35; processes of equifinality in development of, 32–33; radical respatialization of, neoliberalism and, 164–65; resilience of inhabitants and conditions of larger, 35–40; as sites of imposition, 117, 215

Clark, Gordon, 243

class(es): coexistence of different, vii, viii, 72–79, 170, 199, 215; increasing gap between, 25; Indo-Chinese, 14, 184; political, economic crisis and realignment of, 13–14; Thompson's notion of, 85; working, 14, 63, 89, 154, 184. *See also* middle class; professionals/professional class; urban majority

clientelism, 87

Cochrane, Allan, 37, 166

Coe, Neil M., 25

Colebrook, Claire, 160, 241

collaboration(s), 3; attribution of difference to neighbors and, 115–16; constellations' coming-into-formation, emergent property

inadequate, 250; spatial development plans needed for, 246–47; transitions requiring, 197–98; underutilized buildings in older commercial and residential areas, 52; water supply systems in Jakarta, 245; working around deficiencies of, 199–201

inheritance of property: disputes over, 66. *See also* land

interdependencies, 19

interstices/interstitial space, 162; in cinema, "power of the false" in, 225; collective, in megacomplexes, 194–95; created by limits of available management, 228; near-South as, 34, 35, 162

inventive policy, 250–56; enrolling residents in work of city, 256–60

investment(s): environment performance adaptation and socioeconomic adaptation underpinning urban strategies for, 247; Indonesia's need to identify more creative forms of productive, 62; megadevelopment units geared toward, 70; multiple initiatives by households, 110–11; productive, challenge of engineering, 64–67; signs of gentrification, 61; in technology of printing industry, Chinese control through, 203–4

Isin, Engin F., 215

Islam, 15–16, 265; as "brand," 15–16; mosques, 176; Muslim-Christian conflict, 123–24

Islamic organizations, 14, 94, 140; in Nasakom, 11; youth groups, 127

Islamic travel agencies, 49

Islam Liberal Network, 94

Jacobs, Jane M., 29, 102

Jakarta: absence of any municipal democratic politics until 2008, 248, 249–50; accommodating new and temporary residents as major economic activity across, 112, 126, 209; as ambiguous landscape, 1; city left behind, 64–67; contradictions of, 40; deceptive appearance of, 220–22; declining physical circulation across, 143–44; developers with dominant role in, 41–42; forging sense of the common in, 206–8; government's efforts at enrolling residents in work of, 256–60; infrastructures of segregation in, viii; intense contiguities of social classes in, vii, viii, 72–79, 170, 199, 215; land, relationship to, 7–9; large-scale needs of, 259–60; metropolitan region, 42; most heterogeneous areas of, 6; new town residential areas, 41–44; official origin of, 6; as part of Global South, 1–2; planning literature on, 7; pluri-districts of, ambiguities of, 72–79; political traumas in, 10–15; population of, 6–7; religion of, 15–16; Sadikin's modernization plans for, 37–38; streets of, 9–10; unemployment rate, 181; urban region encompassing, 7; urgency of, 267; waning of residents' interest in daily life of, 265–66; water supply systems in, 245

Jalam Casablanca (avenue), 57

Jalan Tebet Raya (street), 229

James, William, 190, 192

Jáuregui, Jorge Mario, 29, 215

head-on producing confounding, 229–30; incrementalism in atmosphere of muted, 93; intelligibility and, 227, 251; invisibility rendered by implication of, 241; of *preman*, 234; of residents' assets, expansion of opportunities and, 6; self-fashioning for, 61; survival vs. endurance and, 213, 214; of Tebet residents, concern for future and, 146
volatility of urban life, 61, 216–17

Wachter, Susan, 28
Wallbaum, Holger, 54
Wang, Yanglin, 169
Wang, Ya Ping, 169
Ward, Kevin, 26, 37, 63
water supply systems in Jakarta, 245
Weber, Samuel, 131
Whelan, Robert, 37
Whitehead, Alfred North, 116; notion of lure, 153
Whitson, Risa, 29, 168, 171, 219
Widodo, Joko, 256, 257
Wie, Thee Kian, 88
Wieringa, Saskia, 120
Wigle, Jill, 29
Williams, Gavin, 171
Williams, Karel, 243
Wilson, Ara, 168
Wilson, Ian Douglas, 10, 13, 120
Wilson, Robert, 31
Winarso, Haryo, 7, 41, 42, 68
witnessing, 149–50, 207; of intersections of individuated performances, 192–93; by *preman*, 234, 235; social housing developments facilitating sense of mutual, 193
Wood, Andrew M., 30
Woodward, Keith, 161
work: capacity to resiliently become many different things as standard, 212; dynamism of local district economies dependent on mixtures of, 196–97; efforts at tending needs of relational economies, 192; enrolling residents in work of city, 256–60; formal and informal, blurring between, 196; growing professionalization of workforce, 266; heterogeneity creating, 170; Kebayoran Lama as expanding opportunity for, 155–56; process of creating, 153, 154, 206–7; service jobs, 170, 182–83, 258; uncertainty as incentive for, 168–72; urban majority's capacity to stretch and provide, 181–84
working class, 14, 63, 89, 154, 184. *See also* urban majority
working majority, 3. *See also* urban majority
World, The (film), 241–42
World Bank, 101, 220
Wright, Gwendolyn, 27
Wu, Jiansheng, 169

Yeo, Wei-Wei, 163
Yeoh, Brenda, 32, 168
Yeung, Henry Wai-chung, 25
Young, Douglas, 166
youth: drug dealing and elders' loss of control of, 124; migrant, 126–27; resilience of, 6; *tawuran* (violence) by, 120, 122–30; using plurality of opportunities as means of creating space, 127

Zaki, Saeed, 169
Zhang, Li, 165
Zhang, Zhanxin, 169
Zhangke, Jia, 241
zoning regulations, 51, 106–7

AbdouMaliq Simone is research professor at the University of South Australia and professor of sociology at Goldsmiths, University of London. He is the author of *In Whose Image? Political Islam and Urban Practices in Sudan*, *For the City Yet to Come: Changing African Life in Four Cities*, and *City Life from Jakarta to Dakar: Movements at the Crossroads*.